The Writer Writing

✣

Jan Vermeer, *A Lady Writing* (Washington, D.C.: National Gallery of Art).

The Writer Writing

PHILOSOPHIC ACTS IN LITERATURE

✜

Francis-Noël Thomas

PRINCETON UNIVERSITY PRESS

PRINCETON, NEW JERSEY

Library of Congress Cataloging-in-Publication Data
Thomas, Francis-Noël, 1943–
The writer writing : philosophic acts in literature / Francis-Noël Thomas.
p.   cm.
Includes bibliographical references and index.
1.Criticism. 2. Literature, Modern—History and criticism.
3. Literature—Philosophy. I. Title.
PN81.T47   1992
ISBN 0-691-06955-7 (acid-free)
801—dc20   92-14220   CIP

For Michael Murrin,

fellow intellectual traveler;

and for the Necessary Angel

Ζῶν γὰρ ὁ λόγος τοῦ θεοῦ καὶ ἐνεργὴς

⁜ Contents ⁜

CONTENTS

✥ *Illustrations* ✥

✤ Foreword ✤

BY WAYNE C. BOOTH

In *An Appetite for Poetry*, Frank Kermode tells of seeing on the door of a laboratory at UCLA a posted quotation from the *Carnets d'un biologiste* of Jean Rostand: *"Les théories passent. Le grenouille reste."* Kermode comments, "There is a risk that in the less severe discipline of criticism the result may turn out to be different; the theories will remain but the frog may disappear." In redefining the study of literature, recent theorists in the traditions of structuralism and post-structuralism have offered sophisticated abstract concepts intended to replace our pre-theoretical commonplace experience of literature. Often self-consciously "scientific," these theories have explicitly questioned the ties of "the text" to any individual human agency. The true agency may be class, or the unconscious, or the nature of language or *écriture*, or the bipolar structures of the mind, or history at last properly understood, or gender, or genre—anything but *this* poet, *this* musician, *this* painter, creating this particular work of art, realizing specific intentions and purposes. Indeed, the very existence of *this* artist as in any sense responsible for the work of art has been frequently questioned.

Frank Thomas's deeply original book recalls us to the full force of Rostand's observation about those enduring frogs: theories can dazzle us in ways that obscure the wondrous riches of that frog. After a while they can lead us to forget all about the very frog that the theory, at least at the outset, was supposed to explain. The theory, after all, has the beauty and power of simplicity and comprehensiveness, the poor frog is covered with warts in unpredictable patterns, and in itself it seems to explain nothing, not even itself. When ravished by the unmistakable appeals of marvelous theory, we need someone like Thomas to come along and repeat over and over until our reverie is broken: "Look at this one frog, and next really look at this surprisingly different one, and then again at this really quite strange one over here in a pond that your theory has totally ignored."

To some readers that voice, heard in full eloquence in *The Writer Writing*, will seem like the voice of reality crashing through the fog of controversy; to others it may seem like a philistine intrusion. The point to stress is that Thomas's subject cannot be considered genuinely old-fashioned for the same reason that frogs can never become old-fashioned to biologists. His subject is human actions, human makings, as the bedrock for the study of literature. It is thus hard to say whether he is conservative or radical when he insists, through example after example, that "people do things. One of the things they do is write."

Indeed, careful readers will soon recognize that Thomas is not a pre-structuralist troglodyte concealing a reactionary message with his unusually clear and engaging style. Though fully informed about current theories, he is a reader in love with a grand, never-dated conception of literature, passionately engaged with individual works. If, as Thomas Pavel says in *Le Mirage Linguistique*, "the fear of singularities ... haunts all philosophies inspired by structuralism ...," books like *The Writer Writing* are badly needed. Abandoned is the fashionable hope of knowing in advance of reading that the next work, like the previous one, will necessarily be about power relations, or about problems of gender, or about the infinite deferral of determinate meaning—though for all one knows in advance the next work might be precisely "about" any such matters.

Thus reading this book, after reading in the varieties of contemporary criticism, is a little like moving out of the no-man's-land in some war zone and meeting someone standing in the line of fire who says, "Don't bother to duck; there's no real killing going on here, and the two warring sides do not exist as sides. Now what I'd like to do is introduce you to *this* fascinating general—she's nineteen and the agent of God sent to work His will in contemporary politics. And meet this private, who has discovered the real life of past and present in a biscuit, and this philosopher, who has discovered the depth of human folly in a ..."

In lumping many current theories together as what his project must bypass, Thomas might be accused of engaging in the very kind of theoretical violation of individual qualities he deplores. But his lumping of theorists is not based on a claim that they are all identical in their theoretical aspect, but that their consequences for the practical reader are too often the same. As he says, whenever a critic's theory "resituates agency to impersonal or suprapersonal sites where an individual writer's plans, projects, and purposes are meaningless or irrelevant," the consequences will be similar, regardless of the differences in internal logic or in theoretical or political motivation: the artist's original contribution (if any) will be understated or ignored. Many a theory tells us just what the next work will be doing, and why. In contrast, any reader who follows Thomas will become as open to new and unpredictable experience as some readers who know no formal criticism: they can just let the powers of that next work determine how to live with it.

Thus the book's success is measured by whether Thomas has been able, with his combination of formal analysis and historical reconstruction, to reveal riches we had previously ignored. And it is here that his work on Shaw and Proust becomes quite wonderfully central. Critics have tended to see writers like these as opposed: they see Shaw as a writer with professed purposes, creating almost in spite of himself aesthetic objects that could be admired for reasons not his own, and Proust as the idol of aesthetic critics for whom pragmatic interests are thought to be corrupting. As Thomas says of Shaw, "Against his vociferous, insistent, unmistakably clear, and lifelong objections, they [some prominent critics] have persisted in trying to accommodate his dramatic achievements to their own concepts of art because they cannot deny the quality of his writing but cannot accommodate such quality to a concept of literature that envisions writing as a practical activity, an engagement with life that is meant to affect its course by changing the way people think and act."

By placing Shaw and Proust in juxtaposition and by revealing both the similarities in their contemporaneous pursuit of the uses of art and the radically distinct quality of the purposes each pursued, Thomas in effect presents us with the lovely gift of two refurbished giants, cleansed of our inherited clichés about them. Those readers who move beyond anxieties about Thomas's rejection of theory and look again at these two extraordinarily imaginative writers in the way Thomas suggests may well feel, as I did, that they are, in a sense, encountering these eccentric folk for the first time.

Thomas's celebration of the particular is underscored by the quite marvelous range of his explanations of other unique achievements: explanations of why the stained glass at Chartres was organized precisely as it was by its medieval creators (Emile Mâle receives here the kind of homage he deserves); of how and why the organization of

Vermeer's interiors is brilliantly original; of just why the the precise organization of *Macbeth* is both unprecedented and effective; and many another brief but telling revelation of the distinctive acts performed by genius.

Perhaps the sharpest way to distinguish what Thomas has achieved here from the work of most other intelligent critics on our scene is this: Let us imagine a young reader who, with no experience of criticism or theory, has learned to love a miscellaneous list of art works—novels, plays, poems, and works in other media. This budding art lover has so far read no criticism. Suppose now that I must decide what kind of criticism will be useful to her. I assume that she will believe what she reads, because when you read your first book of criticism you tend to believe it, especially if it is, like this one, elegantly written. Should I send her to someone who will teach her just the one right way of reading and the one agency that all art works are produced by or illustrate? If I do, and if she accepts uncritically what she reads, she will come away from the criticism with no reason whatever for reading another novel or poem or looking at another painting—except perhaps as further illustration of the truth she already has learned from the critic. Would I not do better to send her to a critic who teaches that you cannot predict, on any grounds whatever, what the next "art work" will do to or for you? Knowing that it is called a novel will not help you; indeed, it may render your reading pointless if you try to shoehorn the work into your notion of what a novel is or should be. Knowing that it was written in a given period cannot help you much, and may destroy your reading if you begin with fixed notions of how the period determines what the individual artist is allowed to do. Knowing some theory of language or culture or class or gender or genre will only blind you if, as will be true if the work is really powerful, it refuses to fit that theory.

After reading Thomas, all that the young reader will know about the next book on the shelf is that it may very well be something marvelously new, and that it will reveal its original qualities only to the reader who slows down and brings her whole soul to the reading moment.

In short, with a few "commonplace" concepts and an unlikely assortment of facts, Thomas engages the actions of writers writing. He has allowed the artists themselves, not a theory that supersedes them, to yield access to diverse experiences that could not have been predicted in advance by even the shrewdest of theorists. No one, certainly not Thomas, needs to be told these days that there are many other ways of reading books. But the "old-fashioned" notion that art works are individual projects of individual artists, inviting us into *diverse* worlds, in this book feels refreshingly new. Even readers who ultimately choose to turn from the frogs back to the theories should carry with them the kind of respect for specific achievements that alone can protect us from pointless warfare in the clouds.

✣ *Preface* ✣

Explanation, the philosophic act I consider in this book, is a uniquely human action. To explain is inseparable from being conscious of what we are, what we do, and the environment in which we live. Explaining is not simply the same thing as being conscious, but it is impossible to be conscious and follow Oscar Wilde's advice: "Never explain." Everyone explains—all the time. If we did not, it would be impossible to maintain our very sense of self. We work unconsciously and continually to explain to ourselves who we are, how we got to our present state, and how it is that we are the same person that we were when we were five years old, or two months old, or five minutes old, despite the pervasive and evident differences.

Explanation accounts for apparently static phenomena by seeing them as the results of actions and events. When I call explanation a philosophic act, I do not mean to restrict it to philosophers; it belongs to the core of human mental activity. It is too important to be left to the philosophers because it is so fundamental to what it means to be human. Explanation is a philosophic act when it is formal and conscious, but even then it is not always or even usually restricted to philosophers. It belongs to philosophy in the sense that the most fundamental subjects belong to philosophy: action, knowledge, being.

Since explanation is a fundamental human activity, it should come as no surprise that writers of imaginative literature explain, but I am not thinking here about explanation *within* literary texts. The narrator of *Pride and Prejudice* explains why Charlotte Lucas schemed to get Mr. Collins to propose marriage to her although she thought he was a fool and found his society irksome. Macbeth explains why he wants to kill Banquo. This is not, however, the sort of thing I am concerned with when I refer to philosophic acts in literature. I am thinking of the *writer's* act, and I argue that literary texts are the acts of the individuals who wrote them.

I do not deny that it may sound a little odd to call a text an action performed by its writer, although we are comfortable calling a speech an action performed by its speaker. If my conception of texts as acts seems odd, it is owing, in large measure, to an impressive body of contemporary critical theory in which texts are seen in ways that separate them not merely from speech but also from an individual writer's action. These theories are sophisticated because they violate a presumed relationship, derived from common experience, between a text and a writer. The traditional concept of this relationship is derived from no theory of literature or texts; it is a commonplace model that belongs to everyone in our culture. We are used to seeing people do things, and we ordinarily take them to be agents rather than instruments. A great deal of literary theory for most of the past fifty years has encouraged us to think that this traditional conception of writers as agents is naive. Agency has come to be situated in language, in the subconscious, in the culture, and in other places remote from individual writers. I have taken the traditionally presumed relationship between writers and texts with full seriousness—not out of piety, nor because I am unfamiliar with recent critical theory, but because of the traditional concept's irreplaceable power to give full scope to the original ideas of great writers. These ideas are not normally found in their texts but are rather the writer's conceptions of what a text might be and how it might be used to address an issue, answer a question, solve a problem—in short, how it might *do* something. Consider this reflection by Chinua Achebe.

> I did not know I was going to be a writer because I had no notion that such beings existed until relatively late. The folk stories my mother and elder sister told us had the immemorial quality of the sky and the forests and the rivers. Later at school I got to know that the European stories we read were written by Europeans—the same fellows who made all the other marvellous things like the motor-car. We didn't come into it at all. We made nothing that wasn't primitive and heathenish.
>
> The nationalist movement after the Second World War brought about a mental revolution which began to reconcile us to ourselves. We saw suddenly that we had a story to tell. . . .
>
> Although I did not consciously set about it in that way my first book, *Things Fall Apart*, was an act of atonement with my past, the homage of a prodigal son.[1]

The concept of literature I propose, traditional and theoretically unsophisticated as it is, allows us to take such statements seriously. Alternative concepts—when they rest on sophisticated theories of agency—render these statements, if not completely meaningless, irrelevant to the interpretation or understanding of literary texts, since their claims are impossible. Sophisticated theories have a way of placing artificial constraints on the sophistication of writers, making their most original ideas disappear. This is the price of their sophistication. Although the concept of literature I propose here no doubt has its own price to pay, it allows us to look at something that more sophisticated concepts of literature miss, something conventional in our lives: texts are actions performed by writers.

The idea that a novel can be an act of atonement, a moral act, is an unusual one among contemporary novelists and a sophisticated one. The act of atonement—once we recognize its existence—is an aspect of the whole text conceived of as an individual's action, not something embedded in the text as one of its parts. If we conceive of Achebe as the author—not merely the writer—of *Things Fall Apart*, then the act of representation, common to so many writers of imaginative literature, has a special character in this text because the whole text is an act of atonement. I call explanation a philosophic act in part because it too can give a distinctive character to the whole of a representation considered as an individual's action. The philosophic act of explanation as such is disinterested. In practice, however, great writers who explain are frequently also great rhetoricians engaged in acts of persuasion as well as great artists engaged in acts of representation. Texts that are the record of such complex action require analysis so that their elements can be seen clearly enough to be identified.

Such analysis, however, cannot be meaningful unless we reconsider the power and scope of commonplace concepts of agency, intention, and purpose. These concepts have been cast aside by many specialized theories of literature whose self-conscious theoretical sophistication has become a kind of mask for critical technology: a way of suppressing or eliding the plain fact of authorial agency and the specific historicity of an individual writer's project.

These specialized theories have made individual human agency and the human projects of individual writers disappear in a variety of ways and for a variety of reasons, none of which I examine in much detail. I merely draw attention to something the theories have in common. They have reversed the commonplace concept that individual writers write texts. For them, the concept of individual human agency is an illusion or a sign of naïveté against which they have defined their own sophistication. In the specialized theories it is the text that writes the "author." The "author" is a secondary phenomenon that requires analysis because what commonplace concepts take as an elementary fact—what I have called the plain fact of authorial agency—sophisticated theoretical analysis takes to be a complex secondary product of language. This product is sometimes seen in a theoretically sustained historical context as little more than a meeting place of institutions and power, primary agents that produces both the author and the text.

To reconsider the scope and force of the commonplace concepts that so many specialized theories have discarded, I have made a sharp distinction between concepts of literature and interpretation that are grounded in specialized and self-conscious theory and those that are corollaries of commonplace concepts and may therefore be considered pretheoretical or naive. I have considered all sorts of theoretically informed approaches to literary criticism that resituate agency to impersonal or suprapersonal sites where an individual writer's plans, projects, and purposes are meaningless or irrelevant as essentially the same—not in their internal logic or in their theoretical or political motivation, but in their consequences.

All theoretically informed concepts of literature that situate agency somewhere other than in an individual writer are particularly blind to original ideas in original writers; such theoretically sophisticated concepts will assimilate what is original to something that is much more common because these concepts of literature have incorporated at the outset a kind of conversion program that flags both "original ideas" and "original writers" as a form of, usually politically motivated and reactionary, illusion. Achebe's concept of his writing *Things Fall Apart* as "an act of atonement with [his] past, the homage of a prodigal son," will not survive the denial of agency to an individual writer; it will ordinarily make it impossible to consider such a claim seriously or at all.

Because I want to clear a space for specifically practical engagements with literary texts, my discussion of concepts such as intention and purpose as they relate to the more specialized concepts of interpretation and of literature itself may sound at times like a polemic against most of the prominent theoretical criticism of the past fifty years. Polemic always runs the risk of being unfair, and mine may seem to be particularly so, not because it distorts the positions of theories that make my practice impossible—it is the most common response of any object of polemic to claim that the polemic has distorted its object's views—but because it does not engage in a systematic analysis of them at all. Now and then I may seem to have personified the whole complex of critical theory as "Derrida" without having taken the trouble to separate the distinctive elements of Jacques Derrida's considerable and idiosyncratic project from the distinctive elements of other theoretical critics, some of whom are not even named.

I define my position against critical theorists, especially those like Derrida, Paul de Man, Hillis Miller, Roland Barthes, and Michel Foucault, who are the core thinkers of what has become practically a new orthodoxy in some of the more prominent literature departments in American graduate schools. My energies are not, however, taken up with analyses of their positions; I concentrate, in the main, on characterizing my own position. To analyze their theories would force me to defend my own practice on theoretical grounds and would simply take me further and further away from putting that practice in the foreground, as I want to do. The theories against which I define my practice, after all, declare that practice to be impossible, so they are the most inevitable of antagonists. In my view the most effective argument against them is not an analysis of their details and motives, but a comparison between the consequences their theories have for particular texts and the consequences my practice has for particular texts.

The Writer Writing, then, is neither a technical nor a theoretical argument. Even in the Aristophanic fantasy in my final chapter I am not attempting to show that Hillis Miller's position is absurd; I merely try to demonstrate how limited its scope is even for those, like Miller himself, whose own critical practice it defines.

For readers who have kept current with the critical wars of the recent past it will be clear that Jacques Derrida's concept of language is not mine, that Michel Foucault's concept of history is not mine, that the critical projects of Roland Barthes, Hillis Miller, and Paul de Man are projects that I cannot take seriously in practice. If I did, I should have to abandon the practical engagement with individual writers' actions that defines my own concept of interpretation.

It will also be clear that my position has some broad affinities with the work of such critics as Gerald Graff, John M. Ellis, Steven Knapp, Walter Benn Michaels, and M. H. Abrams, but while I share their general conceptual framework, my project is distinct from theirs. I do not question the value of their role in the recent debates about "theory," but inasmuch as they have engaged the theorists on theoretical grounds, they have been required to offer something like full-blown theoretical defenses of their own positions. I do not say that this has been a mistake, although, as a rhetorical strategy, it has not been more than a limited success. I should like to suggest that these critics have not engaged the theorists on the most favorable ground because the general conceptual framework they have argued for is not at heart a theoretical one at all. It is a practical one.

I think that my differences with the theorists—and perhaps those of Graff and others as well—are best presented not as an argument that opposes one theory to another but as the juxtaposition of the consequences of one concept of theory and the consequences of one form of practical engagement with texts. My "argument" against theory, so to speak, is my detailed engagement with two highly original texts considered as practical actions, in the sense that Achebe's claim to be engaged in an act of atonement as the writer of *Things Fall Apart* is a practical action.

My procedure, now becoming distinctly unusual among contemporary literary scholars from the best clubs, is less unusual in other disciplines where practical acts of writers writing are still commonly engaged. Both the reasons for practical engagement with specific cases and the usual suspicions about the usefulness of such engagement are incisively discussed in an essay by the cultural anthropologist Clifford Geertz called "Local Knowledge: Fact and Law in Comparative Perspective." It appears in *Local Knowledge*, a collection of essays in which Geertz also discusses the value of commonplace concepts in "Common Sense as a Cultural System."[2] In his more recent *Works and Lives*, in which he considers four anthropologists as writers, Geertz finds the sophisticated concepts of Foucault and Barthes to be approximately as useful as I do.[3]

I have heard the work of Abrams, Graff, and the others described as "neoconservative," and, from certain vantage points, that may be an accurate description, and one that could be applied to my own project. But I would not want any reader to think that I am engaged in a battle of ancients and moderns, as if individual agency and the historicity of an individual writer's project are concepts that have only a kind of museum value—as if they were once, in a simpler age, central concepts in humanistic inquiry and today remain merely as vestigial debris in the queer mixture of old rubbish that operates as "common sense" in an illusory world that "common sense" itself generates.

In at least one area of contemporary theory, feminist theory, these concepts are as much an issue as they are for someone like Bernard Shaw precisely because so much feminist theory is an advocacy form of theory, just as Shaw's drama is an advocacy form of drama. In current feminist theory, it is as plain as it is to the so-called neoconservatives that suprapersonal agency is unsatisfactory in any project that clearly belongs to individuals trying to affect existing conventions. The aim of such projects is, after all, action of a broadly moral, social, and political kind. What would be the point of advocacy in theory or in drama if human agency and the projects of individual writers were illusory or irrelevant? The issue of agency that I address is an issue for feminists such as Judith Butler and Denise Riley as much as it is for Abrams and Graff.

The issue is neither conservative nor avant-garde; it is not the property of a faction, a party, a cult, or a gender. Individual human agency is not, like the pikeman after the invention of the bayonet, obsolete and a matter of interest merely to erudite antiquarians or entrenched power elites. It cannot be obsolete as long as individuals attempt to do things and experience the impact of their own strategies against established convention and received ideas. It is fundamental to human self-consciousness to regard agency as an individual human attribute. We should find it impossible to retain self-consciousness if we were to regard individual human beings as no more than temporary intersections of impersonal powers embodied in institutions—as if these institutions are not themselves human inventions, other people's successful projects, subject to revision by anyone sufficiently tenacious and intelligent to revise them.

Just as I have accepted a traditional view of the relationship between writer and text, I have also assumed a particular conception of the humanities. It is neither novel nor idiosyncratic, but since it is no longer commonplace, I think its explicit articulation is warranted.

In the fifteenth and sixteenth centuries, the humanities stood for a decisive revision of prevailing views about what it means to be human. At that time the humanities were enveloped by a sense of discovery; poetry and rhetoric, painting and music seemed to be at the very center of philosophic and scientific inquiry.

In contemporary discourse—especially as represented in textbooks and required college courses—this sense of discovery has disappeared. The humanities now often mean certain discrete subject matters: philosophy, art history, literature, music. Since a great deal of stress is put on taxonomy and definition—Is this column Ionic, Doric, or Corinthian? Is this music baroque, classical, or romantic?—these subjects can seem far removed from the excitement of discovery, far distant from the center of contemporary inquiry into what it means to be human. Certain of the biological sciences and the contemporary study of language and human cognition seem to have taken over that role.

The difference between genetics or cognitive linguistics, on the one hand, and the degenerate concept of the humanities that I see in textbooks, on the other, is the difference between an inquiry that expects to make discoveries and the placing of inert material into a schema. There is all the difference in the world between asking a question such as: How do human beings acquire language? and asking a question such as, Why is Caravaggio a baroque painter? or, How does *Macbeth* fulfill the function of tragedy?

These questions are different at a fundamental level. When we are able to answer the question about the acquisition of language we will know something more about language, to be sure, but we will also know something more about human cognition and therefore about what it means to be human. We cannot imagine that language is somehow autonomous from human beings and can be studied without taking human beings into account. That would be as if we were to attempt to study dancing while dispensing with dancers, as if laws of dance could somehow exist without reference to the possibilities of the motion of the human body.

The other questions—Why is Caravaggio a baroque painter? and, How does *Macbeth* fulfill the function of tragedy?—each in a somewhat different way have separated an activity from human beings. They suggest that a culture or a style is the agent of painting; that a form is the agent of a play. If we answer these questions we manage to treat Caravaggio's paintings and *Macbeth* apart from their human authors, apart from human possibilities, apart from human action. We know, perhaps, something more about abstractions called "baroque painting" and "tragedy"; we know nothing more about what it means to be human.

My own approach to my materials places an insistent stress on the conception of the humanities as activities peculiar to human beings, activities that involve desire, intelligence, invention, imagination, and discovery—in short, human experience. These activities are fluid and capable of almost infinite nuance. The products of these activities are marked by human consciousness—that is, they are products of human agents aware of themselves as agents. Can anyone pretend to know the "field" when it is conceived in this way?

The interpretation of imaginative literature, so conceived, tells us something about the possibilities of literature. I do not recall any textbook suggesting that a novel might be an act of remorse, might be a way for a prodigal son to recognize the value of an African culture he once despised because he thought it was inferior to the culture of the Europeans who destroyed it. To see *Things Fall Apart* in this way requires us to consider it as the action of an individual writer affected in a distinctive way by a particular set of circumstances.

I maintain that much of the greatest modern literature deserves to be considered in just this way: representations meant as actions by their writers—actions that are marked by an individual perception of a situation and an individual response to it. The great writers have mastered common techniques. They may share marks of style, and they may share conceptions of subject matter, but how they deploy these common achievements and conceptions and to what purpose are what give their writings vital interest as human documents. The pre-eminent subject matter of the humanities, on this view, cannot be techniques, styles, conceptions of subject matter, or even artifacts regarded as autonomous things, but human activities. We can catalogue techniques, marks of style, and conceptions of subject matter, but the purposes, convictions, and authority that belong to individual human beings and reveal our own human possibilities must always be discovered. Discovery of this kind is the product of a reader's practical engagement with particular texts seen as the actions of their writers.

⁙ *Acknowledgments* ⁙

THE CONCEPT of a text as the act of its writer does not imply that the act in question is a solitary one. Writing this book has been a complex social activity involving the attention and talents of quite a large number of people. To name them all is impossible, but I do want to acknowledge some of those whose advice and assistance influenced this writer's writing most decisively.

Mark Turner read an earlier version of chapters two through six, urged me to add chapters one and seven, and was their original reader and unofficial editor. Wayne Booth and Robert von Hallberg read all of an earlier draft. Peter Dembowski, Gerald Graff, Frank Kinahan, Martin Meisel, Richard Strier, William Veeder, and Jane Upin read parts of a working draft. I am grateful to all of these readers, whose responses helped to shape the final version.

I appropriated, with his permission, the best phrase and most of the best ideas about intention from "Intentions and Things," an unfinished essay by the late Robert Marsh, who first started me thinking about the whole topic of agency in "literature."

One of my anonymous readers for Princeton University Press offered a shrewd assessment of my project and insightful suggestions about how to make its scope and purpose clearer. Her suggestions seemed so right and were so well expressed that I adopted almost all of them and in several cases borrowed her very words since I could not improve on them.

Lany Jansen made available to me her native competence in Dutch and her personal and professional knowledge of Dutch culture. Jude Lucier was generous with his time and his masterful command of Greek.

I had an opportunity to consider some of the relationships between literary interpretation and the interpretation of painting as a participant in a 1987 NEH Summer Seminar, "Portraiture: Biography, Portrait Painting, and the Representation of Historical Character" at Northwestern University. I want to thank Richard Wendorf, the director, who encouraged this project, and the other participants, especially Jerry Eager and David Kievitt.

ACKNOWLEDGMENTS

I am grateful to all the libraries that allowed me to use their collections and resources: the Bibliothèque d'institut pédagogique national; the Bibliothèque publique d'information; the Bibliothèque de l'institut néerlandais—whose librarian, A. van Leeuwen, found me a photocopy of H. Meidema's article from *Proef*, a publication that could not be traced by conventional methods—the Bibliothèque du musée des arts décoratifs; the incomparable Bibliothèque Nationale in Paris; the Universiteitsbibliotheek in Amsterdam; the British Library in London; Perkins Library at Duke University; the Newberry Library in Chicago; and especially the Joseph Regenstein Library and the Computing Organization Central Users Site at the University of Chicago.

I want to thank Robert E. Brown, literature editor at Princeton University Press, for his resourcefulness in handling the problems, large and small, that this project encountered from first manuscript submission to published book.

The Writer Writing

✛

The Writer Writing

Today the author is no longer in good repute. . . . Chimera,
phantom, mirage; a simple linguistic sign, a deconstructed
and rejected simulacrum which no activity, no construct, no
writing can ever bring into existence and to which criticism
wrongly attached itself in its first wanderings. . . .
(Gérard Defaux, *Montaigne: Essays in Reading*)

THE INTERPRETATION of any text is fundamentally and pervasively affected by the interpreter's concept of what a text is and how it comes to be. To have such a concept is to have a concept of literature. The interpreter may tacitly accept a conventional concept of literature and may be unaware that a choice has been made, but no concept of literature is a simple given. A concept of literature is rarely original to the interpreter, but original or conventional, commonplace or sophisticated, *some* concept of literature must serve as a foundation for any specific understanding of a text. One of the issues that such a concept resolves is the relationship between the writer and the text. There is no need to attempt to establish from historical sources that this relationship can be conceived of in many ways. All we have to do is look at contemporary rival theories actively engaged in trying to advance specific concepts of literature—usually under a special designation such as *écriture*—and we can see a respectable variety of possibilities.

Increasingly since about 1970, the theories that have received most attention in elite circles of academic discourse are those that, broadly speaking, conceive of writers as having an instrumental relationship to what they write. In these theoretical perspectives, the *agent* of the act of writing is not the writer.[1] That is why, among those who adopt such perspectives, there is so little interest in such "traditional" issues as intention and purpose.

This book is concerned with understanding texts in terms proper to their writers' intentions and in a manner that takes account of how writers' particular choices are meant to affect and exploit the ordinary

assumptions, prejudices, and knowledge of their original readers. It is an approach that embraces the fundamental and commonplace concept that people do things. In this conception of things, people are agents; when they write, their texts are actions. Although this commonplace concept applies to texts in general and is not restricted to the past, I call the concept of interpretation that follows from it "historical interpretation," as it has been called by others in the history of interpreting texts.

Historical interpretation—that is, attempts to understand a literary text by situating agency in its writer—can be seen as an antiquarian discipline by those theorists who situate agency in something more abstract, diffuse, or inaccessible than an individual writer, such as culture, class, or language itself. Theories of this sort do not, of course, bother much with the action of the writer writing. They do not assume such action to be uninteresting; they *assure* that such action is uninteresting because they have situated agency somewhere else.

If there are advantages to considering abstract or corporate agents as authors of texts, there are some disadvantages as well. These disadvantages are most evident when we are dealing with texts that are strongly original. Historical interpretation does not demonstrate its strengths in the study of texts so conventional that they might be considered conceptually derivative even if they are masterpieces, texts like "The Dead," for example, a beautifully articulated work of realistic fiction conceived in the manner of Flaubert, in contrast to *Ulysses*. Such texts might be interesting for many reasons, but they will not be interesting as the deliberate record of a human action—the action of a writer writing.

It is the special strength of historical interpretation to focus on just that action. What makes a writer's action interesting, in this perspective, is precisely that it is open. When we conceive of a writer as the agent of his text, writing a text is neither a fixed action nor a single action. It is not something we start off knowing; it is something we might end up discovering. If a writer is an agent rather than an instrument of another agent, writing itself takes on a different meaning and affects our concept of the text we are trying to interpret. There is a world of difference between seeing a text as the manifestation of a culture and seeing it as the action of an individual.

What an individual does in writing a text is not predictable. The action may be a completely conventional one. Writers sometimes imitate

other writers, or adopt their purposes, or write something that conforms to conventions established by editors. It can be a memorial action, with the purpose of fixing impressions or information. It can be a provocative action meant to create controversy or frame debate. It can be an attempt at self-definition or self-discovery.

It is, of course, true that most writers are not original even when they are accomplished. They frequently try to meet the expectations of editors, publishers, and readers. They quite often adopt subject matter, techniques of representation, and marks of style from other writers. They adopt all sorts of conventions, including conventions about their role as writers.

For example, the writer of a certain kind of troubadour poem is obliged to take on the persona of the unrequited but devoted lover. A current convention of authorship is that a story about the ordinary experience of contemporary characters needs no special justification; it is not meant to demonstrate or even illustrate any general truth; it is not meant to change the reader in any particular way; it makes no claim to illuminating something we already take to be important.

This book does not address such cases; it is about writers who have mastered conventional skills but who have not adopted conventional authorial roles. They sought to do things with their writing rather than in their writing, and the things they wanted to do were—if not completely original—at least distinctive. They were, nevertheless, accomplished masters of techniques that had been developed by other writers for other purposes. What they broke with most notably is a convention about purpose. They broke with realistic conventions in which the representation of a character's self-consciousness and dense description of physical and social setting are their own justification.

Consider for a moment one of the foundation texts of realistic fiction, *Madame Bovary*. In writing it, Flaubert practically invented the convention of authorship in which the text is self-justifying. It is a convention so widely adopted afterward that it requires an effort today to try to understand the objections of readers, such as Henry James, who complained that Emma Bovary is not a suitable heroine for a novel.[2] Even Sainte-Beuve, in a review that catalogues Flaubert's departures from conventional fiction and recognizes this novel's potential as a classic expression of a new mentality, complains that there is no justification for the remorseless detail, that Emma's experience fails to do justice to provincial life.[3]

It is, in a way, Flaubert's seriousness and effort that bother these eminent readers. Flaubert adopts a convention of responsibility to his material with a rigor that was unusual if not unprecedented for a novelist. He does not offer his reader any reason for his choice of subject. The reader who chooses to follow Flaubert in his study of provincial mores (his subtitle, *mœurs de province*, is worth remembering) is tacitly asked to treat the action of reading the text as complete in itself. It is not supposed to change in any basic way either the reader or the writer. It is considered to exist in an area of its own apart from the rest of one's life.

Madame Bovary established these conventions as norms. They have been so widely adopted that it is hard now to think of them as conventions. Flaubert spent five years writing the book; the seriousness of purpose and the application of intelligence are transparently evident, yet it is only with effort that anyone can ask today, What is the justification for all this work? Was all the skill, energy, time, and labor well spent to tell the story of a foolish woman's course of illusions? Flaubert offers no justification at all, and the whole performance discourages such questions. Flaubert engages his materials. If the reader wishes to look over his shoulder, the writer has no objection, but the writer disclaims any relationship with the reader. He suggests that he would write if no one wished to read. He refuses to recognize prevailing conventions; he refuses to acknowledge that he is violating those conventions. He is not writing *for* the reader.

It is part of Flaubert's achievement to turn us away from asking the questions that seemed to make sense to Henry James and Sainte-Beuve. Why did he choose such a person as his heroine? She is not morally serious enough to justify her role. Her *role?* we can almost hear Flaubert say indignantly. She has no role. She *is*. Flaubert does not want to be seen as choosing to follow this woman's experience; that would make him a moralist. He presents himself as a naturalist.

In many respects Marcel Proust will seem to be a writer like Flaubert. In the description of places, in the creation of a character's interior life, in his understanding of complex and irrational lines of motivation, Proust might seem to be Flaubert's successor. He went to school to Flaubert; he learned his techniques, in great part, from Flaubert. These things are the inheritance of verbal representation, refined from generation to generation. They are what make it possible to see lines of continuity from the Homeric epic to twentieth-century European fiction.

To see such continuities, however, we are obliged to assume that there is something like a literary providence that subsumes the purposes of individual writers. In the most famous and perhaps most detailed of all articulations of these lines of continuity, Erich Auerbach's *Mimesis*, there is really no place to consider the actions of individual writers as such. *Madame Bovary* marks a point in the progress of the "impulse of style," whose purpose is to represent reality in Western Literature. The writers Auerbach discusses—and this selection is a self-conscious canon, a secular Old Testament assembled in Istanbul during what Auerbach thought was the destruction of European culture—are privileged participants in a superhuman movement, a line traced by the impulse of style whose text is a work of History and only in the most superficial sense the works of individuals. The agent at work here, the impulse of style, is a Historical agent dignified by purposes beyond the powers and conceptual range of individual writers, an agent unconstrained by human purposes or human follies.

Auerbach does not present himself as a theorist; he does not discuss agency, he simply proceeds on the assumption that the impulse of style is the agent not of individual texts exactly, but of the great composite text called Western Literature, something that subsumes individual texts and gives them a dignified and almost transcendent purpose. With respect to Flaubert and *Madame Bovary*, Auerbach can be seen to provide an answer to James and Sainte-Beuve, who were too close to Flaubert's text to see that it accepted a legacy from Balzac and Stendhal, advanced it, and passed it on to Proust and Virginia Woolf.

I do not mean to deny for a moment that *Mimesis* is, in one sense, a work of historical interpretation, but the concept of history and the concept of agency it assumes are Romantic versions of medieval concepts, closer to the thought of someone like Augustine than to the beginnings of historical interpretation as humanist historians understood the term. Auerbach addresses a composite work effected by the impulse of style; this composite work is almost a secular reflection of the medieval conception of Scripture conceived as a unified work whose concepts must be consistent from book to book, whose author is divine. The distinctive—and contrasting—mark of humanist history is the idea that history is about the actions of human beings. It is a

7

concept Spinoza wanted to apply to the understanding of Scripture when he suggested that the sacred canon ought to be interpreted "in the light of its history."[4]

Spinoza was objecting to the practice of taking a word or concept in a canonical book of Scripture and glossing it by reference to what the interpreter thinks is reasonable, orthodox, or true. When Spinoza says that a text ought to be interpreted in the light of its history, he is thinking about "history" as the understanding of specifically human actions understood in the same way that the human agents who performed them understood them, as things individual people do in human time. The "action" of language, culture, the subconscious—when these are (metaphorically) conceived as agents—are not the actions of individuals and do not take place in human time. They are not historical because they are inhuman—superhuman, if you like—and timeless. They are not historical for a second reason as well: they cannot be documented.

When Auerbach ascribes a common purpose to Western Literature, even one so broad as "the representation of reality," he subsumes the actions of the writers whose texts he discusses to a particular concept of literature. For some of these writers, such as Flaubert, this concept is at least broadly appropriate. It is a concept congruent with Flaubert's claim of being transparent. Auerbach's concept of literature has touches of the sublime; it envisions writers as instruments of "the impulse of style" engaged in a work that transcends the time scale of an individual life, a generation, even a civilization. Its romantic medieval aspects make it tacitly antagonistic to the humanist concept of history that shifts agency from superhuman or subhuman forces to human beings themselves. Flaubert is equally hostile to humanist concepts, but not because he envisions the sublime actions of benevolent impulses. His characters rarely have the moral strength to be much more than passive victims of social, political, or perhaps natural forces.

Flaubert shares with Auerbach a concept of literature that removes it from what we might call the writer's engagement with practical activities. In Auerbach's case that is because literature is the work of an abstract force engaged in a task that transcends the engagements of individual writers. In Flaubert's case, it is simply because he does not envision writing as a way of engaging the practical world, literature is a retreat from the world. Its virtue is exact observation of precisely what Flaubert hates but cannot imagine that anything—certainly not writing—will change. For both Auerbach and Flaubert, although for different reasons, the writing of imaginative literature is something apart from other human activities that cannot be understood adequately by applying conventional concepts of action; it requires a theory that removes it from ordinary human action, even from other kinds of writing.

Concepts of literature that create a special and separate space for at least some kinds of writing (outside of sacred canons) were never widely accepted in Europe until the nineteenth century. Once such concepts were widely accepted, a fissure was created between practical writing and literature. Any writing that was meant to move readers to particular actions, any writing meant to bring about practical effects was not "literature" but, at best, "rhetoric," at worst, "propaganda."

With conventions of this sort well established, the careers of Bernard Shaw and Marcel Proust, the two writers on whom I focus in my examination of the concept of writing as a writer's action, unfolded. Among writers after 1880 who have achieved canonical status, Shaw is unusual because he is so articulate and unrelenting in his claims that his art is fundamentally "rhetorical." He does not hesitate to call it propaganda, and he adds that all great art is propaganda. He is not in the least shy or ambiguous in claiming that he wrote precisely to move his readers to definite and particular actions. He is unambiguously a moralist who disdains any relationship to Flaubert's concept of literature. He is not included in Auerbach's canon, but he would have heaped scorn on the idea that he is the instrument of anything like the impulse of style or that his plays are to be understood as aspiring to represent reality. To the degree that Shaw represents "reality," it is for the purpose of changing it. He conceives of literature not as a retreat from life but as an engagement with life—and he is concerned not primarily with private experience but with the organized life of social and economic communities on the scale of nations.

It would not be hard to find writers among Shaw's contemporaries with similar ideas, but few of them expressed their thoughts in traditional art forms such as drama, and none of the others won acceptance as a major figure within such forms.[5] Drama critics and academic writers have always carped a great deal about Shaw's plays because they fit current conventions about "art" so badly. But Shaw's plays cannot be dismissed even by critics who don't like them. Shaw has won a large *readership*, a most unusual achievement for a playwright. His plays held the stage too; they include characters that have entered both popular culture and the literary pantheon: Barbara, Joan, Eliza Doolittle, Professor Higgins.

Shaw has inspired a number of prominent critics, some of whom I cite in chapter five, to attempt to save his plays from their author. Against his vociferous, insistent, unmistakably clear, and lifelong objections, they have persisted in trying to accommodate his dramatic achievements to their own concepts of art. They do not deny his quality as a dramatist, but they cannot accommodate such quality to a concept of literature that envisions writing as a practical activity, a serious effort to change the way people think and act. For most of them, to recognize Shaw's action—as opposed to the plays, regarded as artifacts to be considered apart from his action—compromises the plays.

These attempts by critics to overrule the author have been largely successful and were probably necessary to establish Shaw's place in the dramatic canon. For a dramatist of his power and energy, he had an extraordinarily difficult time getting his plays produced. It is only because generations of critics insisted on misunderstanding him and found ways to twist his texts into something sufficiently close to their idea of acceptably disengaged and suitably impractical "art" that he was dragged into the canon, albeit kicking and screaming. His canonization is closely analogous to what happens to great religious painting when it is secularized by museums, especially museums founded by states ideologically hostile to religion: it was the French revolutionary government that established the museum of the Louvre and appropriated, for example, Jan van Eyck's *Virgin of Autun* and Philippe de Champaigne's *Ex-Voto of 1662* for its collection.

I do not mean that Shaw objected to being canonized. He objected to having the status of his work changed, to having his plays systematically distorted by concepts of art hostile to his own. He resisted the conventions we associate with his time and did everything he could to make himself understood as a dramatist in the tradition of something like Old Comedy, closer to Aristophanes than to, let us say, Sean O'Casey or even Oscar Wilde. He conceived of his plays not merely in a certain social and political context but as answers to social and political questions.

The English philosopher and historian R. G. Collingwood expresses a fundamental principle of historical interpretation whose application prevents just the sort of systematic distortion under discussion here.

you cannot find out what a man means by simply studying his spoken or written statements, even though he has spoken or written
with perfect command of the language and perfectly truthful intention. In order to find out his meaning you must also know what the
question was (a question in his own mind, and presumed by him to
be in yours) to which the thing he has said or written was meant as
an answer.... A highly detailed and particularized proposition must
be the answer, not to a vague and generalized question, but to a
question as detailed and particularized as itself.[6]

To understand a text in this way, of course, assumes the traditional
and commonplace concept of agency. Collingwood makes this remark
in a passage that describes his concept of historical understanding. It
is a twentieth-century restatement of Spinoza's suggestion that Scripture be interpreted "in the light of its history" made general for all
texts. Neither Spinoza nor Collingwood is talking about knowing
what is sometimes called "historical background"; they are not talking
about information arbitrarily extrinsic to the text. They are talking
about information needed to understand what sort of thing the text is.
Both assume that there is nothing in the "nature" of a text that can tell
us what sort of thing it is, and that the writer determines what sort of
thing it is. If the writer conceives of a text as an answer to a question,
then the interpreter must know that and must know the question as
well in order to achieve "historical" understanding.

The force of the term *historical* here and in the associated concept of
"historical interpretation" goes back to the fifteenth-century humanist
historians who reoriented history away from sacred or natural forces
and redefined its agents as people.[7] People do things; history is understanding the things people do; one of the things people do is write.
To interpret the resulting texts "historically," the interpreter must
conceive of them as things writers have done. If a writer conceives of
a text as the answer to a question, then for the historical interpreter,
it *is* the answer to a question; what the writer has *done* is answer a
question—the writer's question, not the interpreter's.

Shaw is probably close to the limiting case of a writer whose work
can be accepted as great art according to concepts of art contemporary
with it but hostile to his purposes for it and to his informing intention.
The play that convinced many of his contemporary dissenters that
Shaw is really a great artist in spite of himself is *Saint Joan*. It is not

hard to see why. *Saint Joan* requires relatively little change to make it the kind of play Shaw's critics prefer to the ones he wrote. It owes its acceptance to the relative ease with which it can be misunderstood.

If we take all his writing into account, it is easy to see that Shaw's concept of dramatic art is very different from those of almost all of his contemporary playwrights and drama critics. Unlike *Saint Joan*, most of his plays cannot easily be accommodated to the period's more conventional concepts of dramatic art, and Shaw himself is exceptionally articulate and insistent on the subject. It is easy to understand why some of the early New Critics wanted to ignore everything but the writer's text. Perhaps, as Collingwood says, you "cannot know what a man means" if you restrict your field of evidence this way, but those critics really did not want to know what people like Shaw meant. The leading New Critical theorists diffused portentous statements asserting that what writers say outside their texts—and what they *do* inside them as well—is irrelevant to interpretation. To fit *Saint Joan* into *their* canon required dealing with a writer who tried very hard to prevent it. I suspect Shaw owes his place in the canon partly to the dearth of great dramatic literature in English in this century. There were slots to fill in textbooks and course outlines.

Marcel Proust is much easier to accommodate to the concepts of literary art that were firmly in place when *A la recherche du temps perdu* finally found a (subsidized) publisher, but to do so requires a similar determination to ignore what the writer says about his own conception of his text as a way of solving a problem. Proust's concept of literary art has surprisingly little in common with Flaubert's and a great deal in common with Shaw's.

Proust has been widely accepted as a great writer, and he quite clearly is a technical virtuoso, but, seen as a whole, his fiction is instrumental in much the same way that Shaw's drama is instrumental. He shares with Shaw an attitude that writing is not detached observation; it is neither a retreat nor a consolation; it is not something separated from the rest of life. It is an active engagement with life. Like Shaw, Proust means to change what he finds unacceptable; what he finds unacceptable is not, however, social and economic structures, but the self he has become.

There is a sense in which Proust is bolder and more optimistic than Shaw. Yeats's image of Shaw as a perpetually smiling machine is not one we associate with Proust, whose icon is the languid young man leaning on a sofa. There is a Victorian briskness and vigor in Shaw's fantastic project of talking and writing a diseased and degenerate capitalist society into hygienic socialism; a morbid Christianity into the life-affirming religion of creative evolution, and a cockeyed democracy into the clear-sighted rule of the capable. His project is so obviously impossible to most of his critics that they cannot take it seriously, and so they have decided to do a talented writer a good turn and pretend that he did not take it seriously either.

Shaw's large and eccentric claims for what can be expected from writing are no more extravagant, however, than Proust's. The languid young man leaning on a sofa is really a very poor icon for Proust. As a writer, he is ambitious and energetic. He was no more a tepid reformer than was Shaw, and he expected the act of writing to do quite remarkable things, things very few other people ever thought writing can do. The difference between Proust and Shaw is not so much in their view of writing—a practical and instrumental activity impossible to separate from the great engagements of life—or the scale of their expectations as writers but in the locus of their activity. Shaw looked outward to the political and economic structure of society; Proust looked inward to the psychological and intellectual structure of the self.

Writing is, for each of these ambitious dissenters from contemporary conceptions of art, the point at which they engage problems. They engage different sorts of problems, but they expect results. They cannot hold the conception of writing that they do and adopt the role of a writer like Flaubert, who sees himself as transparent. Compared to almost any of his contemporary dramatists, Shaw will seem intrusive. His plays are accused of being "explanatory" and undramatic. The second half of that charge is especially interesting given Shaw's frequently demonstrated ability successfully to dramatize the most unlikely subjects: phonetics, for example. Compared to almost any novelist active between 1890 and 1914, Proust too will seem intrusive; his commentary is, like Shaw's, apt to draw upon academic subjects. He is never content simply to record or represent; he records the way a diagnostician records, first to explain a condition and then to cure it.

Once we see how similar these two writers are at a fundamental level—their sense that writing is an effective way to engage life, to solve human problems—many of the surface differences that normally prevent us from thinking about their similarities can be seen to result from the institutions of literary criticism, whose taxonomies make these writers seem very different. We can begin with simple differences: one is a dramatist, one a novelist. One is overtly "rhetorical," the other lyric, introspective, "poetic." In subject matter Shaw is political and outward looking; Proust is self-involved and nonpolitical.

Proust is easier to assimilate to current critical categories than Shaw, but the basic means of assimilating either is the same. It amounts to systematically severing the connections each of these writers articulated between his writing and the role that writing played in the solution of carefully conceived problems. It flies in the face of current critical categories to say that Proust has more in common with Shaw than he does with Flaubert, but once we get past the surface and take someone like Collingwood seriously, we can see a great division between a writer who means his text to be seen as a way to solve a problem and a writer who wants to record a set of careful observations without conceiving them as "responsive" in this way.

For Proust, as for Shaw, writing is part of a strategy, but it does not make much sense to talk about Flaubert's "strategy" in writing *Madame Bovary*. He did not conceive of it as instrumental to the achievement of any practical end. He was not trying to subvert the values of the French bourgeoisie—the idea that moved the government to bring legal charges against him and his publisher. It is true that he despised bourgeois values and the mentality of those who lived by them, but he did not for a moment think that his novel was going to change them, nor did he write it in the forlorn hope that it would do so. This is one reason that he merely presents Emma's unhappiness and does not try to account for it. There are moments when he touches on subjects that Proust will treat too: at Vaubyessard, for example, where Emma's eyes "come back of themselves to this old man with the hanging lips." Emma sees something very different from the old duc de Laverdière dribbling sauce on the napkin tied round his neck like a child's bib. It is as if this old wreck who had squandered his fortune in debauchery were something remarkable and attractive. "He had lived at Court and slept in the bed of queens!"[8]

Consider how similar this skewed perception of Emma's is to the Narrator's in *A la recherche du temps perdu* as he tries to turn contemporary degenerate aristocrats into the artifacts of the middle ages come to life. But Emma's perceptions are not errors to be accounted for, and they are certainly not errors to be overcome. They are not "experimental" in the way the Narrator's are; they are not "useful"; they are not the data one analyses to arrive at the sort of knowledge that leads to change.

Flaubert has a concept of writing that discloses what amounts to detached observations; Proust, like Shaw, wants to announce a discovery, not as a detached observation but as a form of knowledge that, if acted upon, will bring change in human circumstances. The difference between Flaubert's concept of writing, on the one hand, and Proust's and Shaw's, on the other, is like the difference between knowledge in the sense of formal mathematics—something that exists in a self-contained world that has no direct reference to the conduct of human life—and knowledge in the sense of economics or neurophysiology—something pursued in the first place because it will be able to affect the conduct of human life.

There are differences, then, in the concept of writing, in motive, in expectation. Since both Proust and Shaw resisted the conventions of writing that Flaubert helped to establish, since they wanted to be regarded as in some sense "scientists," by which they mean people who possess knowledge that can bring about practical consequences, they each adopt a kind of scientific costume that calls attention to a relationship between what they do as writers and actually existing forms of knowledge.

What I call Proust's and Shaw's "scientific costumes" are an important element of their "intrusiveness" as seen from the conventions of disengaged and impractical art. It has been deplored, in Shaw's case, as self-indulgent crankiness; in Proust's case it has been ignored where possible and treated as original thought expressed in an unconventional form where it cannot be ignored.

The "costumes" take the form of what I call parodies of disciplines, in the first instance, and paradigms of explanation in the second. I attach a meaning to the word parody that is a little unusual. I mean that both Shaw and Proust borrow the protocol of actual academic or scientific disciplines in the works I discuss—evidently for purposes different from those of the disciplines' regularly accredited practitioners.

They have borrowed these protocols for complex reasons, but one of those reasons is to establish their texts' relationship to problems that they want to address in the manner that the disciplines they borrow from address *their* problems. For both writers, this means addressing a problem with a view to solving it and affecting some important area

15

of life outside of their texts. Shaw, a more theatrical writer, poses as a historian in *Saint Joan*. It ought to be evident that he is not actually addressing properly historical questions by properly historical methods. He expects questions to be raised about why he presents himself as a historian, why he claims to give an explanation of Joan's failure, why he mimics a particular paradigm of historical explanation in doing so. He is, as always, serious about something and trying to offer a genuine explanation, although it is not about Joan of Arc.

Proust borrows the protocol of a now-obsolete concept of psychology in *La recherche*, and his Narrator is not a mere commentator on his earlier self but a systematic one. The narrative itself is shaped according to a borrowed paradigm of psychological explanation, and it is meant not merely to account for a transformation in the Narrator but to be a kind of scientific demonstration of a principle that can be applied to lives outside the pages of his text, beginning with his own.

Both Shaw and Proust wanted to connect their writing with what they conceived to be the proper work of science. Neither of them was especially interested in abstract knowledge; they shared a notion of useful knowledge. The problems that engaged them were problems they thought could be solved, and each came to see the solution to these problems as the purpose of his activity as a writer. When we examine their conceptions of writing, it will be important to see first of all that each of the texts under consideration is formally an explanation, that the models of explanation really belong to contemporary concepts of history and psychology respectively, and that these explanations are purposeful—although they do not have the same purpose they would in the literature proper to the disciplines in question.

In examining how Shaw and Proust conceived of their activity as writers, what sort of questions they raised, what constituted an answer, and how this activity fit into the model of knowledge they adapted from contemporary intellectual disciplines, we will also see how and why they adopted the roles they did with respect to their writing. In doing so, we will learn something about what happens when we accept conventional categories that do not take into account these aspects of writers' concepts of what writing is. Shaw and Proust have each inspired a very large bibliography of secondary works; each has received a great deal of critical and scholarly attention. I am not aware, however, that they have ever been examined together, or that any academic critic has ever suggested they have anything significant in common.

This is partly because we have been encouraged by critical convention to neglect the sort of commonplace considerations that Collingwood advanced. We have not been encouraged to interpret literary texts "in the light of their history," we have not typically tried to see whether literary texts should be seen as part of a strategy, as answers to questions, as ways of solving problems, as an activity chosen by the writer. We have been much more likely to accommodate the texts we admire to critical conceptions that regard all such considerations as irrelevant to the nature of texts, to the nature of writing. One result of disregarding the writers' conception of writing, in the case of the two writers with whom I am mainly concerned, is the difficulty we ordinarily have in even remembering that they are contemporaries. Someone fluent in both French and English might have read *Du Côté du chez Swann* as a new book and seen a performance of the first London production of *Pygmalion* in the same year; even someone who could read English but not French might have read the first English translation of *A la recherche du temps perdu* and the text of *Saint Joan* as new books simultaneously.

Louise Brooks, the silent film actress whose performance as Lulu in G. W. Pabst's *Die Büchse der Pandora* (1929) is often regarded as classic, read and admired both Shaw and Proust. Her biographer mentions them together with Goethe and James as writers "in whose works she found keys to her own life and family."[9] Consider how odd Shaw seems in that company today, how naive her reason for linking these four writers seems. Louise Brooks is an example of a naive reader who could and did read both Shaw and Proust as contemporaries in the hope of better understanding her own life and family. This sort of assistance is not, of course, what academic critics are likely to seek from canonized writers today, but Louise Brooks's expectations were more congruent with these writers' concepts of what they were doing than are those of many contemporary critics. Shaw and Proust seemed to her to have affinities precisely because she assumed they wrote texts to assist readers who sought to understand themselves and their families—texts, in other words, that addressed problems of general human interest, texts meant to be useful in intellectual and psychological discovery. As criticism has moved further and further away from concepts of literary art that might include such purposes, as the very concept of purpose as it applies to individual writers has lost its place in literary interpretation, these writers have ceased to present any affinities to sophisticated readers. They seem to belong to separate worlds.

The naive insights of readers such as Louise Brooks deserve and have begun to receive scholarly attention. Despite the suggestion of a great deal of recent theory that naive ideas about texts as a writer's action ought to be superseded even when these ideas are held by writers themselves, these ideas are widely held by nonacademic readers. There is recent precedent in scholarship for seeing what happens when such naive insights are treated with scholarly precision and rigor. In *Renaissance Self-Fashioning* (1980), Stephen Greenblatt gathers under the rubric of self-fashioning such writers as Thomas More and Edmund Spenser, writers nearly as far apart when seen from the point of view of conventional literary taxonomies as Bernard Shaw and Marcel Proust. The concept of self-fashioning makes sense not only to Greenblatt but also to the sixteenth-century writers he discusses; moreover, it is precisely a human purpose. It is an activity. This is a traditional topic that—special theories of epochal agency aside—suggests that writers are agents, that their texts, if we want to understand them in the light of their history, are actions. Since this is the way I proceed here, it is important to take a fresh look at two fundamental and related concepts: intention and purpose. It is impossible to understand human action—textual or other—without them.

'Intentions' and 'Purposes'

> ... the design or intention of the author is neither
> available nor desirable as a standard for judging the
> success of a work of literary art.
> (W. K. Wimsatt, Jr. and Monroe C. Beardsley,
> "The Intentional Fallacy")

> The interpreter who rejects intention is forced covertly to
> supply an informing principle analogous to it in order to
> make coherent interpretation ... possible. ... Intention is
> unavoidable. The only question is whether we use the
> artist's intention or supply one of our own.
> (Walter A. Davis, *Theories of Form in Modern Criticism*)

INTERPRETATION AND ACTIONS

THIS BOOK BEGAN with an image of the writer writing, an icon for a concept of literature based on a commonplace concept of human action. It is a concept of literature that situates agency in an individual human being. Texts, in this perspective, are the actions of individual writers. They can be understood in the same way that we understand other human actions undertaken by individuals. Writing, looked upon in this way, is one of a range of things that people do. It is better documented than many other human activities, but it is not isolated from them. On the contrary, writing can be affected by other human actions in any number of ways and can in turn affect them in ways limited only by the writer's skill and imagination.

In chapter one, this concept of a text as a human action was juxtaposed with concepts of literature that situate agency somewhere else, making the writer the instrument of an abstract or impersonal agent such as style, language, or culture. These concepts of literature are not based on commonplace concepts and, for that very reason, do not reflect common experience; they are based on special theories that supersede commonplace concepts and remove literature from the normal range of individual human action. What critics see in these special perspectives requires a theory to be seen at all. "Western literature" taken as a single text governed by a single purpose chosen by no individual writer, for example, is inaccessible to ordinary experience shaped by commonplace concepts. The theories that allow access to sophisticated concepts of literature beyond the scope of the commonplace concept of individual agency often find it necessary to introduce impersonal agents and, to a greater or lesser degree, as a consequence, to isolate writing from human action, placing it in a special category of its own. This chapter is a synopsis of such theory-based concepts of literature and the inadequacies of the kinds of interpretation they warrant.

In some cases the replacement of commonplace concepts with specialized theory is straightforward and obvious. The original New Critics, for example, advanced theories about "the language of poetry" that allowed them to draw distinctions between imaginative literature and other kinds of writing. Poetic language, for example, is ironic and ambiguous by nature, not because a particular writer wrote in an ironic or ambiguous manner. We can know that we are dealing with poetry—and not some other kind of writing—by asking if its language is ironic and ambiguous. This is a question about language conceived as something essentially unconnected to an individual writer's action. The language of poetry is *always* ironic and ambiguous no matter what an individual writer does. This is why New Critics regard literary texts as autonomous. These New Critical concepts of poetic language and autonomous texts are, then, explicit parts of an explicit theory of literature.

Interpretation always depends on some concept of literature, but not every such concept is theory-based, even after we take into account those based on an implicit theory. The distinction between theory-based and commonplace concepts of literature is important because our concept of what a text is and how it comes to be affects what we mean by interpretation and tells us what kinds of issues are relevant to interpretation. When Wimsatt and Beardsley proclaimed the intentional fallacy, they spoke as if there were a single conception of literature, the one based on the New Critical theory of poetic language that led to the concept of autonomous texts. Their successors, the Deconstructionists, see more clearly than they did that the author, in such a theoretical perspective, cannot be equated with the writer. The poem writes itself, so to speak. Intention belongs to the language because, in the theoretical perspective of both the New Critics and the Deconstructionists, that is where agency is situated; it is not an issue for them since the intention of the language (to be poetic) is the same in every literary text. The writer's intention is both inaccessible and irrelevant since it leaves no trace in what he writes.

What Wimsatt and Beardsley say about intention is limited to a particular group of conceptions of literature grounded in theories that relegate individual writers to instrumental roles and locate agency somewhere else. Language, style, history (in the Hegelian sense, in which it has a will of its own), culture, archetypal forms, and human nature (variously conceived) have each replaced individual writers as the locus of agency in theoretical conceptions of literature advanced since the eighteenth century.

In any of these conceptions of literature interpretation means looking at the text in the context of its agent. If agency is in the language, for example, then we will have to know the character of the language. When we know the character of the language, we will naturally find that character in every literary text.

Not all theories that warrant concepts of literature are, like those of the New Critics and the Deconstructionists, explicit. Quite often in critical practice the theories are implicit, but they are no less controlling. Even critics who *never* directly discuss theoretical issues can practice interpretation that depends upon an implicit theory. Someone as temperamentally "empirical" as Samuel Johnson, who, Boswell relates, refuted Bishop Berkeley's "ingenious sophistry to prove the nonexistence of matter, and that everything in the universe is merely ideal ... [by] striking his foot with mighty force against a large stone, till he rebounded from it,"[1] can be shown to hold a theory-based concept of literature.

In the *Preface to Shakespeare* (1765), Johnson explains that various "faults" in Shakespeare's plays are to be understood not as things for which Shakespeare is responsible but as indications of the "barbarity" of the age in which he lived. But then he considers a more serious charge: "[Shakespeare] seems to write without any moral purpose. . . . This fault the barbarity of his age cannot extenuate; for it is always a writer's duty to make the world better. . . . [The] greatest graces of a play . . . [are] to copy nature and instruct life."[2] How does Johnson know that no matter what else writers do they are obliged *as writers* to make the world better? How does he know that it is possible to make the world better by writing plays?

The answer to questions of this sort is that Johnson's judgments are

21

based on an implicit theory that warrants his knowledge of the nature and value of literature. It is true that this example involves a question of evaluation, but for a critic like Johnson it is unintelligible to talk about having a knowledge of literature apart from a knowledge of morality and impossible to "interpret" a work of literature without making a value judgment.

Johnson's implicit theory regards literature—all of it—as primarily a kind of action with a universal purpose, not one chosen by an individual writer. Because Johnson begins the act of interpretation with this knowledge, "interpretation" and "evaluation" are no more distinct for him than the "text" and the "interpretation" are for Deconstructionists.

The fact that most critics, even such unsystematic ones as Johnson, can be shown to make tacit reference to theory has led some scholars to affirm that the terms and concepts used by *all* critics of whatever sort are, without exception, derived from "theory." There is, on this view, no such thing as interpreting a text without recourse to theory of some sort—whether the interpreter realizes it or not. Accordingly, all of the knowledge that results from interpretation ultimately is warranted by theory.

This view finally rests on the claim that theory is inevitable because there simply is no realistic alternative. The only alternative, according to the usual formula, is to approach our texts with a tabula rasa and to confront every text as a thing absolutely unique and, therefore, absolutely unintelligible. But claims of this sort ignore an obvious and much less drastic alternative to "inevitable theory."

We cannot, of course, come to a text with a blank mind, but neither do we need to know anything more about a text than that someone has written it, and in order to know that we do not need a theory. All we need is the commonplace concept of human action according to which people do things. It is quite possible to understand a text it as something "done" rather than something "natural." We can, in other words, proceed on the commonplace concept that there is a relation of identity between the writer's action and the "text." If we choose to regard the text as the writer's action, we will address a historical rather than a natural phenomenon. The choice has consequences for the diversity of things we can see writers do.

A discipline of interpretation that is "theory-free" in the sense that it depends on a commonplace concept rather than a specialized theory can do no more at the outset than designate its objects precisely because it has no way of knowing its objects' specific characteristics prior to the act of interpretation. If we interpret a text as an act performed by its writer we cannot know, for example, that the text is ambiguous or ironic or unrelated to practical concerns before we have interpreted it. We cannot know what the writer's act *is* at the outset. In this way of regarding a text, interpretation is an inquiry into a person's action.

"Theory-based" disciplines of interpretation are different. They begin by knowing something specific and essential about the nature of what is to be interpreted. Consider that whenever a traditional designation such as "tragedy" or "comedy" or "novel" is given a substantial definition—not a merely conventional one—the knowledge that the definition represents has nothing to do with an individual writer's action.

There is no difference in principle between Samuel Johnson's designation of Shakespeare's faults warranted by a theoretical moral purpose for all "writing" and the large number of critical works claiming that restricted categories of writing, let us say novels, have essential properties in common regardless of what the individuals who wrote them thought they were doing. For certain kinds of genre critics, *Lolita* is more like *Tom Jones* than it is like the *Mémoires* of the Cardinal de Retz because the designation "novel" is not just a cataloguer's convenience; it really means something. Such critics do not have to consult historical evidence about what Nabokov, Fielding, and the Cardinal de Retz were doing. What they were doing as individuals is irrelevant; what they were doing as writers *of novels* is already known because as writers they are instruments of another agent, the generic form itself. We need a theory to tell us that writers are instruments of forms. We need a theory to tell us that writing a novel is not an ordinary human action that we can hope to understand through our commonplace concepts.

Claims like these cannot be made part of an interpreter's equipment except on the warrant of a theory, since it is impossible to begin with what, in the absence of a theory, we can know only after we have completed our interpretation. But an interpreter so equipped rarely claims to interpret actions. If he does, they are not actions whose ends are within the range of an individual's choice. They are rather like the action of making the world better, which according to Johnson's tacit theory all writers are obliged to perform. That is why, in this perspective, it is irrelevant to refer to the commonplace concept of human agency.

When a discipline of interpretation makes intention "fallacious," then it may be true that it will require an analogous principle to make interpretation possible, but the principle need not be one that applies to an *individual* writer or an *individual* text as such. It may apply to a text only insofar as the text belongs to a "class" of texts.

Whenever the intentions of individuals are replaced by concepts of genre or form, a particular text need not be what it is because the person who wrote it made it to be such. It may be what it is because of the properties of the class to which it belongs, not conventionally, but essentially. In such cases, both the class and its properties must be knowable by reference to a theory, for they are not perceivable by ordinary "empirical" means. On such a view, when critics go wrong it is because they are mistaken about the class to which a text properly belongs. For, if agency is situated in genre, putting a text into the proper class *is* interpretation.

Whether interpretation is warranted by theory is a crux that every specific discipline of interpretation must face because "interpretation" will mean drastically different things in each alternative. If we take the position that literature means "texts" that come into being and are actually caused to be what they are by the actions that specific individuals chose to do, there is no need to have recourse to theory for interpretation to be possible. The interpretation of a text depends upon ordinary historiographic methods whose warrant is our commonplace concept of human action: People do things that they choose to do. From this perspective Flaubert is not obliged to make the world better when he writes *Madame Bovary*; Shaw is free to attempt to convert Great Britain to Fabian Socialism and the religion of Creative Evolution by writing plays about imaginary teachers of speech and historical warrior saints; Proust can try to replace his past by writing about how his Narrator became a writer; and Chinua Achebe can perform an act of atonement to his own African heritage by writing about the destruction of traditional tribal life.

If, on the other hand, we take literature to be a natural product of the human imagination, for example, we *must* have recourse to theory since without it we can never come to know what all literary art has in common as such. Neither can we know that literature is a natural product unless we replace our commonplace concept of action with something else—a theoretical concept that removes literary texts from the category of things people do. In this perspective, of course, we find that the enterprises described above, if these are the things that Shaw,

Proust, and Achebe set out to do, are impossible. Instead these writers, like all other writers, have reflected a certain archetype or were the occasion of the language engaged in an inevitable slippage of signification, or of the impulse of style refining its representation of reality, or of the embodiment of a form. In short, the acts performed in literature are the acts not of individual writers but of language, culture, archetypes, or Hegelian impulses.[3] What is involved is a choice of assumptions. We must make one; there is no logical or empirical basis on which to choose.

In recent years nearly all of the most prestigious academic critics who address modern texts have adopted specialized concepts of literature that supersede commonplace concepts. In one way or another most have come to agree that individual writers' intentions are unknowable, irrelevant, or both, and that a special theory about the nature of language, the nature of culture, the nature of history, or of human nature itself is a necessary preliminary to interpretation. How it came to be accepted so widely that it is easier to know human nature or one of its analogues—such as the nature of language—than it is to know an individual's intention, I cannot explain. It is, however, easy to see the generalizing power of the disciplines of interpretation warranted by theory, and that power is one of their most attractive qualities.

Without the warrant of a theory, critics seem to face chaos. Imagine the difficulty of trying to generalize the intentions of individuals who write books by taking up specific cases. Consider how many writers make claims that would test our ingenuity and stamina if we felt bound to consider them. How can we know that Achebe is telling the truth when he says that *Things Fall Apart* is an act of atonement? What does it tell us about "literature" (or novels, or colonial novels) if we determine that the statement is true?

Faced with apparently hopeless diversity, there is charm in the idea that the writer and her "intentions" have no effect on the finished work of literature—which should be regarded as autonomous and essentially caused by principles more permanent and more universal than the private, provincial, eccentric, childish, or mad "intentions" of every individual who ever took pen to paper. Unfortunately, like so many other charming things, these "autonomous" texts are deceptive. To free ourselves from writers we must bind ourselves to a theory of literature at the least and, quite often, to theories of culture, style, history, language, and human nature as well. There are temperaments that find this situation preferable to dealing with writers, but it is an overstatement of the case to claim that what is preferable to some is necessary to all.

It is not only unnecessary, it is impoverishing. Theories take a terrible toll of writers' originality by making purposes universal for all literature or for a certain class of literature. Many of the theories I have referred to would make it impossible for Shaw and Proust to write plays and novels that explain the way institutions or individuals change. Some of them would say that Shaw and Proust do the same thing as one another and the same thing that every other writer does. This sounds unlikely on its face.

Like many other writers, Shaw and Proust regard what they *do* in writing—or sometimes by means of writing—as essential to their art. Categorically to dismiss such claims as private illusions on the strength of a theory seems to border on superbity and has the unhappy consequence of making what such writers claim to have done inaccessible. To insist that the text is "autonomous" and consequently to declare the writer's act irrelevant can mean refusing to read the *writer's* text altogether.

Let us consider an example of how the writer's text can depend on his sense of what he does. Jorge Luis Borges presents what seems to be an extravagant and paradoxical case of this kind in "Pierre Ménard, Autor del Quijote." In this story Ménard's career as a writer is crowned by a singular achievement, the partial writing of *Don Quijote.*

> He did not want to compose another *Don Quijote*—which would be easy—but *the Don Quijote.* It is unnecessary to add that his aim was never to produce a mechanical transcription of the original; he did not propose to copy it. His admirable ambition was to produce pages which would coincide—word for word and line for line—with those of Miguel de Cervantes.

Ménard's task, "complex in the extreme and futile from the outset," results in a "fragmentary *Don Quijote* . . . more subtle than that of Cervantes."

> It is a revelation to compare [them]. The latter, for instance wrote (*Don Quijote*, Part One, Chapter Nine):
>
> > . . . truth, whose mother is history, who is the rival of time, depository of deeds, witness of the past, example and lesson to the present, and warning to the future.

Written in the seventeenth century, written by the "ingenious lay-man" Cervantes, this enumeration is a mere rhetorical eulogy of history. Ménard, on the other hand, writes:

> ... truth, whose mother is history, who is the rival of time, depository of deeds, witness of the past, example and lesson to the present, and warning to the future.

History, *mother* of truth; the idea is astounding. Ménard, a contemporary of William James, does not define history as an investigation of reality, but as its origin. Historical truth, for him, is not what took place; it is what we think took place. The final clauses—*example and lesson to the present, and warning* to the future—are shamelessly pragmatic.[4]

Since the words are the same, only the design and intention of the author—Ménard—allow us to understand that his book is subtler and more astonishing than Cervantes's. Indeed, without access to his design and intention we could have no access to his action of writing *Don Quijote*. We could not know that *his* book exists at all.

The case is extravagant and paradoxical only because of the weirdness of Pierre Ménard's project. Any "admirable ambition" or individually selected purpose—Flaubert's , Shaw's, Proust's, Achebe's—will be subsumed by a universal or generic purpose that makes an individual's action as invisible as Ménard's unless writing is conceived as an action performed by an individual in the first place. Another contemporary of William James—his brother Henry—maintains that, of all the things we do, writing is the thing most "done." A literary act, in Henry James's formulation, is "conduct with a vengeance, since it is conduct minutely and publicly attested."[5]

As long as we forgo theories that deprive writers of their presumptive role as causes of their books, we will need to know their designs and intentions—their admirable ambitions—not to make interpretation possible, but to be able to interpret the right object.

INTENTION AND HISTORICAL INTERPRETATION

If we are willing to consider a text as its author's "conduct minutely and publicly attested," we cannot avoid being concerned with that author's intentions and very likely with her purposes as well, which are much more elusive things. Such concerns will force us to consider

27

the author's claims too. For if we have no theoretical warrant allowing us to limit the kind of action or conduct that results in a text, we have nowhere else to turn.

This conception of literature as action determined by the writer grounds what I call "historical interpretation." It is historical in the sense that it seeks to understand particular actions performed by individuals in human time rather than natural human behavior not greatly affected by individual agents or the time in which they live.

This concept of interpretation is not apt to be confused with that held by "people who think that the less they know about the historical background of a work of literature the more likely they are to achieve what they call 'the relevance of response.' "[6] Such interpreters avoid the writer's action for the same reason they avoid "historical background." They begin with a theory—usually about language—that renders both irrelevant. Some of these theories enjoin the cultivation of historical ignorance to the extent of regarding knowledge of the writer's identity as a contaminant. Whatever the merits of such practice, it is hardly likely to be thought of as historical.

But there are kinds of history warranted by theories. And since historians—whether theory-based or not—frequently view their domain as including everything that anyone has ever done, there are theoretical historians of literature. What they do is commonly, and quite properly, thought of as historical interpretation, but in such cases the term has a meaning very different from mine because the theories frequently situate agency in forces outside an individual's control. When the writer claims to be doing something that conflicts with the interpreter's view of things, the writer is overruled.

One example from a distinguished work of this sort may illustrate the difference. In chapter fourteen of *Mimesis* Erich Auerbach considers Don Quijote and Sancho Panza in Cervantes's *Don Quijote* as representative of "a very old motif. . . . Two partners who appear together as contrasting comic or semi-comic figures." Auerbach begins then to consider what Cervantes made of this motif but immediately interrupts himself to say:

> Perhaps it is not quite correct to speak of what Cervantes made of it. It may be more exact to say "what became of the motif in his hands." For centuries—and especially since the romanticists—many things have been read into him which he hardly foreboded, let alone intended. . . . A book like *Don Quijote* dissociates itself from its author's

intention and leads a life of its own. ... Yet the historian—whose task it is to define the place of a given work in an historical continuity—must endeavor ... to attain a clear understanding of what the work meant to its author and his contemporaries. I have tried to interpret as little as possible ... I yet cannot help feeling that my thoughts about the book often go far beyond Cervantes' aesthetic intention. Whatever that intention may have been ... it most certainly did not consciously and from the beginning propose to create a relationship like that between Don Quijote and Sancho Panza as we see it after having read the novel.[7]

Auerbach is a learned reader of Cervantes and plainly has a deep affection for him; he is much less diffident with Tacitus in an earlier chapter of *Mimesis*. Yet when faced with a conflict between his understanding of *Don Quijote* and what he thinks Cervantes intended, he overrules the writer. Furthermore, he claims that his understanding is not anachronistic but historically accurate. Cervantes may have intended something else, but "what became of the motif in his hands" is what Auerbach sees. The case seems very curious. It is as if someone says, I am looking at a painting by Rembrandt. What I see represented is an airplane crash. Now I know perfectly well that whatever Rembrandt's intention is, it could not possibly be to paint an airplane crash. But that's what I see. And that's what's there.

There is no question here of historical ignorance. It is precisely Auerbach's historical knowledge that allows him to recognize the conflict. To an historical interpreter in my sense, knowledge that an understanding of a text is in conflict with the writer's intention rules it out. The history my interpreter seeks to know is the history of an individual's action, and intention is more than a characteristic of action. It is *the* characteristic of action.

But Auerbach seeks to know a different history. When he speaks of "[placing] a given work in an historical continuity," he is not thinking of the continuity of an individual's actions. The main actor in the historical continuity he envisions is "style"—an impulse whose activity he traces in "Western Literature" from Homer to Virginia Woolf. It is not Erich Auerbach who overrules Cervantes, but the impulse of style. This impulse is the author—although not the writer—of Western Literature. It is a force whose intention supersedes the intentions of individuals, just as the Holy Spirit, to interpreters of the Bible such as Augustine, supersedes the intentions of the prophets and evangelists.

Consequently, the books that individuals write cannot be seen in their historical reality except as parts of a gigantic historical œuvre that Auerbach calls Western Literature. Only a theory giving a substantial definition to this term and establishing the impulse of style as its author can assure us that when we read Western Literature, instead of books, what we see really exists.

Scholars as sensitive and intelligent as Auerbach know all the risks involved in committing themselves to such a theory but are temperamentally inclined to take those risks in order to achieve—however imperfectly—goals that cannot otherwise be attained at all. For such things as the impulse of style cannot be seen at work without a specialized theory, while the actions of a writer writing can be seen with commonplace concepts. Theory-based critics may think they have greater range, since they see impersonal agents. In some cases these agents are the texts themselves. But interpretation based on commonplace concepts can recognize far more range and scope in the *human* agents, who are never limited to instrumental roles.[8] It is true that the texts that can be seen without the warrant of specialized theory are never so grand as "Western Literature," but they can show remarkable variety, including vast stretches that theory-based criticism never can perceive.

Critics whose concepts of literature, informed by tacit theories, restricted form and unity to its post-medieval models, for example, could understand certain medieval texts only as botched modern texts. These critics tacitly accepted a theory that situated agency in the forms themselves. When they recognized that certain texts could not be accounted for by these forms, they felt forced to regard them as incoherent because their theory could not accommodate what the writers did.

Consider the thirteenth-century French romances that served Sir Thomas Malory as sources for "the book of King Arthur and his knights of the Round Table." Although from one point of view Malory is no more than a translator and redactor, there can be little doubt that he rescued the *matiere de Bretagne* from cultural oblivion, since the "bookes of Frensshe" that Malory "reduced . . . into Englysshe" were incomprehensible to almost all readers by the sixteenth century.

Montaigne mentions these books in the first edition of the *Essais* (1580), where he considers it a mark of superior upbringing that he did not occupy his youth with such trash. About fifty years later the academician Jean Chapelain gives this judicious appraisal of one writer of romance: "The author is a barbarian who wrote during barbarous times and solely for barbarians." A few years earlier, Don Quijote's friend the canon of Toledo expressed what had already become a standard view. "I have never yet seen a book of chivalry complete in all its parts, so that the middle agrees with the beginning and the end with the beginning and the middle; but they seem to construct their stories with such a multitude of members as though they meant to produce a monster rather than a well-proportioned figure." It was, after all, these very books that drove Don Quijote mad. From the canon's point of view it is a wonder that they did not drive more people mad, for they are composed "in such a way that one could never find one's way about them."[9]

After serious and prolonged study, most nineteenth-century medievalists arrived at similar conclusions. Eugène Vinaver cites Gaston Paris and Gustav Gröber, who found the so-called "Vulgate Cycle" of Arthurian romances to be "without shape or substance."[10] Vinaver continues:

> Both [Gröber] and Gaston Paris belonged to the generation of scholars who had set themselves the task of rehabilitating the literature of medieval Europe; but "rehabilitation" as they understood it was, as it still is to most people, a matter of finding in a forgotten text something resembling their own artistic ideal; and nothing could have been more remote from that ideal than the Arthurian prose romances and the tradition to which they belonged. For all the changes of taste and fashion that occurred between the end of the 16th century and the end of the 19th, the concept of poetic perfection had remained fundamentally the same, and Montaigne's reaction to medieval writing had lost none of its significance in the intervening three hundred years.[11]

Modern readers, from Montaigne's day to our own, prefer progressive narrative and a literature informed by a concept of separate "works" complete in themselves. Indeed, to speak of preference in this matter is misleading. Most modern readers, knowing no other concept of narrative structure, have come to look upon the one they know as the whole art of narrative. But as Vinaver observes, "the real question is . . . whether neglect of *structure* in the modern sense of the term necessarily implies absence of a *method of composition*."[12]

The question is both real and important, but—in this form at least— it is also loaded. It is, after all, the interpreter's task not to invent or

31

discover a method of composition that puts the best face on our authors' conduct, minutely and publicly attested, but to determine what that conduct is.

If the authors of the Vulgate Cycle attempted the kind of composition that Malory achieved, they certainly failed to attain it. The mere existence of another structure of coherence or method of composition cannot mitigate that failure or, *a fortiori*, turn it into success. But if they attempted another kind of composition—and Vinaver has made it impossible to doubt that other kinds are available—then Montaigne and the others misinterpret the romances by ascribing an historically inappropriate concept of narrative to them. The concept is historically inappropriate not because later chronologists have decided that it belongs to another "epoch" but because, as a matter of historical fact, it is not the one that the Vulgate authors intended.

There are critics who consider this way of looking at things fallacious, not to say heretical, but it is merely sound and orthodox history. So long as historical interpreters address themselves to writers' actions rather than to the actions of theoretically warranted agents, intention determines both the writers' actions and the things written. It is simply nonsensical to say—as Auerbach does—that a writer intended one thing but, as a matter of historical fact, the text turned into something else because it dissociated itself from the author's intention. Auerbach is saved from nonsense only because he addresses himself not to human action but to the action of higher and more elusive agents.

Yet if it were left to critics who supersede writers with impersonal agents, the French romances would remain to this day an unintelligible maze of adventures without beginning or end in which nothing follows from anything else. We should not be able to see Malory's progress from adaptor of an alliterative English poem to the virtual inventor of modern prose narrative, a progress that rests on the historical evidence of his revisions. Instead, Malory might survive as the author of adventure books for children.

The Malory that Vinaver portrays is not only greater but truer. Best of all, from an historian's point of view, Vinaver's Malory is not the product of mysterious forces or texts that dissociate themselves from writers but merely the result of an intelligent look at historical evidence. Nor is there any great difficulty in establishing the intentions that define Malory's actions and distinguish them in kind from those of his sources. Once an author's intention is admitted to be relevant at all, only rarely is there any serious doubt about what it is.

The role played by intention in improving our understanding of Malory and his thirteenth-century sources is normal for all historical interpretation, but there is some danger that it will be regarded as a special case. In looking to the thirteenth century, even from a vantage point as remote as the sixteenth, we are looking across a famous and self-conscious division in human art and thought. In these circumstances many critics who normally subsist on theory will grant that historical inquiry has a place. They may think that in dealing with an age that perhaps produced literature, although not literature "as we know it," a little history can do no harm.

Yet as long as we are interested in what a writer *did*, historical inquiry into that writer's intention is always pivotal, even when the writer and the interpreter are contemporary—even when they belong to the same well-defined and self-contained order of society. The *matiere de Bretagne* was exotic literature even to Montaigne and Chapelin. But members of a text's original audience, the very people we might imagine they were written for, people who understand every nuance of the culture, can also make the assumption that somehow the writer must conform to a pre-existing concept of form or genre.

I know of no better illustration of this point than the famous dispute about the "avowal" scene in part three of Madame de Lafayette's masterpiece, *La princesse de Clèves* (1678). The scene is carefully prepared, although the avowal itself is made with dramatic suddenness. The princess, who has developed what her husband thinks is a peculiar desire for solitude, asks M. de Clèves to let her stay in the country. She suggests, in fact, that she be allowed to retire from court.

The idea of someone as young as Madame de Clèves retiring from court is too odd to be considered. M. de Clèves, quite understandably, asks her to explain herself. She is reluctant to give her real reason, but she is determined to retire from the society of the court. Seeing no alternative, she confesses to her astonished husband that she has fallen in love and wishes to avoid being at court so that she can remain his faithful wife.[13]

La princesse de Clèves was placed on sale toward the middle of March 1678.[14] Very soon afterward the author's intimate friend Madame de Sévigné sent a copy to her banished cousin Roger de Bussy-Rabutin. On 26 June 1678 Bussy wrote to Madame de Sévigné telling her that he has "at last read *la Princesse de Clèves* in an equitable spirit and without any information at all about the good things or bad things that people have written about it."

Although he has (mild) praise for the first volume, he finds the second marred by the avowal scene: "the avowal by Madame de Clèves to her husband is extravagant, and is possible to say only in a true story; but when one writes [a story] to give pleasure, it is absurd to give one's heroine such an extraordinary feeling. The author, in doing it, took more care not to look like other novels [*sic*] than to follow common sense."[15]

To seal his case, the author of the *Histoire amoureuse des Gaules* observes, "A woman rarely tells her husband that someone is in love with her, but never that she is in love with someone aside from him."[16] *La princesse de Clèves* caused an immediate sensation and inspired prolonged debate about whether Madame de Clèves should have made her avowal. The debate frequently failed to distinguish the characters in the book from real people in contemporary society; it encompassed moral and practical considerations as well as aesthetic ones, but Bussy's point, variously put, was argued about for years.

During that prolonged debate no one mentioned—perhaps because it is only too obvious—that the author was quite aware of how unusual this confession is. She knew that readers familiar with the life of the court could scarcely imagine any woman in their circle doing such a thing. For that matter, Madame de Clèves herself acknowledges that "such a confession was unheard of."[17] A few pages later, she makes the same point much more emphatically: "there could not be another story like mine, no other woman would be capable of such a thing! It cannot have been invented or imagined by chance, nobody but me has ever conceived of such a thing."[18] The avowal scene, then, is intentional. The point is self-evident to Bussy. It is precisely because the scene *is* intentional that he considers it such a serious blunder.

Bussy assumes that both form and purpose are independent of individual writers and that they govern—or ought to govern—the choices that individual writers make. The purpose of novels is to give pleasure; the introduction of wild improbabilities into the action detracts from pleasure. There can be no justification for putting something like the avowal scene *in a novel*. Such a thing can be justified only in a book with another purpose—one written to record actual events, for example.

Like many other theory-based critics, Bussy is always ready to substitute a "natural law" for a convention.[19] Perhaps most novels before Madame de Lafayette's *were* written "to give pleasure." But it requires a theory to warrant the proposition that no one can choose to write a novel for any other purpose. Only a theory can establish that purpose belongs to the "form," not to the writer.

But Bussy, bold as he is ungallant, also offers to account for the avowal scene on historical grounds. Its jarring presence, he contends, is the result of its author's misplaced desire to stand out from other novelists; "nobody but me has ever conceived of such a thing."

This account of the avowal scene is not only ungallant but historically unwarranted and probably wrong. Many things about the composition of *La princesse de Clèves* remain obscure, but it seems to have grown out of Madame de Lafayette's *salon*. This *"cabale du sublime,"* which at one time or another included Segrais, Bossuet, Madame de Sévigné, and the duc de La Rochefoucauld, liked nothing better than to discuss such matters as the relationship between passion and personal integrity.

It is, of course, well known that the novel provoked widespread and serious discussion of just that question. The surviving evidence does not quite allow us to state as an historical fact that to provoke that discussion was the purpose of *La princesse de Clèves*, but there is plenty of support for such a view. Georges Poulet's conclusion, "The work of Madame de Lafayette has only one purpose: to find the connections between passion and existence,"[20] may be overstated, but it is far less extravagant than Bussy's and suggests a more likely reason for the inclusion of the avowal scene.

Yet for all its unlikeliness, Bussy's argument makes an assumption about the relationship between intention and purpose that is worth pursuing. That the avowal scene is intentional can be taken for granted as far as Bussy is concerned. In Madame de Clèves's phrase, "it cannot have been invented or imagined by chance." Nor could it have found its way into a book "by chance." But Bussy makes the interesting supposition that such intentional actions as the inclusion of a scene in a novel are themselves governed by purposes.

Since Bussy has a tacit theory that allots purposes to literary forms, the appropriateness of an author's intention can be judged—and rightly judged—by the purpose of the form. But Madame de Lafayette allowed her intention to be governed by another purpose: to distinguish herself from other novelists. Given Bussy's theory, this purpose is illegitimate.

Historical interpreters, unwarranted by theory, cannot know the purpose of literary forms, or even that such forms can have purposes apart from and superior to the purposes of writers. Inasmuch as they are trying to understand the actions of writers, these interpreters are interested in writers' intentions because intentions distinguish action from mere behavior better than anything else. But if intention is pivotal to historical interpretation, it is not always sufficient. Sometimes we must know the extent to which purpose is responsible for or determines intention.

PURPOSE AND LITERARY ART

Although the words *intention* and *purpose* are sometimes indifferently applied to the same concept, it is not difficult to show that each of these words has a proper conceptual turf.[21] It is possible to wonder if something is done intentionally or—let us say—inadvertently. But for historians the interesting cases usually involve trying to determine whether something is done purposefully or *merely* intentionally.

If, for example, I go to the Louvre and see Rembrandt's "Bathsheba with King David's Letter," it is almost meaningless to ask whether I went to the Louvre intentionally. It would be quite extraordinary to go there any other way. It is just possible that I could have gone there inadvertently—that is, as if I did not know what the Louvre is—or mistakenly, as if I thought I was going to the Galeries Lafayette. But the fact that we have to imagine such unlikely circumstances indicates that "intention is too intimately associated with ordinary action in general for there to be any *special* style of performance associated with it.[22]

Again, once I am standing in front of the painting it is superfluous and almost nonsensical to ask if I am looking at it intentionally. How else *can* one look at a painting? But to ask whether I went to the Louvre on purpose or for the purpose of seeing the "Bathsheba" is not a peculiar question. It is quite easy to imagine that I had never heard of the painting before I saw it or that I didn't know it is in the Louvre. It is no more difficult to imagine that I had read about it or heard someone talk about it and came to the Louvre for the purpose of seeing it.

In a posthumous and partly reconstructed paper that he called "Three Ways of Spilling Ink," J. L. Austin distinguishes the concepts of intention and purpose in these and other ways, and he distinguishes both concepts from deliberateness. His concluding remarks make a particularly good case for the importance of intention in historical interpretation.

we can assess [human activities] in terms of intentions, purposes, ultimate objectives, and the like, but there is much that is arbitrary about this unless we take the way the agent himself did actually structure it in his mind before the event. Now the word 'intention' has from this point of view a most important *bracketing effect:* when the till-dipper claims that he *intended all along* to put the money back, what he is claiming is that his action—the action that he was engaged upon—is to be judged *as a whole*, not just a part of it carved out of the whole. Nearly always, of course, such a contention as this will carry with it a contention that his action (as a whole) is not to be described by the term chosen to describe (only a part of) it: for example, here, it was not 'robbing' the till, because the action taken as a whole would not result in the absence of any money from the till. *Reculer pour mieux sauter* is not to retreat.

Quite distinct is the use of the word 'purpose.' Certainly, *when* I am doing something for a purpose, this will be known to me . . . and will guide my conduct. Indeed . . . a purpose will influence the forming of intentions. But my purpose is something to be achieved or effected as a result of what I'm doing. . . . I need not, however, have any purpose in acting (even intentionally); just as I need not take care or thought. I act for or on (a) purpose, I achieve it; I act with the intention, I carry it out, realize it.[23]

It is possible to imagine situations in which writing a book is not an intentional action, but these situations are decidedly weird. If there are actual cases, they are too rare to shake our confidence in the presumptive truth that writing a book is intentional. But unless we have theoretically warranted knowledge to the contrary, we cannot know that in every case "writing a book" requires the *same* intention.

In his observations on *La princesse de Clèves* Bussy, either arbitrarily or on the warrant of a theory, but not by considering Madame de Lafayette's intention, brackets the action of "writing a novel." There is only one relevant intention or conception of "the novel," known to Bussy from unspecified sources. All he needs to know about Madame de Lafayette's intention is whether it corresponds to what he might have called the universal intention of novels.

But this "universal intention" can have no historical warrant. Historical interpreters, then, must address themselves to the writer's act of writing without assuming that she is obliged to intend a "form" that exists independently of the act of writing. Unless they look to the writer's conception of the thing written (his intention), they can hardly avoid addressing an action whose "brackets" they have themselves arbitrarily determined instead of the action the writer achieved.

Austin's distinction has further implications for historical interpretation. If we regard writing as a human action, and if the writer's intention brackets that action, then the thing written *is* what the writer intended. Intentions—as Austin and I are talking about them—can be separated from actions analytically but not experientially or historically. We are not talking about contemplating one action but actually doing something else. Intention brackets the thing *done*. In this conception of things, intention is the identifying quality of an action and is always realized since it has no existence apart from the action intended.[24]

In *La princesse de Clèves*, Madame de Lafayette intended to write a book that includes the avowal scene, and, as a matter of course, she did. It is nonsensical to say that she intended her book to include the avowal scene but, when she finished writing, she discovered it was not there after all. This is very much like saying that Rembrandt intended to paint an old man wearing a feathered hat but somehow ended up with Bathsheba.

Purposes are something else. Since they depend on the *result* of what we do (intentionally), they need not be—and in many cases are not—achieved. Moreover, our actions may have results that are no part of our purpose or that even are contrary to our purpose. That is why purposes are so much more elusive than intentions. If the purpose of *La princesse de Clèves* is to provoke discussion about the connections between passion and personal integrity, that purpose affected the author's intention to include the avowal scene. But we cannot know that Madame de Lafayette had such a purpose on the evidence of the discussion that actually followed her book's publication. We cannot know that she had *any* purpose without knowing her concept of what she did in writing her book. Since historical interpreters cannot claim that the "form" has a purpose that controls the author's intention, they are left with the difficult problem of trying to determine whether the author had a purpose or merely an intention.

Many texts will make coherent—if quite different—sense under either aspect. Some have been seen alternately under each aspect by successive generations of readers. The history of their interpretation is a kind of weather vane of interpretative fashion. *Macbeth* is one such text. Most recent readers, especially those trained as literary critics, regard it as self-contained rather than purposeful. For some the play is a portrait of a man with (some) noble qualities drawn to fulfill a great ambition by criminal means and torn to pieces by his ensuing consciousness of guilt.

To read this work or see it performed can be moving. It will, however, lose much of its power if Macbeth's noble qualities are not clearly kept in view. A reading or performance of the play so understood requires a distribution of emphasis that keeps those qualities prominent. Macbeth's noble qualities are not the invention of the interpreters, of course, but they recede steadily into the background as he progresses in his career of "deeds." It may be true that the most serious of his crimes is the murder of Duncan, his kinsman, his guest, and his king. But he is driven mad with horror in contemplating that murder and is sunk in grim remorse afterward. In his own eyes, his guilt is beyond remedy (2.2.60–63); his life is in ruins.

> Had I but died an hour before this chance,
> I had lived a blessed time; for from this instant
> There's nothing serious in mortality:
> All is but toys: renown and grace is dead,
> The wine of life is drawn, and the mere lees
> Is left this vault to brag of.
>
> $(2.3.90–95)^{25}$

The crime that causes him the greatest political damage is the murder of Banquo, his old friend and one of the council of thanes. A thane need not condone the murder of Duncan to understand it. Duncan had what Macbeth coveted and was holding it by Macbeth's sufferance. But what did Banquo have? Thanes may not worry overmuch when a thane kills a king. That is, after all, the way of the world. But when a king starts killing thanes, that is another story. Macbeth does not, of course, kill Banquo himself. But his plans and the manner in which he realizes them discredits him more than anything we actually see him do or hear him say in the murder of Duncan.

His self-deception in the soliloquy "To be thus is nothing" (3.1.47–71); his treachery and deceit in dealing with the thugs he has brought to him (3.1.72–141); the fear unmixed with remorse he shows afterward; and the monstrous if magnificent resolution he shows after the catastrophic banquet: "For mine own good / All causes shall give way . . . (3.4.35–36), all make him inevitably less noble than he was during and just after his initiation in the course of "deeds."

But by far his worst crime, as it affects our attitude toward him, is the slaughter of Lady Macduff and her charming little son in act four, scene two. From the perspective of a contemporary expert in law and morality—such as the learned king for whom the play was written— this crime is the least serious of the three. It is not a sacrilege like the murder of Duncan; it is not a violation of a king's obligation to a vassal like the murder of Banquo. Moreover, if the danger of leaving Banquo alive is the product of Macbeth's self-deception, Macduff actually is seeking to overthrow him. In a sense, then, Fife is fair game. The slaughter of his wife, babes, and servants will teach Macduff what it means to raise arms against a king.

But no casuistry can mitigate the horror of this most ignoble crime. No anguish precedes it.

> From this moment
> The very firstlings of my heart shall be
> The firstlings of my hand. And even now
> To crown my thoughts with acts, be it thought and done:
> The castle of Macduff I will surprise.
>
> . . . .
>
> No boasting like a fool;
> This deed I'll do before this purpose cool.
>
> *(4.1.146–50, 153–54)*

Again, from a casuist's point of view, the seriousness of the crime cannot be affected by whether Lady Macduff is the gracious, intelligent, high-spirited, and delightful woman she is or an old shrew. Nor can it matter whether her son is the immensely winsome and charming little boy he is or a snivelling, cowardly, and unloving little brat.

But Shakespeare has included a preliminary dialogue between Lady Macduff and her little boy that makes their slaughter the most wanton and vicious of all Macbeth's deeds. Kings who can preserve their thrones only through the prowess of other men's arms are naturally in trouble. Thanes who serve as chief counselors to kings who sit on thrones of blood had better watch their step. But what worldly wisdom can mitigate the horror of Macduff's wonderful little boy, who has stood up for his father against an invading ruffian, saying, "He has killed me, mother: / Run away I pray you"(4.2.84–85)? The reader who can recollect Macbeth's, noble qualities at this point is not, I think, one to whom this play is addressed.

The scene leaves a painful and horrible impression. It casts shame on Macbeth, shame unqualified by either pity or admiration. For these reasons, it has always been something of an anomaly in productions of *Macbeth* that represent the ruin of a noble character. Perhaps that is why the murder of Macduff's little boy simply was omitted from stage productions beginning with D'Avenant's in 1674 and continuing through most of the following two hundred years.[26] Of course, a reader cannot use such crude expedients to mark the distribution of emphasis. There are, to be sure, ways to treat this scene as falling outside the main action of the play without violating the text. Yet there is reason to question such treatment.

Interpreters of *Macbeth* for whom this scene is not central tend hardly to mention the fact that Macbeth has a peculiarly naive, almost childish belief in the operation of justice.[27] As a warrior-lord who finds himself more powerful in fact than the king to whom he owes allegiance in law, it is only natural that he should think about taking for himself what he has just now preserved from Macdonwald. Certainly Duncan thinks about it. That is why he makes haste to shower Macbeth with praise, thanks, honors, and goods. That is why he names Malcolm his heir. Above all, that is why he visits Dunsinane. Duncan knows that no one can regard the challenge to his throne as settled until Macbeth shows his hand. After watching Macbeth's reactions in act one, scene four, Duncan decides to demonstrate that Macbeth has accepted the situation by offering him his best opportunity to dispute it.

Duncan is neither an amateur nor a fool. We can infer that he has discussed the situation with his sons. Notice that they show no horror or amazement when they are told that their father is murdered. They keep cool heads, put two and two together in an instant, and take advantage of the confusion to get away from the danger that confronts them. Nor does Malcolm expect the thanes to take up arms to dislodge Macbeth. He thinks it far more likely that one of them will take up arms to eliminate *him*, since he is a convenient rallying point for the inevitable political enemies that Macbeth will acquire during his (presumably long) reign.

Banquo knows what happened, and the other thanes at least suspect the truth by the time Macbeth leaves for Scone. Certainly it would take a fool to accept the official account. But Macbeth seems to imagine that the thanes *do* believe the official account. For if they do not, how is it that they tolerate him? He knows the truth, and he will not rest until he destroys himself. Remember that this is a man who thinks that

> ... pity, like a naked new-born babe,
> Striding the blast, or Heaven's cherubin, horsed

> Upon the sightless couriers of the air,
> Shall blow the horrid deed in every eye,
> That tears shall drown the wind.

(1.7.21–25)

He is a man who fears that the earth itself will rise up in witness against him (2.1.58), for surely nature cannot stand idly by while he commits unnatural acts.

> Stones have been known to move and trees to speak;
> Augures and understood relations have
> By maggot-pies and cloughs and rooks brought forth
> The secret'st man of blood.

(3.4.124–27)

It is impossible not to agree with Lady Macbeth's appraisal of such notions, "O proper stuff!" (3.4.60)

Macduff is the only other person in the play sufficiently unsophisticated to share such sentiments. He is an easy target for Malcolm's teasing in act four, scene three. But when he is told that his wife and children have been slaughtered, no one can have the heart to say his sentiments are "proper stuff," even if they are as childish and naive as Macbeth's.

> Did heaven look on,
> And would not take their part?

(4.3.223–24)

Rather than give up the idea that heaven protects the innocent, he takes the slaughter of his family to be heaven's punishment for his own sins.

> Sinful Macduff,
> They were all struck for thee! naught that I am,
> Not for their own demerits, but for mine,
> Fell slaughter on their souls . . .

(4.3.224–27)

But Lady Macduff knows better. She is incensed to learn that Macduff has left her unprotected. "His flight was madness" (4.2.3). She has more practical sense than to think that heaven either protects the innocent or punishes the guilty.

> I have done no harm. But I remember now
> I am in this earthly world; where to do harm

Is often laudable, to do good sometime
Accounted dangerous folly: why then, alas,
Do I put up that womanly defence,
To say I have done no harm?

(4.2.73–78)

There can be no doubt that Shakespeare expected his audience to regard Lady Macduff's views as perfectly sensible and to regard Macbeth's (and Macduff's) moral vision suitable for "a woman's story at a winter's fire / Authorized by her grandam" (3.4.65–66). Only a critic unusually innocent of history could imagine that King James did not regard Macbeth as morally naive.

But if we emphasize Macbeth's naïveté rather than his noble qualities, act four, scene two is the very heart of the play. Until that point, we might regard Macbeth's views in much the same light as Lady Macbeth does. But only the most jaded reader can maintain such a position after this scene. Macbeth's concept of the world remains as naive as it ever was, of course, but who cannot feel the pity that it should be so? What kind of a world is this in which the man responsible for the slaughter of Lady Macduff and her son can positively prosper unless, like Macbeth, he happens to be so naive that he will not allow himself to prosper?

Shakespeare certainly intended to make Macbeth naive, but our question is whether that intention is determined by a purpose. Is *Macbeth* purposeful? Did Shakespeare write it to cut through our "practical wisdom" by making us feel with tremendous affective force what a pity it is that we live in a world so much worse than the one Macbeth insists on living in? If he did, he wrote a very different play from the one that simply represents the destruction of a man not quite worldly enough to enjoy the fruits of crime.

The text will support either of the two *Macbeth*s I have considered and no doubt many others as well. Disputes about which of these plays is, as a matter of historical fact, bracketed by Shakespeare's intention are endless because we simply cannot determine from the surviving evidence his conception of what he did in writing *Macbeth*. As a consequence, we cannot determine how to distribute emphasis to (intentional) features of the text. This is an historical question, and to answer it we should need historical evidence. We have to make do with clichés of our author's time, if nothing else is available. But knowledge of the author's concept of what a play might be made to do and of his purposes and strategies in writing this one are what we need to settle the question.

Without knowledge of these things both actions and texts remain forever ambiguous. In recent times, it is true, we have not lacked for academic critics who claim that the very nature of literary art is to be ambiguous and even that this ambiguity is its chief value.[28] But that takes us back to theory, the historical interpreter's hell, where a writer who chooses to make us weep that we live in a world where evil is laudable and goodness folly is rendered unable to do so because a theory has declared his purpose to be without effect.

My analysis of *Macbeth* is meant to illustrate a feature of historical interpretation—its dependence on evidence. When we inquire into an individual's action—we are not guaranteed a decisive answer. Theory-based concepts of literature, as we saw in the examples of Pierre Ménard, Auerbach's analysis of *Don Quijote*, the baffled amateur and professional readers of thirteenth-century French romances, and Bussy's objections to the princesse de Clèves' avowal, run other risks.

Adherents to those concepts may be unaware of the author's text because they concentrate on the words as if they were independent of a writer's action rather than the evidence for it; they may find themselves creating their own books because their theories allow them to see texts dissociated from what their authors did. The juxtaposition is an odd one. Ménard wanted to write *the Don Quijote*; had he waited two years to read Auerbach, he would have learned that even Cervantes didn't write *the Don Quijote*. The book apparently wrote itself.

Montaigne, Chapelin, the canon of Toledo, Gaston Paris, and Gustav Gröber all had a concept of coherence to which the French romances did not conform, so they all concluded that these books are incoherent. None seems in the least indecisive on the point. Neither does Bussy in his criticism of Madame de Lafayette. These readers keep writers on a short leash. They know what romances and novels do, and these texts fail to do what they are supposed to. For them it is the *texts*, not the writers, that do things—so these texts are incoherent or extravagant.

With no theory to tell us what we *must* see, or to extend our vision beyond the commonplace world of human action, or to give us comprehensive standards of appropriateness, historical interpreters are sometimes left with insufficient evidence to decide among possible interpretations. Theories are eternal, but historical evidence disappears after a while.

The historical interpreters' world of discourse is less sophisticated than that of the literary theorists. Without a theory to tell them otherwise, historical interpreters assume that the nature of literary art is as varied as the possibilities of human action because every work of literary art *is* what its author has determined it to be. In this world of discourse no text ever frees itself from its writer to lead a life of its own. As a result, we cannot hope to understand Literature or even Western Literature. Neither can we hope to understand "the novel" or "tragedy." But, from time to time, we can hope to understand some books.

'Parody' or the Imitation of Disciplines

T HE BOOKS that I hope to understand at present, Shaw's *Saint Joan* and Proust's *A la recherche du temps perdu*, each present a represented author in scientific or academic costume. Before I discuss how these authors use a special technique that helps them associate their work with knowledge of the sort that might affect the way their readers act, I shall identify that technique more thoroughly.

The English language, to the despair of foreigners trying to learn it, already has what seems to be an endless vocabulary. It is hard to believe that there is an important literary concept or convention left unnamed. I am, therefore, embarrassed to say that at this late date I find it necessary to extend the word *parody* in order to discuss this prominent feature of my chosen texts.[1]

Etymologically a parody is something set beside—parallel to—an ode. In ancient Greek the term designates mock odes, which apparently were once a conventional form of comic literature. But whatever conventions govern this lost form have long ago fallen into disuse. Modern parodies have no special reference to odes, songs, or verse of any kind.

The *Oxford English Dictionary*'s first citation is from 1598. The word is there said to mean "a composition in prose or verse in which the characteristic turns of thought and phrase in an author or class of authors are imitated in such a way as to make them appear ridiculous, especially by applying them to ludicrously inappropriate subjects; an imitation of a work more or less closely modelled on the original, but so turned as to produce a ridiculous effect." Almost as an afterthought, but still within the first definition, the word is said to apply to "a burlesque of a musical work."[2]

But if we look at some parodies with an eye both to what is being imitated and why, I think we will find that this definition is not wholly a satisfactory one. Perhaps my extension of the term is just a special case of what we mean by parody when we distinguish it from burlesque.

Consider a schoolboy imitating his teacher. A characteristic turn of phrase and perhaps a characteristic tone of voice are the most common objects of imitation. The performance often is topped off by the imitation of physical mannerisms to complement the verbal and oratorical ones. If we isolate the verbal part of such an imitation and write the words down, the result conforms to the *OED*'s definition of parody, although we are here speaking of burlesque. But is parody simply verbal burlesque?

Max Beerbohm's parody of Bernard Shaw serves nicely to suggest that this concept of parody is deficient in recognizing a distinction that most experienced readers actually make in practice. "A Straight Talk" (Preface to "Snt. George: A Christmas Play.") is a parody of Shaw, not of a particular text. Like many parodies of this sort, it incorporates elements of burlesque. "Snt." is burlesque. Beerbohm imitates Shaw's eccentricities in orthography, his straightforward "scientific" stance, his characteristic subject matter, and his impatient rhythms. "Mr. Shaw," he once observed, "wrote ever as one who had two thousand words or so of printed matter to wake the dead in."[3] The result is very funny burlesque—burlesque of perhaps the highest order but still burlesque because the fact of imitation is impossible to miss. Exaggeration, the hallmark of burlesque, is everywhere apparent. But two-thirds through "A Straight Talk" come three extraordinary sentences that are parody free from any suggestion of burlesque.

> In my nonage, I believed humanity could be reformed if only it were intelligently preached at for a sufficiently long period. This first fine careless rapture I could no more recapture, at my age, than I could recapture hoopingcough or nettlerash. One by one, I have flung all political nostra overboard, till there remain only dynamite and scientific breeding.[4]

These three sentences are parody and not burlesque because there is nothing to distinguish them from authentic products of Shaw's pen. In them we encounter not so much an imitation of Shaw's "characteristic turns of thought and phrase" as a simple use of Shaw's thought and style. There is a joke here and a particularly delicious one, but is it true that such parody makes Shaw ridiculous? Not, I think, unless his own writing makes him so, because when parody is unambiguously achieved, as it is here, it is impossible to tell the difference between the original and the parody. *That*, of course, is the joke.

One of Nabokov's narrators says that "literary style . . . constitutes the only real honesty of a writer."[5] Certainly literary style is what gives a writer her literary identity. To achieve an individual and recognizable voice in writing is an arduous business. Beerbohm says, in effect, Oh, to write like Shaw is not so hard; why *I* could do it. And he does. A brilliant trick and undoubtedly an excellent joke, but the trick is brilliant and the joke excellent just because Shaw is a virtuoso stylist. The joke would not be nearly so funny if he were a pedestrian writer. The joke, moreover, is best appreciated not by Shaw's detractors but by his admirers. And no one can think worse of Shaw for having read Beerbohm's parody.

True parodies, in contrast to burlesque, require the kind of attention to thought, syntax, rhythm, and vocabulary that we commonly give only to writers we admire. It would take a real snt.—or perhaps a real dvl.—to have the requisite patience with writers one finds ridiculous.

Marcel Proust perfected his singular style in parodies of writers he admired. He accomplishes the same miracle with Saint-Simon that Beerbohm does with Shaw, producing sentences that the object of the parody very well could have written word for word.[6] Ridicule, in this case, is out of the question. The encyclopedia entry for *pastiche*—one normal French equivalent of the English *parody*—in the *Nouveau Larousse Illustré* includes some alternatives worth considering.

> There are two kinds of parodies: those which one does seriously for the purpose of modeling one's own writing on the style of a famous writer, and those that one composes with the intention of satire, criticism or simply in order to demonstrate the flexibility of one's own gift. Thus La Bruyère amused himself in writing a page in the style of Montaigne. . . .[7]

This is, in some respects, better than what the *OED* has to say about parody, but it is dangerous to include purpose in the definition of a technique. Proust, for example, claimed that the main purpose of his parodies—his "overt parodies," as he calls them—is to free himself from the danger of unconscious imitation that can so easily follow intense reading of an author like Saint-Simon.[8]

The comments in the *Larousse*, like the definition in the *OED*, apply best to the imitation (or reuse) of turns of thought *and* phrase. But not all parodies involve turns of phrase to any significant extent. James Thurber, a master of the art, had a good ear for turns of phrase, especially turns of phrase he disliked. He was, however, even more alert to turns of thought he disliked and could make them objects of parody with devastating malice. In "The Macbeth Murder Mystery," for example, a woman who requires a paperback mystery to get through the night mistakenly picks up a copy of *Macbeth*. In reading the play, she applies the conventions of her favorite kind of literature. *Macbeth*, it turns out, is a most unsatisfactory mystery because its author is inept.

"In the first place," the woman confides to the narrator, "I don't think for a moment that Macbeth did it. . . . I don't think the Macbeth woman is mixed up in it either. You suspect them the most, of course, but those are the ones that are never guilty—or shouldn't be anyway." Showing far more adeptness at following clues than Shakespeare, the woman concludes that the killer is Macduff. The narrator then reads *Macbeth* as a mystery and proves to be even more adept than she at following clues. He concludes the killer is not Macduff, who is as innocent as "Macbeth and the Macbeth woman," but Lady Macbeth's father, old "Mr. Macbeth."

"The Macbeth Murder Mystery" parodies a convention of reading, not conventions of writing: a turn of thought, not turns of phrase. It does not achieve its ends by imitating turns of phrase. The narrator's references to Lady Macbeth as "the Macbeth woman" and to her father as "Mr. Macbeth" are the only instances of verbal imitation in the piece; the use of a mentality is what counts here. When the narrator decides to "solve" *Hamlet* next, he has adopted the woman's mentality but not her "turns of phrase." Only he is capable of the concise eloquence with which he answers her question.

"But who . . . do you suspect?"
"Everybody."[9]

It is true that Thurber's parody applies the conventions of mysteries to something "ludicrously inappropriate," but this is not characteristic of all parodies and is, in certain respects, more appropriate to a definition of burlesque. Beerbohm, for example, applies Shaw's mentality and literary style to precisely the subjects that Shaw does.

The terms "parody" and "burlesque" are not as distinct in English usage as *pastiche* and *burlesque* are in French. In English parody seems to have become a synonym for burlesque. "Burlesque" is a French word that comes from the Italian *burlo*, to ridicule, and it is the name of a conventional form of comic verse. Burlesque verse was a fad first in Italy and then in France during the first half of the seventeenth century. Scarron's *Virgile travesty*, published between 1648 and 1652, is a landmark of French burlesque. In an attempt to establish the original

French meaning of burlesque, Antoine Adam cites Scarron's contemporary Gabriel Naudé on burlesque style: "[it is] low and comical, not artlessly, but by affectation (that is to say by study) and delicacy of wit. . . . [It is] the explanation of the most serious things in the most ludicrous and ridiculous . . . terms."[10]

This sounds a good deal like what the *OED* says of parody. The confusion is complete if parody is used—as the *OED* says it is—to refer to a burlesque of a musical work. But the *OED* does not mention a more common and less eccentric meaning of parody. In music, parody is the name of a common baroque technique that involves neither ridicule nor comparison. In hearing a parody, an audience hears a text given *appropriate* emotional or expressive force by music originally composed for an entirely different text.[11]

J. S. Bach is a conspicuous practitioner of this technique. He parodied about 20 percent of the 936 choral movements, accompanied recitatives, arias, and other eligible compositions he wrote during his tenure as cantor of the Thomaskirche in Leipzig. He often took a setting originally composed for a "secular" text and reused it for a "sacred" one.[12] It is this sense of parody—the reuse of a form with new material—that is furthest from burlesque and closest to the literary device I want to discuss.

Consider *Pale Fire*, for example. It does not imitate a book or an author. Neither does it imitate a class of authors, for the notes of annotators do not ordinarily form a narrative as Charles Kinbote's do. The poem in four cantos by John Shade is not a ludicrously inappropriate object of commentary, nor is the book's purpose to ridicule annotated editions of poems. But *Pale Fire* looks like a kind of book it is not because it uses the decor if not the techniques of another kind of book.

Nabokov's novel is both funny and original, but getting one kind of book to resemble another is an old trick that is not always meant to be funny. In his 1954 Terry Lectures Pieter Geyl gives some examples of writers using the decor of history in order to pass off their religious or political views as something less personal, less arbitrary than they are.

> They looked to the past for prefigurations, for symbols, of contemporary events or personalities. Not only—not even in the first place—to decry, but to do homage. History was to them a treasure house from which could be taken beautiful and dignified images fit, by way of similitude, to elevate the present. . . . And it was not national history which furnished the most shining examples, but the history of Israel

and the history of Rome. . . . The Estates party in Holland appealed to the Judges in Israel, while the Orangists loved to recall the Kings—instituted by God in his wrath, as they were reminded by the republicans.[13]

Geyl relates that one famous seventeenth-century controversy about the constitution of the province of Holland takes on "a look of unreality" because the political problems of the moment are discussed almost wholly by reference to past events—some of them quite remote.[14]

Both Nabokov and the Hollanders who dress up their political arguments in the trappings of historical analysis are disguising one kind of book as another. But I am interested primarily in writers who borrow more than decor. Bernard Shaw in *Saint Joan* and Marcel Proust in *A la recherche du temps perdu* borrow a little decor from history and psychology respectively. But more to the point, each borrows a way of arguing or a way of organizing and explaining material—and some of the material as well—from these *genres savants*.

I am not claiming, then, that *Saint Joan* looks like history instead of dramatic fiction and that *La recherche* looks like a psychological treatise instead of narrative fiction. They do not. But it seems that these books purport actually to *do* something proper to history and psychology respectively. They can be shown to use paradigms proper to one kind of history and one kind of psychology.[15] In using these paradigms, they imitate learned disciplines. It is this imitation of disciplines that I call "parody."

The use of this technique is easy to see in *Saint Joan*. On its face, the play claims to offer answers to historical questions. We might say as much for the pamphlets of Professor Geyl's Hollanders, of course, but Shaw's parody is especially thoroughgoing and much more self-conscious. Unlike the Hollanders, Shaw begins with a discussion of historiographic method and reviews some of the previous accounts of Joan's career in order to establish the need for his own.

Once we observe that Shaw's discussion of previous historical literature on Joan of Arc is confined to that great scholarly tradition that begins with Shakespeare and Schiller and culminates in the work of Andrew Lang and Mark Twain, we can safely dismiss the idea that *Saint Joan* is authentic, if amateur, history. Even so, Shaw's purpose is not immediately apparent, even though anyone familiar with him will (rightly) expect that we are in for a sermon on Fabian socialism in medieval costume.

Familiarity with Shaw's politics aside, the play presents itself as an explanation of why Joan was burned, and Shaw claims that his answer to that question is better than previous ones because his historical method—which he calls scientific—is superior to the methods used by what he calls matter-of-fact historians. It is a little unusual, of course, for the fruits of historical inquiry to be presented in dramatic form, but then Joan's history is a little unusual.

Shaw borrows historical subject matter, but that is not what makes *Saint Joan* a parody. It is a parody because he borrows a historical discipline. It is true that Shaw's method of gathering data cannot easily be confused with the activity of a historian, no matter how "scientific," but his method of explaining his main datum is another matter. Not only does Shaw's discussion of historiography echo Comte, Hegel, Nietzsche, and Theodor Lessing, but his paradigm of historical explanation is the same as that used by Augustine, Condorcet, Henry Buckle, Marx, and Toynbee, among others, with what they conceive to be "real" facts.

This use of an identifiable historical paradigm may help to explain why *Saint Joan* was mistaken for an authentic attempt at history by the British amateur J. M. Robertson, who was sufficiently annoyed with it to take its author to task. In 115 pages of vigorous rejoinder, Robertson's book *Mr. Shaw and "The Maid"* convicts the accused of being an incompetent historian and concludes that "the reader who would know the truth about the age of Jeanne, then, will do well to dismiss Mr. Shaw's assurance that *Saint Joan* tells him all he needs to know."[16]

Robertson's objections may suggest that he is an earnest simpleton, but his understanding of *Saint Joan* was shared by at least one distinguished scholar. Johan Huizinga, professor of history at Leyden University, read the play and decided that if one more miracle were needed to clinch the case for Joan of Arc's canonization, *Saint Joan* is it. He says he can read the preface with "hardly a shrug of the shoulders." Shaw, of all people, "that man with the utterly prosaic mind . . . who appears so alien to everything that seems to us to be noblest in the Middle Ages and most essential to the history of Joan of Arc" has, in a word, got it right.[17]

It may be true that Huizinga's disinclination to be interested in politics made him especially prone to take *Saint Joan* for an effort to dramatize historical conclusions. But it is also true that Huizinga is not merely a trained historian but a historian of eminence. He may have misunderstood the play, but he is not wrong to see something in it that belongs to history—something beyond mere subject matter.

Of course Shaw scatters plenty of clues to prevent irrelevant evaluations of *Saint Joan* as history, either incompetent history or miraculous history. To begin with, when he gets past the initial scenes of exposition to the real business of explanation in scene four, he invents everything. Then he refuses to end his play with Joan's death. He actually brings her back so that he can hammer home his "lesson" about the danger of trying to effect revolutionary change with nothing more than the force of personality.

Whatever we may think of the lesson, it is surely not a legitimate historical conclusion derived from the study of Joan of Arc's career. But since Shaw uses Joan's career to discuss contemporary politics (just as the Hollanders use the history of ancient Israel to discuss contemporary politics) serious history is useless to him precisely because it will not yield his lesson.

For Shaw parody serves the simple purpose of attracting attention. *Saint Joan* is part of the same old curriculum he had been selling since 1889. Like all mountebanks, Shaw is shameless. If he can get people to pay attention to him in 1924 by calling his heroine Joan of Arc, so be it. If the historians want to help his cause by engaging him in debate or conferring their approval, so much the better. Madison Avenue had nothing to teach Shaw.

Proust's use of parody in *La recherche* is not nearly so easy to perceive, nor is its function so clear. Proust's style is, of course, very different from Shaw's, and so are his specific ambitions as a writer—although, like Shaw, he is insistent about the "scientific" nature of his book. Whatever we make of that claim, each of Shaw's works, with a few exceptions, is designed to teach a single, useful lesson. But the art of *La recherche* is complex and baroque. Proust is in love with his subject matter in a way that Shaw is not in love with his. "Snt. George" has very little interest in the Middle Ages or Joan of Arc for their own sake. That is why people like Huizinga think Shaw has "an utterly prosaic mind." But everything in *La recherche* from the window of Gilbert the Bad in the church of Saint-Hilaire at Combray to the figure of the senile baron de Charlus lifting his hat to Madame de Saint-Euverte because he no longer knows who she is has the texture of reality that even a very great writer can give only to what he loves for its own sake. There has been a huge volume of commentary on Proust in the past seventy years, but I do not believe anyone has accused him of having a prosaic mind.

Once Shaw finds his vocation as a Fabian missionary, everything from phonetics to heresy is grist for his mill. But Proust begins with a vast and unwieldy subject matter. He tried and failed to cast it into the form of an autobiographical novel before he began *La recherche*. That attempt failed in part because the form was too loose to organize his subject, in part because Proust felt that his fictional autobiography lacked an adequate rationale. He could not, to his own satisfaction, answer the question he imagined his reader asking: Why are you telling me all this?

The problem is on his mind even after he found a way to solve it. In 1912, on the eve of publishing *Du côté du chez Swann*, he writes to his friend the art critic Jean-Louis Vaudoyer, "But I also envy your being able to have at such a young age both a forum and an accessible framework."[18]

Proust's own framework is a remarkable combination of borrowed elements ingeniously combined to answer original and specific needs. Only some of these elements are borrowed from a discipline, so parody is only one of Proust's formal principles. He borrows conspicuously from the memoir literature he knows so intimately, and he borrows with unprecedented boldness and inventiveness from painters, but neither of these sources can yield an acceptable rationale.

For his rationale he turns to psychology—structurally the most important, but in all ways the most obscure, of the sources for what he calls his architecture. His parody of psychology is difficult to perceive for at least two distinct reasons. First, it is almost impossible to keep in mind that the largest unit of narrative is the story of the Protagonist's illness and recovery. That narrative is continually interrupted by other narratives, engrossing in themselves, brilliantly told, and at times as long as conventional novels. Consider, for example, the story of M. de Charlus's introduction to the society of the Verdurins, his membership in "the little group," and his brutal expulsion from it. This story has no obvious connection with the story of the Protagonist's illness and recovery, it occupies most of 550 pages in the first *Pléiade* edition, and it is, after all, told by the Protagonist, who seems to be anything but a hopeless neurasthenic. The complex relationship between the Protagonist and the Narrator and the method of interlaced narrative constitute one obstacle to perceiving Proust's parody of psychology.

The second obstacle is the fact that the discipline Proust imitates is no longer practiced, and, in a sense, it never was. Proust put together elements from several quite different schools of psychology: the philosophical psychology of Henri Bergson, the physiological psychology of Théodule Ribot, and perhaps the experimental psychology of Pierre

Janet.[19] The hybrid discipline that results from this synthesis directs Proust's description of the origin and nature of the Protagonist's eventually crippling illness and of its long, painful course of successive obsessions in love and repeated failure in work. Finally, it provides a way to make his dramatic recovery intelligible. Proust is committed to the recovery and must have a way to account for it.

Despite its largely dramatic form, *Saint Joan* echoes the language of textbook historiography. But *La recherche* cannot very easily call to mind the literature of psychological case history. Bergson does not write in this form, and Ribot's cases are rarely more than a page or two long. Janet writes long and detailed case histories, but he is suspicious of the procedure Proust parodies, and his cases do not end in dramatic recoveries. Besides, the mere decor of case history can no more answer Proust's needs than the decor of autobiography can.

What Proust wants is something like one of Freud's exemplary case histories—one that offers the scientist's first knowledge of a paradigm and is especially significant for that reason. But he had no model for such a case history before him. Proust got his decor from memoir writers and fashioned his own scientific paradigm from parts that lay ready to hand.

He combines some of Bergson's concepts with some of Ribot's terms to concoct a dynamic psychology that never was, but one that has stirred some interest among psychologists and historians of psychology. Although they cannot match Huizinga's eminence, Milton L. Miller and Henri Ellenberger among others find Proust's parody psychology interesting as psychology, and both of them have a professional interest in the history of psychological disciplines that inform therapeutic practice.[20]

The scientific apparatus in *La recherche* does not, of course, excite the same kind of response in all of Proust's readers. For Richard Barker, such things as the "unconscious memory" have "some of the elements of the literary hoax."[21] The mechanism of the cure at least leads others, Robert Vigneron and Vladimir Nabokov among them, to speak of the two "halves" of *La recherche*—the first and less explicitly "scientific" half, in their opinion, much the superior of the two.

There is little doubt that Proust intermittently took his parody for something it is not. He sometimes makes claims for his book that suggest it is a work of psychology. He finds it difficult to remember that as psychology the book suffers from a fatal flaw: the data is invented. Psychology as such is as useless to Proust as history is to Shaw. He begins with, and is committed to, his conclusion and cannot afford to have it tested with real data. If his invented data is offered seriously to validate the paradigm, *La recherche* is not a hoax but a fraud.

Proust, however, maintains an unusual distinction between his writing self and his nonwriting self, and that distinction is sometimes worth remembering.[22] The nonwriter may have been capable of fraud, but no one can reasonably accuse the writer of cutting corners.

For the writer, then, the function of the parody is analogous to the function that theological cosmology has for the builders of thirteenth-century cathedrals. When we look at the porch of the apostles at Chartres or the relief sculpture of the Annunciation, these "parts" seem to carry their own interest and justification. That the whole sculpture program even has a rationale need never cross the mind of someone actually studying a single part of it. It is only when we begin to wonder why this scene is depicted, or how this group was selected, or why it is here and not on the other side of the building that we realize that the builder needed a design to encompass the embarrassment of riches to which he is committed. In fact, for 250 years or more the organizing principles of the sculpture and stained glass programs were forgotten. Emile Mâle rediscovered these principles late in the nineteenth century.[23] But people did not find the cathedrals worthless in the meantime.

Nevertheless, the cosmologies organize the buildings and the work of the builders as well; they justified the craftsmen's work by giving it a significance their society found acceptable. There may have been a time when most people took the cosmologies to be deposits of profound truth. Not many do today. Yet even those who find the cosmologies ludicrous can be moved to tears by the cathedrals.

I think something similar is true of the relationship between Proust's science, his book, and his readers. The science still has a few admirers, but most of Proust's present and future readers will surely agree with Barker. No amount of involuntary memory will make a scientist of Proust. Yet it is his science that gave the book its significance in his eyes. And if the value of his book is not dependent on this science, its organization is.

Explanations

Man may smile and smile but he is not an investigating animal.
He loves the obvious. He shrinks from explanations.
(Joseph Conrad, "Author's Note" to *The Secret Agent*)

EXPLANATION IS ALMOST co-extensive with consciousness. "Explanations"—the title of this chapter—is a much less daunting topic. The following discussion is limited to a description of two distinct models of explanation, the "scientific" or "covering law" model and the historical or "processive" model and an analysis of how these two models are 'parodied' respectively by Shaw and Proust in their particular acts as writers, their philosophic acts of explanation.

To this point I have considered a kind of interpretation based on the commonplace concept of texts as their writers' actions. At this point, I turn to the act of explanation in particular, and to two specific acts of explanation by two different writers.

The distinctions I employ and the rhetorical aspects of explanations I discuss are well established. But the distinction between the two models and especially the case for the independence of the historical or "processive" model have been made in the recent past by the philosopher William Dray in *Laws and Explanation in History* (1957) and by the historian and historiographer J. H. Hexter in *The History Primer* (1971). I have given them particular attention because they have focused on the relationship between an explanation's mode of articulation and its paradigm. That relationship is particularly important in analyzing the shaping force of the specific paradigms of explanation that held respectively Shaw's interest and Proust's interest.

It would be helpful to begin with a notion of what in general an explanation is. Fortunately for this discussion, the fact that there is no philosophically non-controversial concept of explanation can be ignored since what is at issue is rhetorical practice rather than philosophic validity.

Let us say, then, that an explanation in general makes something clearer than it was before the explanation was offered. Percy Bridgman in *The Logic of Modern Physics* (1927) puts it this way: "The essence of an explanation consists in reducing a situation to elements with which we are so familiar that we accept them as a matter of course, so that our curiosity rests."[1] Bridgman does not hedge here; he makes the test of an explanation's success rhetorical. It is a test that would be rejected by many contemporary philosophers of science. It is now common to claim that explanations are deduced from "general laws" that "cover" particular cases. Those who accept this view can speak of *the* explanation of something.

Those who do not accept the "covering law" model include philosophers and historians strongly impressed by the rhetorical aspect of explanation. This group dismisses the possibility of a single explanation superior to all others. For them the best explanation is best for someone or for some purpose.

Explanations simplify, reduce the unknown to the known, the less familiar to the more familiar. Dray maintains that an explanation succeeds in explaining what is not understood not only if *it* is understood but also if it is merely accepted. "It is part of the *logic* of 'explanation' that if something can be explained, there is something else which does not require explanation. But the reason it does not require explanation is not necessarily that we know its explanation already."[2]

Explanations, from this perspective, are affected by what question is asked, who asks it, and why it is asked. Not all explanations are answers to "why" questions; not all questions calling for explanations are disinterested requests for knowledge. In this way of framing things, explanation implies local curiosity about something, so in general the best explanations satisfy precisely the curiosity that exists in the questioner's mind. Precision is essential because an explanation that accounts either for too much or too little accounts for the wrong thing and so fails to be an acceptable explanation altogether. This is the typical failing of explanations found in folk wisdom or old wives' tales. "Because it is the will of God" can sound impressive in certain contexts, but of course it explains everything exactly the same way and so fits particular cases poorly. On the other hand, if explanations are entirely unique to every event, how can they ever be known at all?[3] What general concepts of method, then, apply to explanation? In broad terms, there are two. Paradigmatically, explanations are divided between those that are theory-based and those that are not. I refer to them as "scientific" and "processive," respectively.

"SCIENTIFIC" EXPLANATION

"Scientific" explanations require a theory to be intelligible. Popular explanations about how things work, what's wrong with them when they aren't working, and so on commonly refer to theories such as those of electricity or combustion. When scientists change their minds about how things burn, for instance, it is because they have abandoned one theory for another. As long as a single theory commands the field, however, scientific explanations show agreement and consistency.

There are historians, very much impressed with the generalizing power of scientific explanation in this sense, who seek to limit disagreement and inconsistency among their colleagues' explanations by adopting this "scientific" model to their own subject. Whether the scientific model always, sometimes, or never makes sense in historical discourse continues to be contested.[4] It is maintained by "scientific" historians that events in history, such as the French Revolution, can be explained by reference to general sociological laws that govern the process of revolution. Politicians, social reformers, and others who seek to manage situations often are interested in this kind of explanation because of its presumed power to predict events as well as to explain them. Prediction, in this conception, is a sort of inverse of explanation.

Perhaps the heyday of "scientific history" was the late nineteenth century, during much of which "scientific" seems to have been used as a synonym for "valid," "nonsentimental," or "accurate." Karl Marx was one exponent of this sort of science, but the idea is by no means the property of one political or economic party. It has had a powerful influence on twentieth-century historiography and philosophy of history not only among Marxists but also among classical liberals such as Sir Karl Popper, who claims to have invented the "covering law" model for historical explanation.[5]

All forms of this paradigm of explanation put heavy emphasis on what discrete phenomena have in common. All revolutions are, after all, revolutions. The mere fact that the Russian Revolution of 1917 and the French Revolution of 1789 are called by the same name seems significant to some students of revolutions. The common name is sometimes taken to be a reference to a perceived but unarticulated sociological law of revolutions. Once the inquirer knows that law, he can pick out the significant facts from the tumult and chaos of particular cases. Some "local facts" can be discounted because the theory or law renders them unnecessary. Too many "mere" facts can make scientific explanation impossible.

The general procedure is common in recent times, but it is not of recent origin. In the Fourth Gospel, for example, the disciples ask Jesus, "Rabbi, who sinned, this one or his begetters so that he be born blind?" The answer is, "Neither this man sinned nor his begetters, but he is blind so that the works of God be made visible in him."[6] This unexpected kind of explanation is then followed by the "works of God made visible" in the cure of the man born blind. The disciples' question assumes, of course, a scientific paradigm of explanation. The theory is that blindness is a divine punishment for sin; the "normal" scientific question then is *whose* sin? Jesus' explanation is unscientific since it explains why *this* man and no other is blind.

The answer most commonly acceptable today is, in its abstract form, more like what the disciples expected. It eliminates the divine agent and the notion of punishment but refers to a biochemical theory explaining sight. For a medical student something like "his retinas were malformed at birth," with its elliptical reference to a theory defining the role of the retina in vision, would be a perfectly satisfactory explanation. To the disciples, unfamiliar with such theory, it is simply unintelligible and hence no explanation at all. But it fits the paradigm of their question.

The late nineteenth century abounds in "scientific" explanations of biblical miracles. It is the great age of controversy between "science" and "religion."[7] As the prestige of "science" rose, everyone who wanted to change peoples' opinions was soon claiming that present notions about whatever was in question were "unscientific," while what they were offering represented scientific knowledge.

This rhetorical situation and this general strategy are the essential setting of Bernard Shaw's career. If ever a writer of fiction wrote to explain, Shaw—or more properly his narrative spokesman G.B.S.—was that writer. "Let me explain,"[8] occurs early in the first of the trademark prefaces and might well be his motto. He writes "for the vast majority to whom a word of explanation makes all the difference."[9] He is "nothing if not explanatory."[10] "It is your favorite jibe at me that what I call drama is nothing but explanation," he says in the "Epistle Dedicatory" to A. B. Walkley that serves as a preface to *Man and Super-*

man. And he goes on, "I have a conscience; and conscience is always anxiously explanatory."[11]

G.B.S. may have a conscience, but, more to the point I wish to make, he always has a theory. He is nothing if not "scientific." It is true that he often disagrees with prevailing scientific theories and relentlessly ridicules "workers in live flesh," but he does so only because prevailing theories are the *wrong* theories and conventional scientists are not scientific enough.

Shaw's attitude toward history is thoroughly scientific. Its main features are: (1) historians who gather facts indiscriminately—or at all—obscure what really happened; (2) an interest in what happened in the past for its own sake is trivial; (3) what really happened has nothing to do with accidents of time, place, or personality; and (4) the theories that explain past events are valuable to the extent that they make what happened in the past applicable to the solution of present problems.

In *Saint Joan*, when G.B.S. gets down to cases, what *really* explains Joan's downfall is a wholly unhistorical and anachronistic conversation between Pierre Cauchon and the earl of Warwick, personifications of the entrenched institutions she has antagonized, defending themselves. What causes their defense to fail is the "fact" that Joan is riding the waves of Protestantism and nationalism, the "logical" and "lawful" successors of medieval Catholicism and feudalism. The theory of dynamic forces or the laws of political evolution explain both the opposition Joan aroused and her subsequent vindication. The theory and the laws make her a saint instead of a crank.

Shaw as a critic of historical scholarship always argues that historians who pay attention to facts instead of theories and laws treat events as if they are discrete and unique, consequently making them antiquarian and useless. Utility is the ultimate test of truth with Shaw. He has nothing but scorn for what the philosopher Michael Oakeshott calls "genuine history"—an interest in the past for its own sake.[12]

Shaw and Oakeshott are certainly an odd pair, but the issue between them is one of the great dividing points in contemporary historiography. Arguments over who are the *genuine* historians and who are the impersonators show no signs of abating. I am not, at least on this occasion, a combatant in these lists. I merely wish to show that, unprofessional as he is, Shaw's paradigm of historical explanation is an established one. It is actually used by serious historians in ordinary practice. It is pre-eminently the method of schoolbook history. In a broadside against the history of "the educated" written in 1944, Shaw ridicules schoolbook history and the theories—such as the theory of Britain's innate wisdom in government—on which they are based because they offer such propositions as that "the battles of Trafalgar and Waterloo, which substituted Louis XVIII for Napoleon as a fitter ruler for France, were Triumphs of civilization and British good sense."[13] He contrasts this sort of "fabulous" history with his own.

> At last I became a historian myself. I wrote a play entitled *In Good King Charles' Golden Days*. For the actual occurrences of the incidents in it I cannot produce a scrap of evidence, being quite convinced that they never occurred; yet anyone reading this play or witnessing a performance of it will not only be pleasantly amused, but will come out with a knowledge of the dynamics of Charles' reign: that is, of the political and personal forces at work in it, that ten years of digging up mere facts in the British Museum or the Record Office could not give.[14]

The Preface to *Saint Joan* contains similar reflections on the "distortions of Joan's history." "It would be far less misleading if [historians] were wrong as to the facts, and right in their view of the facts."[15] In the end, "it is only through fiction that the facts can be made instructive or even intelligible."[16]

The utilitarian nature of what Shaw regards as good history is shown especially well in the last two quotations. It is one's view of the facts—that is, one's theory—that is important, not the facts themselves. In Shaw's view, "what actually happened" is an antiquarian fetish of no concern to any serious person.

Shaw never took seriously Oakeshott's notion of history or even the kind of humanistic concept held by J. H. Hexter. Particular events are, in his view, unintelligible and unimportant; theories and laws that explain all events as a dynamic system are both intelligible and vitally important. All explanations worth considering must therefore reflect an understanding of something much larger and more abstract than the particular event being explained. The idea is admirably summed up by Shaw's Immenso Champernoon: "Explanation is not a difficult art. I should say that any fool can explain anything. Whether he can leave you any the wiser is another matter."[17] For Shaw, no explanation of the past that does not tell us how to solve present problems can leave us wiser. Scientific laws whose significance is not particular to specific past events leave us wiser.

Shaw's discussion of what can and what cannot be intelligible in historical discourse reflects the epistemological problem of "the whole and the part." Historians who are careful of facts and seek to know what actually happened without recourse to theories or laws end up, in his view, with uncorrectable distortion—a kind of fiction, but one not consciously fashioned. Oakeshott would not endorse many of Shaw's views, but he does take the most uncompromising view of the general problem of knowing detached events. "To know in part is at once to know something less than the whole and know it imperfectly."[18] This is axiomatic among scholars in all fields who argue that valid explanation follows the scientific paradigm.

If we add Shaw's validating principle—the truest theory is the one most useful for the elimination of the twin plagues of the contemporary world: democracy and capitalism—we have his principles of history complete. Writing conscious fictions containing true explanations is his method of making the past intelligible and leaving his audience wiser. That the "facts" are invented is irrelevant. From Shaw's perspective, *all* facts are invented. History is merely a special form of political rhetoric.

It is also wonderfully dramatic. G.B.S. takes an event or cluster of events that seem startling and inexplicable to historians and reduces them to what might be called "what-did-you-expect" phenomena. To the layman or the antiquarian this is astounding and inexplicable. To the scientific historian it is quite everyday stuff.

"Processive" Explanation

It is a feature of scientific explanation that what is "simpler" and better known is something abstract, a law or a theory. What is not understood is less abstract, an event. This feature of scientific explanation—at least as it is applied to history—is most strongly repudiated by adherents of a second major paradigm of explanation.

J. H. Hexter puts the operative notion of this alternate paradigm as succinctly as anyone. Historians who reject the scientific paradigm are not therefore unable to learn the truth about historical events. "In fact, truth about history is not only attainable but is regularly attained ... the whole issue has been confused by a failure to make some rudimentary distinctions, the most important being that between knowing something and knowing everything."[19] Hexter maintains that the regular attainment of truth about "something" is achieved and expressed by what he calls "processive" explanation. What brings curiosity to rest in a processive explanation is not the trimming away of excess and misleading facts so that the phenomenon under investigation can be viewed as a "case" of a general law, but something close to the reverse: namely, the reinsertion of an event in a process of change. This reinsertion is accomplished by marshalling details and following the steps or stages of change at a level sufficiently minute so that no question is excited about any individual stage of change. The accumulated changes, taken together, account for the more or less radical contrast between the starting point and the end of the "process." The questions that this kind of explanation answers well usually begin, How did it come about that . . . ? How did it happen that . . . ? or even, How *could* it have happened that . . . ? In other words, historical questions. It is less frequently invoked to answer absolute Why does . . . ? or How does . . . ? questions.

There may be processes in natural phenomenon, but these are seldom the main focus of scientists' curiosity and never the chief interest of scientific historians. If Joan of Arc's collapse is seen as a "case" to be covered by a sociological law, for example, it is that law that satisfies an investigator's curiosity, not a description of the process of her collapse. Shaw argues that the details needed to describe such a process are both elusive and useless. The laws of institutional and epochal change are what give explanations of such events their force.

Hexter's history of the 1951 National League pennant race as an answer to the question, "Hey, Pop, you know why the Giants won the pennant in 1951?" makes an instructive, as well as irreverent, contrast.[20] It stresses the absence of both laws and generalities that are even remotely satisfying to the questioner's curiosity. The points of the story that are crucial from the historian's perspective—after the event—are almost all heavily influenced by human choice and judgment, but they were neither predictable or governed by laws. It is characteristic of explanations like Hexter's that they emphasize the unusual aspects of what they explain, since it is precisely these aspects that prevent one's curiosity from being satisfied by generalizations or laws.

Joan of Arc's history seems ready-made for this kind of explanation, but Shaw presented her rise and fall as quite typical and even predictable given the "laws" that operate in such "cases." Hexter, of course, would hardly tolerate calling Joan of Arc's career "typical." It is precisely because it is very nearly unparalleled that it cannot be "covered" by laws.

We could say as much for the 1951 New York Giants. Generalities such as "good pitching and a strong bench win pennants" or "strength up the middle tells down the stretch" will do most of the time to explain why a baseball team won a pennant—perhaps. Karl Popper might want to formulate a "trivial law" such as "overwhelming superiority in hitting and pitching always results in a team's winning the pennant" and claim that this is the "law" that covers the cases, but the cases these things "cover" are not the ones that whet a baseball lover's curiosity at all. Epics of the unexpected such as "The Little Miracle of Coogan's Bluff" demand explanation of an entirely different sort. It is achieved by stringing a narrative of events between what Hexter calls "pivot points." These pivot points are as important to processive explanation as laws are to scientific explanation. "Unless the writer has the outcome in mind as he writes his historical story, he will not know how to adapt the proportions of his story to the actual historical tempo, since that is knowable only to one who knows the outcome."[21] The first pivot point, then, is the outcome of the story or conclusion of the process. The second, the "beginning" point, cannot be seen as such at any time during the process. The outcome gives it its significance. Processive explanation cannot be "reversed" to serve as a technique for prediction.

Michael Oakeshott does not use the term *processive explanation*, but his discussion of experience as a completely coherent world of ideas "satisfactory to itself" includes a concept basic to it. Experience *as a whole* gives rise to no questions. It is only because of arrests in experience that explanations are ever called for. The curiosity raised by an arrest in experience is satisfied simply by putting the arrested or abstracted segment back into its place.[22]

Both Hexter and William Dray discuss a form of explanation that might be considered a proper subset of what Oakeshott describes as the general way we comprehend our experience. It is the form or paradigm of explanation that they maintain most historians actually use to write history. Neither Hexter nor Dray requires, as Oakeshott seems to, ultimate coherence as a requisite for explanation. They are, of course, considering explanations as answers to specific questions about "arrests in experience"; Oakeshott is considering how we comprehend experience as a whole.[23]

Marcel Proust does not analyze any paradigms of explanation as Shaw does in the Preface to *Saint Joan*. I should like to see him use the word "explanation" as often as Shaw does, but he does not. Nevertheless, he uses it in one very interesting place, and in doing so he illuminates the machinery of the whole of his vast work. At the very beginning of *A l'ombre des jeunes filles en fleurs* the Narrator says:

> My mother, when it was a question of our having M. de Norpois to dinner for the first time, having expressed her regret that Professor Cottard was away from home, and that she herself had quite ceased to see anything of Swann, since either of these might have helped to entertain the ex-ambassador, my father replied that so eminent a guest, so distinguished a man of science as Cottard could never be out of place at a dinner-table, but that Swann, with his ostentation, his habit of crying aloud from the house-tops the name of everyone he knew, however slightly, was a vulgar show-off whom the Marquis de Norpois would be sure to dismiss as—to use his own epithet—a "pestilent" fellow. Now this attitude on my father's part may be felt to require a few words of explanation, inasmuch as some of us, no doubt, remember a Cottard of distinct mediocrity and a Swann by whom modesty and discretion, in all his social relations, were carried to the utmost refinement of delicacy.[24]

The "few words of explanation" are duly given, not merely in the summary statements that immediately follow but very fully through stories. Telling a story to explain something is characteristic of Proust. Even taking its almost unprecedented length into account, *La recherche* is unusually rich with stories. To mention a few, there is the story of how the duc de Guermantes went from being anti-Dreyfusard to pro-Dreyfusard through the agency of the three charming Italian ladies; the story of how he became implacably anti-Dreyfusard two years later as a result of being passed over as president of the Jockey Club; the story of how the prince von Faffenheim finally was elected to the Academy of Moral Sciences; the story of how Robert de Saint-Loup was granted leave to see Rachel.[25]

But telling a story to explain something is not merely the favorite procedure of the Narrator within *La recherche*; it is also characteristic of the whole book. For how is it, after all, that our wonderfully illuminating and accomplished Narrator came to be himself? It is a curious outcome of the life he began as a morbidly anxious child who grew up to chase after illusions until he collapsed and retreated from the world a delicate and shattered invalid.

It is true that Proust did not claim the merits of an historian but of a scientist. And the Narrator has more theories than his comic counterpart, Tristram Shandy, Gentleman. But having theories does not make a storyteller a scientist, nor does the invocation of theory disqualify a discourse from being paradigmatically processive.

To Proust's way of thinking *La recherche* is not notable for detail. It is not easy to know what he meant by that odd assertion, "I omit all detail, all facts, I cling only to what appears to me some general law."[26] The book is economical in the main, but if Proust means that the only details included are those needed to show the operation of "laws," he is correct only in the case of the Narrator's sudden illumination at the end of *Le temps retrouvé*. And that case is an exception, however important, to his usual practice.

Consider, for example, the Narrator's story about how he came to fall in love with Gilberte when he was a boy.[27] Like almost all of the stories in the novel, it is remarkably sure-footed in scale and treatment, in its choices of description, summary, and representation. It also testifies to the extraordinary observation of internal states of feeling and their elision one into another that is one of Proust's—and the Narrator's—characteristics. This acute and sensitive perception is a trait that Proust shares with many psychologists. Psychologists almost invariably respect this quality of Proust's intelligence. But can this ability to describe from the inside, so to speak, the progress of an adolescent love affair be said to clarify or even to illustrate any "general law"?

Consider the disposition of the story. It begins with the Narrator recalling Balbec, then referring to a time before he had ever been there. He recalls what Swann told him about its cathedral, and then he recounts how that information shaped his image of the place, how it had given substance of a kind to the very name "Balbec." This leads to further examples of a name and some bits of information giving imaginary form to those wonderful and mysterious towns along the route from Paris to Balbec and a similar process with respect to the famous cities of northern Italy.

He recounts, then, what happened as the time approached for him to replace his fantasies of those cities, utterly unlike any he had ever seen, with the cities themselves. The trip to northern Italy that his parents proposed for him caused such nervous excitement that he grew too ill to leave at all.

All this is prelude to his visits to the Champs-Elysées, where he spent the afternoons of his Easter vacation because he was too ill to go to Italy. At first dreary and inadequate substitutes for the trip, these dispirited visits to the thoroughly unmagical public park are actually revealed to be the dawn of a new epoch in the Narrator's life. For it was on one of these visits, an unforeseen consequence of his fantasies on the names of places, that he came to make Gilberte Swann's acquaintance and fall in love with her much as he had previously fallen in love with Balbec and Italy.

Care is taken to emphasize the similarities between the towns and Gilberte as they become objects of his fascination. That Gilberte is said to mark a personal epoch is important because there will be many other such epochs in the novel, each of which derives some of its emotional and rhetorical power from its place in a continuum.

But where is the "general law" in all this? And what knowledge of such laws could possibly have led to the masterful shaping of these apparently disparate materials into the story the Narrator tells? There is no law of unforeseen compensations that determines this new epoch in the Narrator's life. In fact, the story he tells is marked by the contingent and accidental nature of its episodes. It is true that the Narrator shows a regularity in his emotional life, but what law does the story depend upon? The vacuous "law" that a child like this one who goes to the Champs-Elysées and happens to meet a little girl like Gilberte will fix on her as an object of fascination? It is not a "general law" but the point at which the Narrator stands, as he surveys the past, that shapes his story so that the many events he narrates fit together in a continuing series leading to his final understanding of the past.

Shaw's way of explaining things is more lawful. His concepts of "the dynamic forces that shape epochs" and "the common man's fear of superior beings" determine the shape of his history of Joan's career. Almost nothing is contingent in that account. *Saint Joan* does not explain the way things happened to turn out; it explains the way things had to turn out. Moreover, the narrative does not rest on a careful arrangement of detail but on the wholesale invention of events that make laws visible by showing how they operate. The story Shaw tells does not depend for its shape on where he stands in relation to the events. Anyone who knew the relevant laws of dynamics and popular fear could have predicted the outcome from the moment Joan left her father's farm. If Joan could reflect upon the case—and Shaw brings her back in his epilogue to do just that—she *still* wouldn't know what happened to her, really, or why, because she still has no grasp of the laws. Leaving aside the questions of how Shaw came to the knowledge of these laws and what their value is, his explanation has the merit of conforming to them. That is what makes it "scientific."

Proust's data are quite different. They are not consequences of laws. They cannot, therefore, serve as evidence for the laws even in the circular way that Shaw's data do. Shaw treated problems proper to historical process by a method he claimed is "scientific." If Proust regarded the subject matter of *La recherche* as "scientific," as he seems to have done, he treated it processively or historically.

Both Hexter and Dray are emphatic in their claims that history is a significant and intellectually autonomous way of knowing, and each offers a powerful argument for such a claim. It is certain, or as certain as such conclusions ever are, that Shaw never seriously entertained such a possibility. As far as he was concerned, even if such history can reach true conclusions, those conclusions are trivial.

Proust had more respect for the paradigm of knowledge that Hexter calls processive. He was intimately familiar with the writing of one of its classic French practitioners, the duc de Saint-Simon. If he read the 1743 preface to Saint-Simon's *Mémoires*—as he almost certainly did—Proust encountered a famous distinction between scientific and historical methods.

> the arts and sciences consist of a succession of rules, propositions, degrees which follow necessarily upon one another and which are not, consequently, impossible for a brilliant, sound and studious mind which has received only their first principles from other people to discover one after another. . . . But history is of a kind entirely different from all other forms of knowledge. Although all the general and particular events that comprise it are caused by one another and form a succession so delicate that the breaking of one link will destroy it, or at least change the event that follows it, it is nevertheless true that unlike the arts, above all the sciences, where one level, one discovery, leads exclusively to a certain other one, no general or particular historical event necessarily announces what it will cause and very often it will be quite reasonable to expect the opposite [of what actually results]. Consequently, neither principles, nor keys, elements, rules nor any introduction once well understood by no matter how brilliant, sound or studious a mind can conduct that mind by itself to the sundry events of history: this results in the necessity for a tutor continually at one's side who moves from fact to fact by means of a connected narrative from which the reader learns what, without it, will be always necessarily and absolutely unknown.[28]

Proust's stories sometimes seem to be taken straight from Saint-Simon's pages, yet Proust insists on the scientific nature of his book and the central role of the kind of "laws" that Saint-Simon rejects.

Aside from Proust's tendency to disguise his debts, there is a compelling reason for his insistence on the laws. Proust could not claim a reader's attention for the reasons Saint-Simon can. Louis XIV's most unyielding antagonist offers uniquely detailed accounts of the important events of the *grand monarque*'s last twenty-four years and a privileged account of the duc d'Orléans' regency. But if Proust's book is significant, it cannot be so because everyone already acknowledges that the events it describes are important. For Proust there seemed to be only one acceptable alternative—that those events, properly seen, demonstrate general laws of human experience.

To understand this claim is not, of course, to accept it. J. H. Hexter makes a wry objection to claims that historians really follow the scientific model of explanation. Scientific explanations articulated in conventional form, he observes, will look thin. By comparison, historical or processive explanations articulated in conventional form will appear to be "egregiously obese."[29]

If ever a book could be said to be egregiously obese, surely *A la recherche du temps perdu* is that book. The text of *Saint Joan* could be fitted into it at least fifty times. Certainly it is not true that the collapse of Joan of Arc is an event fifty times more simple to explain as the collapse and recovery of the Narrator. We might even recall that *Saint Joan* is a long play and that Shaw was never very attentive to the requirements of producers when he had an important project in hand. *Back to Methusalah*, for example, with its preface and additions is a considerable volume, unproducible in its entirety on any stage.

The dramatic form of the consecutive history of Saint Joan is not what makes it shorter than a traditional historical narrative on such a subject; Shaw's mode of explanation does. Details are irrelevant to that mode. But making connections through filling in relevant detail is, if not the whole art of *La recherche*, at least the dominant method of procedure. The laws are always subordinate to the story. Proust was not altogether wrong when he claimed that there are no unnecessary facts or details in his book—but just look at the number of necessary ones.

In a book fascinating not so much for what it says as for the fact that it was written at all, Milton L. Miller devotes an entire chapter to a comparison of *La recherche* with Thomas French's five-volume work *The Integration of Behavior*—a study of a single individual whose object is to draw some general conclusions about psychological disturbances.[30]

Miller claims striking parallels between French's patient and Proust. The analysis is compromised by historical errors and Miller's persistent collapsing of the fictional Narrator and Proust himself. The parallels, such as they are, seem to me inconsequential. But the *literary* parallels between French's case history and *La recherche* are striking indeed.

The selection and degree of detail, the encyclopedic scope, and the length of Proust's book—in short, its materials and outward appearance—while unusual in modern novelistic fiction, are about normal for a very full case history seeking to draw general conclusions. Full case histories tend to be long because they tend to gather a great many details. Serious works of this kind are seldom content merely to illustrate a theory or law. Particular details might be explained by a theory, but many case histories really are processive histories, and sometimes not very tidy ones because neither the beginning nor the end of the process is always clear.

Not only does *La recherche* look like history, it is first of all and first to last a narrative—a *story*. Why did Proust decide to express himself in such a form? How did he decide where to start? How could he have decided to make the surprising shifts in scale and sequence, so often leading us to expect just the opposite of what happens? These are not questions that can be answered by reference to laws and scientific theories; they are precisely the areas of Proust's genius that make his book impervious to the fashions and revolutions in what counts as scientific, psychological, or sociological knowledge. They are also the gifts that make great narrative historians great.

Proust was very proud of his theories. If they were ever taken seriously, they are not taken seriously today. Yet his reputation stands higher now than ever. What was at first obscure—what he calls his "architecture"—is widely admired today. *La recherche* is much more than a collection of brilliant observations. For all its bulk, it is a tightly organized narrative whose complex sequence of parts is a tour de force of narrative art. To see how it works, that is, to see how the parts operate together as an explanation, it is not to philosophers like Karl Popper or Morton White that we must turn, but to scholars who show how stories can be made to explain. There is no need to go further than Hexter's primer. If we look for philosophic validation of explanation without recourse to "laws," Dray's monograph provides it.

Having described my terms, concepts, and procedures, I am ready to turn, at last, to Bernard Shaw and Marcel Proust, their texts, their acts.

Bernard Shaw: Historical Explanation

*Great works of fiction are the arduous victories of great
minds over great imaginations.*
(Bernard Shaw, *Our Theatre in the Nineties*)

"A FRANKLY DOCTRINAL THEATRE"

BERNARD SHAW has not changed the economic organization of
the world or raised its ordinary level of justice; he has not persuaded
the human race to accept divine responsibilities or even to abandon vengeance. To be sure, few of his critics consider these failures
relevant to appraisals of his art. But Shaw, who hated to follow the
crowd, did.

Today Shaw is widely admired as a dramatic genius, a brilliant wit,
and the master of a plain and energetic elegance that characterizes one
of the great prose styles of his generation. His plays continue to enjoy
unusual success in the theater and as "literature." But Shaw's success,
such as it is, rests on concepts of art alien both to his thought and to his
practice. In his view, dramatic art is an instrument of reform. Its success or failure cannot be measured by what the players do on the stage
but only by what the audience does after it leaves the theater.

Such notions were not fashionable in Shaw's lifetime and are not
fashionable today. In fits of broad-mindedness, literary theorists have
been known to concede that some rhetorical literature is "art," but it is
at best art of a troglodyte variety. On this subject René Wellek and
Austin Warren undoubtedly speak for the many. "We reject as poetry," they decree, "or label as mere rhetoric everything which per-
suades us to a definite outward action." Nevertheless, "it would be a
narrow conception of literature to exclude all propaganda art. . . . We
have to recognize transitional forms."[1] If Shaw is to be accommodated
by such reasoning, his art is second-rate not because it fails to effect
reform but because it tries to.

But Shaw invariably finds such thinking perverse. As early as 1891
he writes, "we want a frankly doctrinal theatre,"[2] and as late as 1933,

"All great art and literature is propaganda."[3] Few of his critics since Chesterton have attempted to understand his plays as a program of reform, yet Shaw could hardly have been more emphatic on this point. His plays are not about his characters; they are about his audience.

> I must ... warn my readers that my attacks are directed against themselves, not against my stage figures. They cannot too thoroughly understand that the guilt of defective social organization does not lie alone on the people who actually work the commercial makeshifts which the defects of society make inevitable ... but [on] the whole body of citizens.[4]

Shaw is, from first to last, perfectly open about the practical and doctrinal character of his drama. His program is simple, even classical. He seeks first to convict his audience of sin, then to move them to "definite outward action." But his current reputation was established in great measure by critics who are not in sympathy with his ends and who baldly deny that his drama is fundamentally practical. The lively admiration Shaw can inspire in people who abhor his ideas encourages efforts to rescue the artist from the reformer. Edmund Wilson's comment is representative: "It used to be said of Shaw that he was primarily not an artist, but a promulgator of certain ideas. The truth is, I think, that he is a considerable artist, but that his ideas—that is, his social philosophy proper—have always been confused and uncertain."[5]

Even critics who admire Shaw's ideas often refuse to treat them as anything but unfortunate obstacles to his dramatic genius. Elder Olson, for example, admires Shaw's "wonderful humanitarian instincts" but continues,

> I do not think much of Shaw as thinker ... he is less a philosopher than a crank; his ideas are neither original nor profound. Despite his great reputation for argument, he is really very poor at it. . . . But he *is* a great playwright; and as long as the playwright has the upper hand of the philosopher and propagandist, his contentiousness makes for freshness, and his extravagance for fun.[6]

R. S. Crane praises Shaw's best plays—unspecified—as "finished and lastingly moving works of didactic art," but the compliment comes at a price that undoubtedly would have moved Shaw to reject it. For, according to Crane, these best plays "subsumed . . . practical aims and deflected them from any easily recognizable party line."[7] Marvin

Mudrick has no more regard for Shaw as a thinker than Olson does, but, far from regarding him as a great playwright, Mudrick regards him as a dramatic misfit. "The point is not that Shaw's plays are tracts, but that they are so much duller, clumsier, more banal than his un-dramatized tracts. . . . The old joke is a statement of fact: Shaw's prefaces *are* better than his plays."[8]

None of these views of Shaw is without value, but none attempts to take Shaw's own concept of art seriously. Even if his ideas are shallow, they always come first. And to the extent that his plays are successful, they cannot be divorced from the ideas that give them their power. That, at least, is Shaw's view: "No doubt I must recognize, as even the Ancient Mariner did, that I must tell my story entertainingly if I am to hold the wedding guest spellbound in spite of the siren sounds of the loud bassoon. But 'for art's sake' alone I would not face the toil of writing a single sentence."[9]

Shaw often equates the power of a work with "style," but his notion of style is not decorative. He is emphatic on the point that no great art is possible except as the product of strong conviction. If it lives on, even after the ideas on which it is predicated are exploded, it still owes its vitality to those ideas.

> Effectiveness of assertion is the Alpha and Omega of style. He who has nothing to assert has no style and can have none: he who has something to assert will go as far in power of style as its momentous-ness and his conviction will carry him. Disprove his assertion after it is made, yet its style remains. . . . All the assertions get disproved sooner or later; and so we find the world full of a magnificent débris of artistic fossils, with the matter-of-fact credibility gone clean out of them, but the form still splendid. And that is why the old masters play the deuce with our mere susceptibles. Your Royal Academician thinks he can get the style of Giotto without Giotto's beliefs, and cor-rect his perspective into the bargain.[10]

It is impossible, then, to understand Shaw as he asked to be under-stood without considering the purpose of his plays, and that must in-volve considering his ideas—not merely his ideas about art but also his ideas about what is wrong with the world and the role of dramatic literature in setting it right. No one can be blamed for wishing to avoid such terrain, but there is no other way to enter the thought of a man who insists that "the best dramatic art is the operation of a divinatory instinct for truth."[11]

G.B.S.

Sometime before 1876, when he first settled in London, Bernard Shaw came to the conclusion that the world is unfit for human habitation. Between 1879 and 1884 he expressed his general disapproval of things in five long novels, not one of which found a commercial publisher.

"Mainly About Myself" (1898), the preface to Shaw's three "unpleasant" plays, offers an account of his failed career as a novelist and his subsequent success as a critic.

> Now it is clear that a novel cannot be too bad to be worth publishing.... I was not convinced that the publishers' view was commercially sound until I got a clue to my real condition from a friend of mine, a physician who had devoted himself specially to ophthalmic surgery. He tested my eyesight one evening, and informed me that it was quite uninteresting to him because it was normal. I naturally took this to mean that it was like everybody else's; but he rejected this construction as paradoxical, and hastened to explain to me that I was an exceptional and highly fortunate person optically, normal sight conferring the power of seeing things accurately, and being enjoyed by only about ten per cent of the population, the remaining ninety per cent being abnormal. I immediately perceived the explanation of my want of success in fiction. My mind's eye, like my body's, was "normal": it saw things differently from other people's eyes, and saw them better.... Had I been a practical commonsense moneyloving Englishman, the matter would have been easy enough: I should have put on a pair of abnormal spectacles and aberred my vision to the liking of the ninety per cent of potential bookbuyers. But I was so prodigiously self-satisfied with my superiority, so flattered by my abnormal normality, that the resource of hypocrisy never occurred to me. Better see rightly on a pound a week than squint on a million. The question was, how to get the pound a week. The matter, once I gave up writing novels, was not so very difficult.... All I had to do was open my normal eyes, and with my utmost literary skill put the case exactly as it struck me, or describe the thing exactly as I saw it, to be applauded as the most humorously extravagant paradoxer in London.... Soon my privileges were enormous and my wealth immense. I had a prominent place reserved for me on a prominent journal every week to say my say as if I were the most important person in the kingdom.[12]

This delightful arioso is a fair sample of Shaw's mature style. Unfortunately, even such exceptional connoisseurs of style as Sir Max Beerbohm failed to give sufficient attention to a notable feature of such passages: they are spoken not by Bernard Shaw, but by his familiar spokesman, the irrepressible world authority on everything, G.B.S.

G.B.S. is entertaining, benevolent, witty, assertive, and extravagantly unrealistic. Although he is good at picking up jargon, he seldom knows what he is ostensibly talking about. But he has a way of giving expression precisely to a party line—the fundamental beliefs of Fabian socialism. Mr. Shaw, on the other hand, was by all accounts a realistic and sensible man whose only point of solid contact with G.B.S. is his belief in the same party line. Unlike G.B.S., however, Shaw does not inadvertently reflect that line; he was neither an unconscious Fabian nor a party hack but, as Martin Meisel says, "one of [the party's] prime shapers."[13]

G.B.S. seems to have led a charmed life, but Shaw knew that it takes a good deal more than normal mental eyesight to obtain a prominent place on a prominent journal. He knew it because he worked as a badly paid and obscure journalist for nine years before he became a famous and successful critic, first of music, then of drama. Even after his privileges were enormous and his wealth immense, he looked with a kind of moral horror on his "desperate days." In his view he was saved from mortgaging his life to the commercial makeshifts of a defective social organization only by his "insane gift" for "conjuring up imaginary people in imaginary places, and finding pretexts for theatrical scenes between them."[14] He determined to use that gift in the interests of the 90 percent of society whose gifts were "sane." The invention of G.B.S. is neither a personal indulgence nor a gratuitous display of wit. It is part of a strategy of reform.

Not everyone who came into personal contact with Shaw understood how different he was from his celebrated literary alter ego. One who did was the celebrity recluse T. E. Lawrence, Lawrence of Arabia, who was himself a considerable authority on invented personalities. "When I met you," Lawrence wrote to Shaw in 1928, "I discovered that the public Shaw wasn't even a caricature, much less a likeness, of the private one."[15]

Although the private Shaw's transition from failed novelist to successful critic was considerably more gradual than G.B.S.'s, it was similarly prepared for by a scientific illumination. In 1884 Shaw joined the Fabian Society, a little group of socialists who interested themselves in the science taught by such specialists as Henry George and Karl Marx. The Fabians were not, however, ordinary communists. They distinguished themselves by their analysis of how the scientific principles of socialist society might be transformed into everyday reality in Victorian England. The Fabians quickly came to regard themselves as practical scientists, nicely distinguishing themselves from their impractical confreres the "impossibilist" revolutionaries.

The distinctive conclusion of the Fabians is that a proletarian revolution cannot succeed in replacing anarchic capitalism with scientific socialism. In England, in the ninth decade of the nineteenth century, they maintained, such a change can come about only through a gradual, step-by-step process. The key to success is not a proletarian revolution but the conversion of the great mass of middling individuals. "Gradualism" and "permeation" became the bywords of the Fabian Society. The group's chief theoretician was Sidney Webb; its effective minister of propaganda, Bernard Shaw.

The merits of Fabian socialism as political philosophy or economic policy are irrelevant to understanding Shaw, but his adherence to Fabian strategy is the foundation of his career as a writer. To read Shaw's novels is to see the proof of this claim. Shaw is the kind of writer who needs a sense of practical purpose before he can rise above what he calls mere correctness. In discussing his first novel, *Immaturity*, some fifty years after he wrote it, he makes two important observations: first, "the lack of . . . a clear comprehension of life in the light of an intelligible theory: in short, a religion . . . set limits to this ungainly first novel";[16] second, there is "nothing of the voice of the public speaker in it: the voice that rings through so much of my later work."[17]

It was not Shaw's eye doctor but his zeal for socialism that led him to abandon novel writing—not for criticism but for platform oratory. It was on the platform, suitably enough, that G.B.S. found his voice. In short, the Fabian Society provided Shaw with his "clear comprehension of life in the light of an intelligible theory," gave him a practical mission, and helped him discover the oratorical style for which he has such a strong artistic affinity. In addressing perhaps a thousand audiences between 1883 and 1895, Shaw learned how to attract attention and how to direct it; what is more, he learned to subordinate his own character to an invented one better suited to his audience.[18]

G.B.S. is a product of Shaw's career as a platform orator. His leading characteristics are determined by the audience to whom Shaw speaks, not by Shaw's own temperament or character. Shaw's audience distrusts visionaries and misfits, so G.B.S. is a disinterested "scientist" and an immensely successful one. His audience respects technical "experts," so G.B.S. knows simply everything. In an offhand way, he can top any expert on any subject.

The character was developed over a period of several years. It was not until 1888, when Shaw began to write music criticism for the *Star*—as Corno di Bassetto—that he began to demonstrate his talent for turning journalism into propaganda and making it palatable to a wide circle of readers. In his own delighted words, "I could make deaf stockbrokers read my two pages on music."[19]

In 1890 Shaw moved to the *World*, where he wrote music criticism until 1894. He signed these columns G.B.S. When he left the *World* to become the theater critic for Frank Harris's *Saturday Review*, he greatly reduced the time he spent on the platform. But Shaw did not abandon oratory for journalism as he had abandoned novel writing for oratory. He merely found a way to be an orator in print. Maurice Valency observes—correctly, I think—that Shaw "[t]o the end of his days ... considered himself a journalist, but from the first his style was oratorical."[20] There is no contradiction here. Shaw merely discovered in practice what a great student of modern vernacular prose style offers as a scholarly conclusion.

> The ancients were very slow to recognize any kind of literary customs other than oral ones; and even in the genres that were obviously meant for silent reading, such as the letter, the form of the style was controlled by the ear. This is a sound principle at all times, and for all kinds of style, and its operation cannot be escaped even though it is forgotten or denied. There is only one rhetoric, the art of the beauty of spoken sounds. In oratory this beauty displays itself in its most obvious, explicit, exfoliated forms; in the *genus humile* in much more delicate, implicit, or mingled ones. But the forms are ultimately the same, and whatever beauty of style we find in the most subtle and intimate kinds of discourse could be explained—if there were critics skillful and minute enough—in terms of oratorical effect.[21]

Shaw's style is obvious and explicit in most respects. Its most subtle feature is the character he invented to speak for him—an achievement that is rarely lost on other writers, of whatever style, who invent spokesmen. "Bernard Shaw educed almost innumerable persons or *dramatis personae:* the most ephemeral of them is, I suspect, that G.B.S.

who represented him in public and who lavished in the newspaper columns so many facile witticisms."[22]

G.B.S. in the Theater

By his own account, G.B.S. turned to the theater when he was no longer able to write journalism.

> In my weekly columns, which I once filled full from a magic well that never ran dry or lost its sparkle . . . I began to repeat myself; to fall into a style which, to my great peril, was recognized as at least partly serious. . . . I listened to the voice of the publisher for the first time since he had refused to listen to mine. I turned over my articles again; but to serve up the weekly paper of five years ago as a novelty! no: I had not yet fallen so low, though I see that degradation looming before me as an agricultural laborer sees the workhouse. So I said, "I will begin with small sins: I will publish my plays."[23]

G.B.S., a man in the business of attracting attention, knows the value of pulling a rabbit from a hat, but, like any good conjurer, he is more interested in concealing details than in revealing them. Matter-of-fact historians may want to consider a few points that G.B.S. does not choose to mention. To begin with, Shaw was not driven to publish his plays because his career as a columnist was in decline. His first play, *Widowers' Houses*, was produced in 1892, when he was still writing music criticism for the *World*. His brilliant stint as theater critic for the *Saturday Review* did not even begin until 1895, more than two years later. It is also worth noting that in the spring of 1898, when Shaw gave over writing for periodicals, he was at the top of his form. Finally, he did not leave one career as a journalist for another as a playwright. He merely stopped writing journalism for a small group of readers in order to write journalism for a large one.

Later on, Shaw would be happy enough to serve up the weekly paper of five years ago—or thirty-five years ago—when there was a huge new audience for it. His problem was to attract that audience; his solution was to write plays. Going to the theater in search of readers is surely a singular tactic, but then Shaw's career in the theater is altogether a singular one. Early on, perhaps from the start, he thought of his plays as books. G.B.S. can say, as if it were the most normal thing in the world, that he decided to *publish* his plays. However well they play—and they play beautifully—they are meant finally to be read. If their production was a device for attracting the attention of the reading public, as distinct from the theater-going public, it was a successful one from the beginning.

Widowers' Houses may have played to small audiences, but almost everyone who read a newspaper heard about it. As G.B.S. relates with evident satisfaction: "[T]he newspapers discussed the play for a whole fortnight not only in the ordinary theatrical notices and criticisms, but in leading articles and letters. . . ."[24]

Shaw's second theatrical venture, *Mrs. Warren's Profession* (1894), played to even smaller audiences but reaped an immensely greater harvest of publicity. The Lord Chamberlain refused to license its performance. It is almost as if Shaw's years on the platform and in print had been a deliberate preparation for just this moment. He certainly took full advantage of the opportunity it offered. The ensuing melodrama of the fearless playwright armed only with his mighty pen and the mindless censor armed with all the feeble powers of the state marks a decisive turning point in Shaw's career. It was not performed on the stage but in the newspapers, where its audience was the great public that Shaw had been courting for ten years—not as a playwright but as a journalist and mob orator. Appearances to the contrary, he was a journalist and mob orator still, for he could never hope to bring his prime audience into a theater.

The Lord Chamberlain had brought Shaw's plays to the attention of the general public, but Shaw faced formidable problems in carving a stable readership out of that gawking crowd. On the whole, these assembled worthies had neither the experience nor the imagination to find published plays interesting or even intelligible; moreover, they could not be trusted to understand the force of Shaw's plays as propaganda. Naturally Shaw has an answer to these problems, and that answer is G.B.S.

G.B.S. prepares his readers to understand the plays as propaganda by addressing the issue—and the readers—directly in his prefaces, a celebrated and wholly undramatic feature of Shaw's theater. Anxious as a mother hen, he hovers over his readers providing descriptions and commentary lightly disguised as stage directions to ensure that they can picture what they read. The "plays" that Shaw decided to publish are, therefore, as much oratory and narrative as they are drama. In this form they cannot be produced on any stage, but they are as accessible as novels to the reading public, lose none of their oratorical drive, and, freed from the mercy of actors, fully meet the requirements of Shaw's "frankly doctrinal theatre."[25]

The role of G.B.S. in this "theatre" is as important as it is unusual. He is not a stage figure, but his voice and mentality, even his personality, dominate the published plays. His job is to prevent them from degenerating into mere drama by making sure they fulfill their high destiny as propaganda. His success can be measured by the objections of traditional theater audiences, whose basic sense of theater is offended by a playwright who seems to confound the stage with the pulpit and the soapbox.

Sir Max Beerbohm, Shaw's successor on the *Saturday Review*, reflects those audiences' outlook and temperament. He loved the theater but did not expect to encounter politicians, reformers, or revolutionaries attempting to sell their nostrums there. It is little wonder, then, that he found Shaw's plays "fatiguing." "It is like being harangued; it is like being a member of one of those crowds he used to exhort on street corners."[26] We might observe that it is also a tribute to Shaw's skill as a publicist that someone like Sir Max Beerbohm, who would never have stood on a street corner to have his ears assaulted with warmed-over Fabianism, finds himself a member of Shaw's audience. Within a few years of his debut as a dramatic author, no street corner on earth—and no playhouse—could accommodate the audience that Shaw succeeded in gathering for his harangues.

Not many of Shaw's critics have seen that gathering such an audience and keeping it was Shaw's first significant *artistic* success. Most of them insist upon keeping the dramatist separate from the propagandist and then dismiss Shaw's ideas as shallow and derivative without ever understanding that his ideas are not *in* the plays; they *are* the plays.

Misunderstandings of this sort are the result of critics substituting their own concepts of art for Shaw's. Art, in Shaw's view, makes the thought of exceptional people—prophets and intellectuals—accessible to the great mass of unexceptional people, whose convictions about what is and what is not possible determine how the world is run. It is not the sublime concepts of Socrates and Jesus that determine the level of justice actually achieved but the middle-class clichés of ordinary suburban commuters. Anyone who seeks to raise the level of justice as actually practiced must change the way those commuters think.

Attacks on Shaw's "social philosophy proper," to use Edmund Wilson's phrase, are misplaced. Shaw is an artist in the service of

81

ideas; he is not a philosopher. For him this means that his work begins where the philosophers' ends. As far as he is concerned, the world's social and economic problems have already been solved—intellectually. Shaw undertakes the artistic task of making those intellectual solutions accessible to the average suburban commuter by turning sublime ideas into middle-class clichés—the indispensable prerequisite for turning them into everyday reality.

Shaw's concept of art is an unusual one for his time and place. Art, as he conceives it, is not distinct from propaganda and must win a popular audience as a condition for its existence. It is simply irrelevant to Shaw's art that Elder Olson thinks his arguments are poor. Shaw is not addressing Elder Olson, an exceptionally intelligent and well-educated man who has spent a professional lifetime analyzing arguments. He is speaking to people of average intelligence and moderate education who cannot tell a good argument from a poor one. When the average suburban commuter has been raised to the intellectual level of Elder Olson, then Shaw's poor arguments will be blunders instead of masterstrokes.

Shaw's writing serves ideas in a sense that Jan van Eyck or Rogier van der Weyden would understand at once. The early Netherlandish masters took ideas expressed by theologians and gave them visual expression in order to make them available to unexceptional and unlettered viewers. Such people cannot perceive the reality of a religious mystery such as the Annunciation unless they can see a Virgin who looks like a Netherlandish lady in a room that belongs in a familiar kind of building—one whose windows look into a street like the streets they walk every day. When sacred events can be seen as literally as everyday reality, they can enter into the fabric of everyday reality and cease to be fairy tales.

Shaw's task as an artist belongs to this general conception of art but is immensely more difficult than the tasks addressed by Jan and Rogier. The painters sought merely to give a visual reality to the idea that the world we live in is enveloped by another world superior to and "more real" than the one we see every day.[27] Their viewers took the truth of such a sacred cosmology for granted.

Shaw's "theology" is not merely different in content; it has a different status with his readers. Far from taking it for granted, they regard it as heresy. That is one important reason for the central role of G.B.S. in the published plays. He must call into question his readers' beliefs, their received opinions, and prepare them to open their minds to a little heresy. Nor is it quite enough for Shaw to persuade his audience to accept his vision of a superior reality; they must themselves bring it into existence. All he asks of his audience is that they replace capitalism with communism, replace democracy with "government by the capable," and replace Christianity with the religion of "creative evolution." These are not the ordinary demands that playwrights put on English audiences in the 1890s. It is not difficult at all to understand Sir Max Beerbohm's sense of "fatigue" when he finds himself confronted with such a program. But then Shaw was always quite forthright about his conception of his artistic task: "I am not an ordinary playwright in general practice. I am a specialist in immoral and heretical plays. . . . I write plays with the deliberate object of converting the nation to my opinions. . . ."[28]

G.B.S. AS HISTORIAN

The scope of Shaw's task as a "specialist in immoral and heretical plays" is so vast that G.B.S. is called upon to give an unusual kind of continuity to the published plays. Shaw's plays are not simply random pieces of propaganda; they comprise something like a curriculum of heresy and immorality. There is, however, a good deal of repetition in this curriculum, for if Shaw's program is vast in scope, his doctrine is neither very long nor very complicated.

He seems to discuss an impressive range of topics, but that is merely part of his act. The journalist must always have—or appear to have—fresh and urgent copy. Appearances to the contrary, once we have heard his polemic against capitalism and his brief for communism, his criticism of popular Christianity and his sketch of "the religion of creative evolution," his arguments against democracy and for "government by the capable," and then add the distinctive element of Fabianism—in Sidney Webb's phrase, "the inevitability of gradualism"—we have had the whole course. Yet Shaw deploys a breathtaking display of invention in keeping these topics fresh.

Shaw taught his lessons in season and out of season for almost seventy years. His career required an almost freakish energy and stamina. It is remarkable to see him display the same energy, the same enthusiasm, the same sense of purpose in a play such as *Too True to be Good* (1935) that his readers encountered in his first plays, over forty years earlier. It is this element of almost mechanical consistency in Shaw's work that William Butler Yeats, whose artistic temperament is very far from Shaw's, said he "stood aghast before." Shaw was a walking contradiction to Yeats, and in time he invaded the poet's dreams as well. He was "the most formidable man in modern letters." He wrote "with great effect [but] without music, without style, either good or bad. . . . Presently I had a nightmare that I was haunted by a sewing machine, that clicked and shone, but the incredible thing was that the machine smiled, smiled perpetually."[29]

Throughout his long career Shaw faced the problem of finding new garb for old lessons. He sends G.B.S. to rummage around the journalist's equivalent of Rembrandt's closet, and his spokesman usually emerges in "scientific" costume, whether mundane or fantastic. He is now a professor of phonetics, now a professor of "metabiology," for the curriculum is, by and large, a "scientific" one. It looks to the future, not the past. History, at least that "matter-of-fact" history that Shaw disdains, smacks of "the dismal pseudo-scientific fatalism founded on the preposterous error as to causation in which the future is determined by the present, which has been determined by the past. Mere accident apart, the true dynamic causation is always the incessant irresistible attraction of the evolutionary future."[30]

The human race, in Shaw's view, is not passive and helpless before that evolutionary future. Shaw stands with the socialist prophets and saints in urging human society to direct its own evolution in a kind of societal soul making. "You imagine what you desire; you will what you imagine; and at last you create what you will."[31] These lines are spoken by the Serpent in the first part of Shaw's "Metabiological Pentateuch," Back to Methusalah, an ambitious summary of the Shavian curriculum written between 1918 and 1920. Rewriting the Pentateuch is perfectly in keeping with G.B.S.'s character, but some of his other postwar activities seem less so. In 1924, after thirty-two years of metabiology and scientific socialism, G.B.S. became an historian. The role is such an odd one for him that many readers of Saint Joan were confused into thinking that the play is actually about Joan of Arc.

G.B.S. is careful to explain that he is not one of those matter-of-fact historians who is right about all the nitpicking details and wrong about everything of real importance. He is a scientific historian, to be sure. But even this sort of history requires something forever beyond his reach: the ability to be disinterested. When, for example, G.B.S., that famous New Testament scholar, begins his "Preface on the Prospects of Christianity" with the question, "Why not give Christianity a trial?" it is surely not to rediscover the teachings of Jesus. Discerning readers, remembering that it is not Albert Schweitzer posing the question but the author of *Man and Superman*, will have a question of their own: What set *him* off in the direction of the four Gospels? The answer is not long in coming. A "scientific" analysis of the New Testament soon reveals that Jesus was a communist who "would have conferred an incalculable benefit on mankind" had he "worked out the practical problems of a Communist constitution."[32] Unfortunately, Jesus died before he had a chance to study *Essays in Fabian Socialism*.

G.B.S. is an expert on a rather odd range of subjects, but, in the end, the result of any scholarly inquiry is that what is wrong with the world is capitalism, democracy, and vulgar Christianity. If the human race is finally too stupid to work out the practical problems of a communist constitution, devise a way of being governed by the capable, and adopt the religion of Creative Evolution, then the irresistible evolutionary future will replace the human race with some better form of life.

It may not be clear at first why Joan of Arc has attracted G.B.S.'s attention, but his strategy in *Saint Joan* is nothing if not obvious. Our celebrated medievalist manages to include no less than six dates in his first paragraph. If that doesn't prove he's a historian, what will? He tops off the case for his erudition by tossing in casual references to women of whom his audience is almost certainly ignorant. "To say nothing of Catalina de Erauso . . ." indeed.[33]

For over fifty pages G.B.S. labors at his new profession to rescue this poor victim of inept historians from the hopelessly inaccurate interpretations of her career that have hitherto filled the pages of history books. Having cleared away the errors of previous scholars, he then gives us a consecutive history in the form of a play. No educated reader can fail to recognize the protocol. It is one that countless works of history repeat: a review of problems followed by a review of the previous literature on the subject divided into main types, objections to solutions previously put forward, new evidence, and finally a new consecutive history.

G.B.S. is, of course, something like a one-man revisionist university; still, we can hardly help wondering why he is interested in Joan of Arc. What does it matter to him if her career has been misunderstood? G.B.S. is certainly not the kind of historian who values mere accuracy. He is not interested in the past for its own sake.

What then is history good for? G.B.S. might appear to agree with Herbert Spencer that "the highest office which the historian can discharge, is that of narrating the lives of nations, so as to furnish materials for a Comparative Sociology; and for the subsequent determination of the ultimate laws to which social phenomena conform."[34] But he is not engaged in furnishing materials to sociologists, nor is he a sociologist himself. To begin with, he is not addressing scholars of any kind. Moreover, he is not trying to determine the "ultimate laws"; he seems already to know them. G.B.S. is hardly offering his learned tome on Joan of Arc for the sake of illustrating those "dynamic laws" to which he so often refers, although, in keeping with his pose of scientific detachment, that is what he seems to be doing. What then of the man who pulls the strings? For whatever G.B.S. is up to, Shaw himself is no more interested in the "laws" for their own sake than he is interested in the past for its own sake. Shaw is neither an historian nor a sociologist but a reformer rummaging through the past for usable parts. What has he discovered in Joan's history and why does it serve his interests to have his spokesman pose as a historian? To understand *Saint Joan*, it is necessary to keep G.B.S.'s project distinct from Shaw's, and to do that we shall have to consider the interplay of preface, play, and epilogue; propagandist and persona; earnest and jest.

SAINT JOAN:
THE ARGUMENT AND FUNCTION OF THE PREFACE

In the second paragraph of *Saint Joan*, G.B.S.'s most considerable venture into history, he offers his major conclusion, here boldly presented as a thing almost too evident to need argument. "It is hardly surprising that she was judicially burnt. . . ."[35] Most of the Preface is spent establishing the "scientific" basis for this conclusion. It is clear from the first page of the Preface that G.B.S. is presenting a "what-did-you-expect" explanation, and it quickly becomes clear that Joan's "case" is useful for the way it illuminates the laws and dynamic forces that shape epochs.[36] Since Joan's destruction ultimately was caused by her ignorance of these laws and forces, G.B.S. can show the superiority of his "scientific" history to "matter-of-fact" history. Joan knew the facts that matter-of-fact historians are so eager to recover, yet her account of her downfall would be worthless as an explanation of what happened.[37] She failed to see that she had created an alliance between her friends, her enemies, the civil authorities, and the ecclesiastical authorities, all of whom found it necessary to be rid of her in order to preserve their power. The matter-of-fact historians are as ignorant of the laws of power as Joan was, and they understood what happened to her no better than she did herself.

A "scientific" analysis of Joan's career will show that her failure is not an anomaly; it is precisely what a scientific historian would expect. G.B.S. wants to bring his readers up to this point of scientific observation because it is impossible for them to understand anything about Joan until they understand why they themselves "might have voted for burning her."[38] Her burning was conventional wisdom; it was also a mistake. Of course, scientists familiar with the ways of "the evolutionary appetite" understand that conventional wisdom is always a mistake.

As G.B.S. presents her, Joan is undoubtedly a heretic, but since no progress can take place without heresy, heretics are immensely valuable people.[39] It is hopeless to imagine that the representatives of the institutions a heretic sets out to destroy will see beyond their own interests. The heretic must be familiar with political institutions and must be clever enough to work through conventional lines of authority until she has established a new one powerful enough to withstand any desperate last gasps of the old.

The "case" of Joan of Arc is a demonstration of how important such knowledge and such skill are—even for a heretic who is riding the leading edge of the future and who is gifted with an attractive and tremendously forceful personality. The matter-of-fact historians have made an unintelligible muddle of Joan by making her the victim of corrupt judges and hence an exceptional case. The scientific historian will establish—mainly by simple postulation—that Joan was not the victim of corrupt judges. In one sense the scientific historian's task is not to defend Joan but to defend her judges. He does not undertake the judges' defense in the interest of historical truth or to do justice to them, but because Joan's history loses its exemplary value and becomes irrelevant to present problems if her failure depends on particular or "local" causes.

The first step for the scientific historian of Joan's "case" is to establish that everyone in a position of authority acted quite reasonably. Civil authorities could not let Joan undermine feudalism; ecclesiastical authorities could not let her undermine Catholicism. The second step is, by all accounts, a more formidable one. Joan herself has somehow to be made typical. Typical of what? we may ask. G.B.S.'s answer is that she is typical of geniuses whose vision encompasses military strategy and politics. If she seems to bear no resemblance to people like Napoleon it is because she belongs to a different variety of such geniuses, the unlearned and saintly.

Joan, in G.B.S.'s account, is something of a "natural." What saves her from being insane is simply that she was among the first to act on the understanding that feudalism had had its day and that nationalism was an idea whose day was about to dawn. It is an important feature of this treatment of Joan that the common people took up her incipient nationalism. Individuals may be aberrant, but the mass movements of human history trace the true course of the Life Force. Joan was, of course, a Protestant because Protestantism is nothing more than the religious complement to nationalism.

Matter-of-fact historians have been thrown into confusion because Joan dealt with these powerful concepts by the "visionary" method—a matter of temperament and style that raises no difficulties at all for a scientist such as G.B.S. Her method of articulating concepts to herself or to others is neither difficult to account for nor relevant to scientific evaluation. Her manner of articulation may interest antiquarians, but the scientific question is, "Are the concepts valuable?" From the standpoint of a Europe that is both nationalist and Protestant—a standpoint our guide to medieval history anachronistically and shamelessly adopts whenever it suits his purpose—the answer can hardly be in doubt.

From this perspective, Joan must be regarded not merely as a military genius but as a political one as well. Her genius in politics is, however, qualified by her ignorance. Her confidence in nationalism was sound enough, but she was too ignorant to realize that nationalism is the mortal enemy of feudalism. On a practical level, she was simply unaware that she threatened powerful vested interests—not merely those whose fortunes she had destroyed but those whose fortunes she had made, including Charles "the very victorious" king of France, who owed his crown to her.

G.B.S. boasts that he presents no melodrama of a pitiful maiden hounded and finally burned by wicked inquisitors. Instead of that old canard, he describes a struggle of a dying order of things vainly fighting against irresistible change, with Joan "the original and presumptuous" caught in the middle. There are no melodramatic villains in the piece. The "tragedy" is not Joan's but society's—that is to say, ours. "We" have always been too ignorant and too frightened to understand the value of today's heretics, who will be tomorrow's saints. Since our ignorance and our fear are "scientific" facts, it is up to the heretics to take them into account and work around them. If they do not learn to do so, change will come anyway, but it will come slowly and inefficiently.

Joan failed because she tried to substitute the force of her personality for knowledge of political institutions and skill in working within established concepts of authority. A visionary who can see quite clearly the next stage of society's evolution is naturally impatient with the cumbersome machinery of conventional authority. Joan had no patience with it and claimed undefined and unlimited authority. She thought these claims provided an efficient way of translating her vision into reality, but she was wrong. She merely raised an instinctive and uncontrollable fear in the many and assured her own destruction.

Must society waste its visionaries in this fashion? "Must . . . a Christ perish . . . in every age to save those that have no imagination?"[40] With these questions we leave the concerns of G.B.S., the medieval historian, and enter the thought of Bernard Shaw in the aftermath of the First World War. He had no new lessons to teach, but the old ones seemed even more urgent. A veteran preacher of heresy, Shaw was convinced that the world needed heretics equipped for survival. *Saint Joan* stands apart from such other post-war works as *Heartbreak House* and *Back to Methusalah* partly because it is addressed to a special audience; it is the advice of a heretic to his fellow heretics.

Joan of Arc suited Shaw's purposes because she was news. The Vatican, after five hundred years of reflection, overruled the Inquisition and made the girl whom its courts had once declared a witch, a saint. The opportunity was irresistible. Shaw, an Irish Protestant, defender of heresy, protector of the oppressed, clearly had to defend what the Vatican had abandoned—the Inquisition. Joan's trial was remarkably fair—far fairer than analogous trials recently conducted by British courts. Her judges had been maligned. Historians had distorted her trial so that society's guilt in killing its saints could be shunted onto a few corrupt judges.

G.B.S. may talk as if he were interested in historical truth, but the truth Shaw wants to preach is not discovered in history, it is merely illustrated there. Since G.B.S. is Shaw's spokesman, he finds reasons to dispense with the facts and embrace a theory, the theory of scientific history that tells us what always happens and therefore what must have happened in Joan's case. Facts are of no use, and what is of no use can be dispensed with. "In real life truth is revealed by parables and falsehood supported by facts."[41]

The real life of Saint Joan is significant for reasons that inevitably escape the petty net of facts. Properly understood, Joan was an early nationalist, one of the first Protestant martyrs, the earliest practitioner of Napoleonic warfare, and a pioneer in rational dressing for women. This may seem to be a strangely mixed list of claims about Joan, but each of the roles that G.B.S. ascribes to her is less romantic than its predecessor, and they all fit into a concept of political evolution that will govern the "history" to follow.

Joan's greatest success was as a general. She was burned for wearing men's clothes, but G.B.S. takes this breach of medieval law as a sign of grace. The romantic image of women to which the stage pays tribute is an obstacle in the way of political progress. Just as Joan forced her king to accept her as a general, she forced her soldiers to accept her as one of themselves, for all practical purposes a man. In these matters she acted intelligently because she understood that she was a soldier and that no one who fulfilled her society's concept of womanhood could expect to lead an army. Unfortunately, she did not understand that she was a nationalist because she was ignorant of the institutions of feudalism, and she went to the stake without understanding that she was a Protestant because she was ignorant of the institutions of medieval Catholicism.

In view of the forces Joan was taking on in her ignorance, what need have we of corrupt judges or villains? Her death was as much a matter of course as that of a man who leaps into a volcano.

This, then, is the argument of the Preface. As it relates to the play, the task of the Preface is to make the action reasonable and coherent. The Preface establishes—or at least proclaims—the essential cause of Joan's failure. The Preface describes the role of the "evolutionary appetite" and the paired forces of feudalism and Catholicism, nationalism and Protestantism. Finally, the Preface makes Joan's history useful by allowing us to see it not as a single unusual career but as the typical failure of a mere visionary. It is not enough to have vision, for the old order will not surrender to the new without a fight.

Once we leave medieval history for this timely bit of practical political wisdom, we can begin to see why Shaw wrote *Saint Joan*. If only Joan had been a member of the Fabian Society and followed its strategy of permeation and gradualism, the world might have been spared the Thirty Years War and the French Revolution. Shaw does not abandon propaganda in *Saint Joan*. For him, Joan is no more than a ship of opportunity. Despite Huizinga's comments, I cannot think that Shaw cared a hang about Joan of Arc as she actually was. If it is not quite accurate to equate Shaw's attitude with Carlyle's, it is ridiculous to equate it with Ranke's. Even if it were possible to write about the past *wie es eigentlich gewesen ist*, the result would be both useless and unintelligible. As far as Shaw is concerned, "events as they actually occur mean no more than a passing crowd to a policeman on point duty, they must be arranged in some comprehensible order as stories."[42] "It is only through fiction that facts can be made instructive or even intelligible."[43] Shaw's attitude toward history, like his attitude toward most other things, was practical and utilitarian with a vengeance. He ordinarily had no patience with the past unless it could be fashioned into an instrument for change.

Shaw commonly spoke as if human life were two hops from being canceled by an evolutionary Life Force whose patience finally had worn away altogether. In his view, World War I might very well have been the last straw. If G.B.S. poses as an historian whose purpose is to offer an improved history of Joan of Arc, Bernard Shaw is after bigger game. He sets out to explain the value of heresy in the evolutionary scheme of human society and the requirements for turning heretical vision into commonplace reality. *Saint Joan* is not an attempt to understand yesterday's saints; it is a primer for today's heretics.

The Scope of the Play

Once we have understood the Preface, the play of Saint Joan is, from one point of view, mechanical. It illustrates the theory already completely worked out in the Preface. The play confirms the theory by a sort of dramatic hallucination. There is nothing original in the play; no new material is introduced; the function of the characters and—especially in scene four—their very speeches are determined by the Preface.

The relationship between the Preface and the play is similar to the relationship between scientific theory and laboratory "experiments" in elementary science courses. The experiment confirms what the theory has already explained. Shaw's elementary course in scientific history reflects the science of historians such as Henry Buckle and Karl Marx.

Scientific history's paradigm of explanation and its interest in laws give G.B.S. a chance to indulge his love for paradox. Joan had typically been presented as a success. She talked her way into taking command of Charles's army and then did what the other generals could not do, lead it to victory. There are no "typical" cases of teenage farm girls taking command of armies on the verge of defeat and leading them to brilliant success. Not surprisingly, this unheard-of achievement is what led to conflicting opinions about her voices, her sanity, her sorcery, and, finally, her sanctity.

Still, G.B.S. addresses a new age with new fashions in belief. The new fashion is "science," and science believes in lawful and regular events. According to G.B.S., there is nothing remarkable about Joan's leap from obscurity to the pinnacle of power. Look at Mohammed, at Napoleon, at any "typical" upstart prophet or conqueror. G.B.S. takes little interest in Joan's rise; he presents it as a matter of course. Her ascent is the smooth progress of a strong personality confronting weak ones, of a determined believer confronting people caught up in doubt and indecision. Her decline receives more careful treatment. When forceful personalities confront one another knowledge and cunning decide the issue, and Joan, ignorant and naive as she is, loses all her contests with the conventional authorities, who know they must fight or perish.

Nevertheless, *Saint Joan* is not a tragedy. It is essential to Shaw's view of politics that today's heretics can succeed where Joan failed. If Shaw had the technical capacity to write tragedy, he was ideologically incapable of it. His almost incredible volume of work during a long career as orator, journalist, and playwright is marked by two convictions: first, that society is so badly organized that the future of the human race is in doubt; and, second, that the course of self-destruction can be changed. The most pernicious of our errors is the notion that there are no alternatives to the way we live at present.

Shaw may have died convinced that things were worse than they were when he was born, but with World War II still raging he could write at the beginning of his political last testament: "Is human nature incurably depraved? If it is, reading this book will be a waste of time ... if we have neither the political capacity nor the goodwill to remedy [our mistake] we had better not torment ourselves uselessly by making ourselves conscious of them."[44] From Shaw's perspective tragedy is an indulgence. It may be art, but it is decadent art—the kind of art for whose sake he hasn't the energy to write a single line. Joan of Arc interests him because, properly presented, her career is instructive, hence practical, but what is the practical use of "inevitable" tragedy?

Joan's burning is "hardly surprising" once we know that she was politically ignorant even as she threatened church and state with two powerful concepts that were about to transform the religion and politics of Europe. Considered in this light, she holds an obvious role in Shaw's curriculum, since he spent a lifetime trying to transform the religion and politics of Europe. The Joan who has excited the popular imagination through the ages—the heroine of melodrama, madwoman, witch, miracle worker—holds no interest at all for Shaw. The Joan who failed by substituting illiterate intuition for knowledge is another matter—if today's heretics can learn from her errors.

The Play of Saint Joan: Structure and Mechanism

The portion of the published play containing G.B.S.'s consecutive history of Saint Joan is an articulate unit separate from his historiographic Preface and from the Epilogue that definitively "places" the consecutive history in a special relationship to the problems of the present. Bearing in mind, then, that the consecutive history is part of a larger work, let us consider its structure and mechanism.

The six scenes break neatly, if unevenly, in the "middle." The first three represent Joan's rise from complete obscurity to the moment she and Dunois begin their move to lift the siege at Orléans. The last three represent Joan's fall from the pinnacle of success to captivity, condemnation, and death.

Each of the first three scenes establishes an important matter of fact about Joan's rise. Scene one represents her complete triumph over Baudricourt, scene two her conversion of the Dauphin and her mixed triumph over the archbishop of Rheims, scene three her winning over of Dunois and his army. The specific details are warranted not by the historical record but by the theories and "laws" G.B.S. discussed in the Preface. Both the details and the proportion of the play allocated to these successes indicate their relative unimportance. Joan's successes are treated as the necessary preliminaries to her failure; it is her failure that dominates this history.

Her only unmixed triumph is over Robert de Baudricourt in scene one, and for all the wonderful verve of that scene the victory is hollow because Robert is a chronic coward who cannot possibly resist someone as self-assured and free from fear as Joan. The novelistic stage directions begin by describing Robert as having "no will of his own."[45] Later they add that he is "self-assertive, loud-mouthed, superficially energetic, fundamentally will-less."[46] Moments after Joan is admitted to his presence, he inflates his chest imposingly "to cure the unwelcome and only too familiar sensation."[47]

Robert's foil is his spineless servant, "whom age cannot wither because he has never bloomed."[48] When Robert storms at him because he failed to get rid of Joan, this coward's servant, selected because he is so easy for his master to bully, finds himself able to say, "we are afraid of you; but she puts courage into us."[49]

This speech points to Joan's main talent. She can inspire the dispirited and demoralized. It is a natural ability, and it is the only prominent aspect of Joan's personality that has never been widely disputed. She was not merely a forceful personality; she had a genuine and valuable ability to inspire. Her military career was founded on this gift. On this point G.B.S. is merely putting the conclusions of matter-of-fact historians into dramatic form. His "science" can be seen in the way he represents Robert, for there is no historical evidence that he was an incompetent commander dominated by chronic fear.

Robert's character is a function of G.B.S.'s essential claim about Joan—that she was completely artless. She believed that she was invincible, and she was wrong. She could succeed only against people who could be intimidated by the force of her personality; therefore, Robert must have been the kind of man who had no defense against a strong personality. For subsequent scenes, it is important to know that Joan failed to understand that her success with Robert was a result of his weakness, not of her strength.

Scene two is a wonderful example of Shaw's ability to dramatize those unimaginable turning points in events. The baffling thing about Joan of Arc to this day is that she somehow convinced the powers of state to let her lead an army. How did she do it? How could she have succeeded even in talking to Charles and his generals? Try to construct a contemporary analogue, and Shaw's genius stands revealed. How would a seventeen-year-old girl from rural Nebraska have talked to the joint chiefs of staff about her strategy for conducting the Vietnam War? It is enough for most kinds of history about Joan simply that she did something that seems to be impossible. The fact that it happened is the best answer to the commonsense objection that it could not. In *Saint Joan, how* she did it is more important. She did not know how she did it, but G.B.S. shows us that she did not do it at all; the archbishop of Rheims did it. This is, again, a departure from the historical record warranted by an a priori disjunction between inarticulate genius and ordinary competence. The disjunction is not necessary for a matter-of-fact understanding of Joan, but it is necessary for the scientific use Shaw wants to make of her.

The Archbishop is as unlike Robert de Baudricourt as he can be. He is the first capable professional in the play, and scene two is built around him. With unobtrusive and brilliant economy, the mechanism of political decision at court is laid bare. The Dauphin can do nothing without the consent of the Archbishop and the Duke de La Trémouille. La Trémouille is less powerful than the Archbishop because he does not understand the nature of political institutions or the relationship between power and office.

The first lines of the scene belong to the Duke. "I don't know how you have the patience to stand there like a stone idol,"[50] he remarks to the Archbishop. The Archbishop's response establishes not only his sophistication but his role as a foil for Joan. He is a man whose power is grounded in conventional office and made effective through self-conscious and deliberately acquired knowledge: "I am an archbishop; and an archbishop is a sort of idol. At any rate he has to learn to keep still and suffer fools patiently. Besides my dear Lord Chamberlain, it is the Dauphin's royal privilege to keep you waiting, is it not?"[51]

Joan does not appear until the scene is just more than half over, but she is the reason the Archbishop and La Trémouille have been kept waiting. She is at court, having arrived with the inevitable sensational flourish. La Hire, an important military commander, has announced her as an angel who has struck dead a local courtier for swearing. The Dauphin is convinced that he has been sent *his* saint as, according to legend, his royal predecessors had been sent theirs. "My grandfather had a saint who used to float in the air when she was praying, and told him everything he wanted to know. My poor father had two saints, Marie de Maille and the Gasque of Avignon. It is in our family; and I don't care what you say: I will have my saint too."[52] The Archbishop is not impressed with any of this. He is irritated that Baudricourt should have had so little sense as to send "some cracked country lass here."[53]

Despite the Dauphin's gratified vanity at having been sent his saint, Joan cannot, at this point, gain entry to see him. La Hire, however, is most reluctant to send her away; moreover, his grounds go beyond superstition. Baudricourt evidently believes that Joan can work miracles. The important point is not whether she can but that Baudricourt, a soldier, believes she can. Will other soldiers believe it?

The Archbishop is too prudent to oppose everyone on the question of whether they shall see the girl, and he takes up the notion that Joan may be useful. Naturally he reserves to himself what shall be done with her, but he decides for the moment that "since his Highness desires it,"[54] she may be admitted to the court. A moment before he was ready to override the Dauphin's wishes, but he knows enough about power and how to keep it to disguise the fact that the decision has been his alone. The careful preservation of official power is something Joan knows nothing about, and something she will never learn.

Yet before Joan appears, the Archbishop in a conversation with La Trémouille must prove that he is prepared to make use of Joan, should she prove useful. He alone sees that the test Charles plans to make of Joan's powers is one she cannot fail. As a professional churchman, the Archbishop is not susceptible to magic, but he is ready to recognize a miracle. It is he who defines a miracle as an event that creates faith. If Joan can create faith in the Dauphin's fight, she will be useful. His question to La Trémouille indicates what he thinks Joan's role might be: "Could you make our citizens pay war taxes, or our soldiers sacrifice their lives, if they knew what is really happening instead of what seems to them to be happening?"[55]

When Joan at last makes her appearance, she impresses the Archbishop as someone he can use to create faith in the Dauphin's cause. She is valuable because there is no trace of cynicism to dilute her personal force. She believes in her mission and in her power; moreover, her belief is contagious.

The audience is never allowed to forget that the Archbishop controls Joan. When La Hire first announces that she had struck dead Foul-Mouthed Frank for swearing, the Archbishop "severely" tries to restore common sense to the discussion. "Rubbish! Nobody has been struck dead. A drunken blackguard who has been rebuked a hundred times for swearing has fallen into a well, and been drowned. A mere coincidence."[56] This, however, is before he decides to use Joan for his own purposes. After he becomes convinced of her worth, he rebukes the court for laughing at her in these terms:

THE ARCHBISHOP: ... this maid prophesied that the blasphemer should be drowned in his sin—
JOAN: [distressed] No!

THE ARCHBISHOP: [silencing her with a gesture] I prophesy now
that you will be hanged in yours if you do not learn when to laugh
and when to pray.[57]

Joan's rise at court results from the Archbishop's changing his mind
about her. He does not, however, begin by assuming she is a lunatic
and end by considering her a saint—although he speaks as if he does.
At first he assumes she is a nuisance and at the end he thinks he can
make use of her. His comments progress from: "[Baudricourt] is sending some cracked country lass here. . . . This creature is not a saint. She
is not even a respectable woman. She does not wear women's clothes"
to his last speech in the scene: "The maid comes with God's blessing
and must be obeyed."[58] As a result, Joan and the Dauphin have their
private audience with predictable results. She wrongly attributes her
success to what she said to the Dauphin and never understands that
her success depended entirely on the Archbishop's decision to let her
succeed.

Because she is too ignorant to know where to look, she does not
observe how the power at court has shifted after her arrival. When the
scene begins the Archbishop and La Hire hold effective power between them. When it ends the Archbishop is the sole power at court,
since Charles replaces La Hire with Joan—something he could not do
without the Archbishop's support. Joan has been the Archbishop's
tool. When she tries to shove him aside, she learns that her naive self-
confidence is useless against such an opponent. At her moment of
apotheosis ending the scene, everyone *except* the Archbishop kneels.
He "gives his benediction with a sign."[59] By the time he next appears,
Joan has played out her usefulness, and he will signal her downfall.

Scene three does not require very close analysis. It is the shortest
and, in some respects, the weakest in the play. It has a few points to
make, all of them simple. The exposition rests almost entirely on a
contrast. Joan is incompetent at ordinary military tasks; Dunois is completely competent. Joan is useful to him at points where ordinary competence is not enough. Joan's specialty is delivering people from fear,
but Dunois does not need to be delivered from fear. He needs a favorable wind and fired-up troops. When the wind changes after Joan's
arrival, he is more than happy to attribute the change to her because he
recognizes her power to inspire his troops. Joan does not recognize her
military limitations, but the scene establishes that her military ability
begins and ends with the extraordinary force of her personality.

97

The first three scenes, then, establish two things about the nature of Joan's success. When it is complete and unambiguous, as with Baudricourt, it is because a weak personality collapses before an unusually forceful one. When it is incomplete and ambiguous, it is because she cannot change her presentation to suit her audience. She has the power to remove fear from the ranks of the army and replace it with a sense of mission; the ordinary soldiers accept her power as miraculous. The Archbishop knows that her power is not miraculous, but she confuses the conditions that make her power effective with the soldiers and the effective source of her power.

She is not capable of making the distinction between her power and the "intuitive method" of articulating it. Her inability to do so limits her success. The seeds of failure already have been planted and nourished by the time the Dauphin is crowned king of France at Rheims. On what ought to be a day of triumph for her, every representative of established authority, including the one she has been responsible for confirming in his office, is ranged against her.

The opposition that she has roused and that she becomes aware of after the coronation is analyzed in scene four. It is the only scene in which Joan makes no appearance at all, but it offers the reasons for her failure.

Cauchon represents the church defending itself against Protestantism. "What will the world be like when The Church's accumulated wisdom and knowledge and experience, its councils of learned, venerable pious men, are thrust into the kennel by every ignorant laborer or dairymaid whom the devil can puff up with the monstrous self-conceit of being directly inspired from heaven?"[60] The earl of Warwick, the secular arm, provides the label: "It goes deep, my lord. It is the protest of the individual soul against the interference of priest or peer between the private man and his God. I should call it Protestantism if I had to find a name for it."[61]

Of course, the aspect of the matter that Warwick finds most dangerous is Joan's "cunning device to supersede the aristocracy." Just as Cauchon sees Joan as a threat to the church, Warwick sees her as a threat to the social order and especially to his own class. "Instead of the king being merely the first among his peers, he becomes their master. That we cannot suffer: we call no man master. . . . we hold our lands in our own hands . . . by The Maid's doctrine the king will take our lands—our lands!—and make them a present to God; and God will vest them wholly in the king."[62] Cauchon gives this doctrine its name. "Call this side of her heresy Nationalism if you will."[63] The point of this Alphonse and Gaston act is to show that these two natural enemies, the church and the feudal state, have seen a common threat in Joan. Cauchon's line, "can we not sink our differences in the face of a common enemy?" is the obvious question.

But there is a third character in this scene, Warwick's impetuous chaplain, de Stogumber. Just as there were signs of Joan's defeat in the scenes that represent her rise to power, so in the scenes that represent her defeat we are not allowed to forget that her ideas were ultimately irresistible. De Stogumber, whose blind nationalism leads him to accuse her of witchcraft, is nevertheless deeply affected by her "heresy." While Warwick is trying to save the aristocracy, his own chaplain has been infected by a concept that will cause its ruin.

In describing her secular heresy, Cauchon complains that Joan sought to replace the international feudal system, "the realm of Christ's kingdom," with nations: "I can express it only by such phrases as France for the French, England for the English. . . ."[64] De Stogumber is present in order to show that it is too late to stop that kind of thinking; its appeal is not partisan. "Certainly England for the English goes without saying: it is the simple law of nature. But this woman denies to England her legitimate conquests, given her by God because of her peculiar fitness to rule over less civilized races for their good . . . [her Protestantism and Nationalism] are only excuses for her great rebellion against England. . . ."[65]

The discussion between Cauchon and Warwick in scene four articulates the theory of institutional forces defending themselves. But Cauchon and Warwick have less abstract reasons for wanting to be rid of Joan. The next scene shows that King Charles and his court are equally eager to be rid of her since they represent the same institutions that Warwick and Couchon do. Scene five also takes pains to show that although Joan's heresy is simply the next step of Europe's political evolution, it destroys her because she is both ignorant and naive.

Like all the scenes except the perfunctory scene three, scene five is subtly orchestrated. In the conversation between Joan and Dunois that begins it, its thesis is announced.

JOAN: Dear Jack: I think you like me as a soldier likes his comrade.

DUNOIS: You need it, poor innocent child of God. You have not many friends at court.[66]

The newly crowned Charles VII has the last speech in this scene: "If only she would keep quiet, or go home!" Charles speaks not only for himself but for the Archbishop and, despite his personal liking for Joan, for Dunois as well.

In the interval, two points are given dramatic representation. First, the essential source of Joan's success with common soldiers and weak-willed leaders, her personal force, cannot succeed with competent and self-assured leaders such as Dunois, Bluebeard, or the Archbishop. But she is too naive and single-minded to use another tactic with them. Second, regardless of their varying personal attitudes toward her, representatives of feudal institutions—be they English, Burgundian, or French—cannot tolerate Joan.

Charles does not speak of nationalism as Warwick does in scene four, but as a newly crowned king he cannot help supporting institutional authority and resisting charismatic claims that leap over all established legitimacy. "Oh, your voices, your voices. Why don't the voices come to me? I am king, not you."[67]

The Archbishop does not speak of Protestantism as Cauchon does, but he knows his office means nothing to Joan. She tries to use him as a kind of sacred drudge when she hears the king talk of a treaty.

> JOAN: [unabashed, and rather roughly] Then speak, you; and tell him that it is not God's will that he should take his hand from the plough.
>
> THE ARCHBISHOP: If I am not so glib with the name of God as you are, it is because I interpret his will with the authority of the Church and of my sacred office. When you first came you respected it, and would not have dared to speak as you are now speaking. You came clothed with the virtue of humility; and because God blessed your enterprises accordingly, you have stained yourself with the sin of pride. The old Greek tragedy is rising among us. It is the chastisement of hubris.[68]

Dunois, whose tone is neither petulant nor stately, nevertheless rejects Joan's claims because he knows how ignorant she is. Since there is no heresy involved, and since he likes Joan, his speech shows how impossible it is to substitute force of personality for knowledge.

> I know how many lives any move of mine will cost; and if the move is worth the cost I make it and pay the cost. But Joan never counts the cost at all: she goes ahead and trusts to God: she thinks she has God

in her pocket. Up to now she has had the numbers on her side; and she has won. But I know Joan; and I see that some day she will go ahead when she has only ten men to do the work of a hundred. And then she will find that God is on the side of the big battalions.[69]

Since Joan has neither institutional authority nor ordinary competence, she cannot translate her visions into common reality. Scenes four and five offer the "real reasons" for Joan's failure. Both scenes are wholly unhistorical, but the knowledge they express makes G.B.S.'s explanation both scientific and important. He understands what neither the matter-of-fact historians nor Joan herself ever did. That is why his explanation is worth more than theirs.

Scenes four and five are the heart of G.B.S.'s explanation—an explanation that no amount of digging through documents, no available or even possible accumulation of "mere" facts about Joan, Dunois, Cauchon, or Warwick could possibly be made to yield. G.B.S.'s explanation is both warranted and made intelligible by the sociological laws of institutions, the dynamics of epochs, the evolutionary appetite, and similar nonhistorical entities. The validity of these abstractions is such that when the available evidence is indeterminate or is actually contrary to what they demonstrate, the mere facts are overridden.

If Cauchon was corrupt, he must be presented as scrupulously fair because Joan, in the nature of things, was not a victim of corrupt judges. If her judges were corrupt, as a matter of historical fact, their corruption can only serve to obscure the real cause of her burning—a burning that no one lifted a finger to prevent. She would have been burned for universally compelling reasons whether or not the judges were corrupt. When J. M. Robertson objects that no one was in a position to save her, G.B.S. in effect replies, That is just obfuscation; anyone in such a position would have done nothing. The virtue of G.B.S.'s history is certainly not that it would satisfy an historian who thinks it is important to understand the past for its own sake. Its virtue is that it leaves his audience wiser—not about Joan but about the value of heretics.

Once we understand our historian's definition of his subject, the protocol of the celebrated trial scene presents no difficulties. Joan does not appear in the first third of this scene. Almost all of the opening segment is spent establishing that the officers of the two courts involved—the bishop's court and the inquisitor's—refused to turn Joan's trial into a political one.

Warwick prods them. De Stogumber is outraged at the scrupulous nature of the proceedings. But the inquisitor takes his office seriously and is impervious to outside pressure. He takes no notice of Warwick's convenience but is earnest about combating heresy: "For two hundred years the Holy Office has striven with these diabolical madnesses; and it knows that they begin always by vain and ignorant persons setting up their own judgment against the Church, and taking it upon themselves to be the interpreters of God's will."[70]

The procedure was not flawed. Cauchon and the inquisitor tried to save Joan from her heresy. Despite his threats, they did not begin her trial knowing they would hand her over to him. The scene takes pains to show that Joan *was* a heretic. It is her heresy that makes her a Fabian saint. The perversity of the trial is not a result of the way it was conducted. Such courts have no need of corruption to function badly; they function badly when they function at all. Although her judges were not corrupt, they deserve Joan's rebuke. "You are not fit that I should live among you."[71]

Indeed, the world is not fit for the saints to live in, nor can it be made so by the policy of doing what was done last time. It is precisely the heretics who must make the world fit for the reign of the saints. But they must be clever heretics, and Joan was not clever. The inquisitor calls her "innocent," and her innocence is what kills her. "What does she know of the Church and the Law? She did not understand a word we were saying. It is the ignorant who suffer."[72]

THE EPILOGUE

The epilogue often has been criticized as a pointless anachronism by readers who have not grasped the purpose of the play—or by readers who wish it had some other purpose. But Shaw's play cannot end with Joan's death and the reasons for it. The six scenes merely complete the explanation of Joan's failure; the epilogue establishes the purpose of that explanation and directs its "lesson" to the contemporary world. To do so, the epilogue makes three points. First, all the principals recognized, in time, that Joan's burning was a mistake. Second, Joan never understood what happened to her. Third, prudent politicians would inevitably do the same thing all over again in the same circumstances. The last point is the most important one for Shaw's real audience.

The problem at the heart of Joan's failure is a current one. Ultimately, it is not her problem but ours. The world runs according to principles of intolerance that lead to errors unrecognizable as such by the prudent.[73] Either we must all become heretics or our heretics must acquire enough knowledge of the church and the law to survive our conventional wisdom.

At this point, it is true, we are a long way from the history of Joan of Arc. But the historical explanation is parody; the lesson directed at heretics is not. The advice to heretics is the very purpose of the explanation offered in *Saint Joan*. The play is historical only in the sense that it uses historical materials—unabashedly and rather roughly. It is dramatic art only with respect to the means of its articulation. If we ask what kind of thing it is and what it is designed to do, we must consider it to be a political harangue. To understand the force of *Saint Joan* as its author's action, both its art and its history must be measured by his "beliefs."

Marcel Proust: Psychological Explanation

> ... you know perhaps, that ever since I have been ill, I have
> been working on a long book.
> (Marcel Proust to Louis de Robert, October 1912)

> ... if it were really a beautiful book, it would immediately
> bring harmony to disturbed minds and calm to troubled hearts.
> (Marcel Proust to Sydney Schiff, June or July 1922)

THE BOOK AND THE MAN

A la recherche du temps perdu is so unconventional that there is no danger of mistaking it for an "ordinary" novel. The demands it makes of its readers are so great that Proust is almost obliged to promise more than the ordinary aesthetic pleasures of fiction as a condition for finding readers at all. He does promise more and has apparently fulfilled his promise. Early critics who accused his book of being form- less, chaotic, and self-indulgent have long since given way to those who see it as a distinguished and serious work, not only a great work of fiction but a distinguished intellectual achievement as well.[1]

That Proust is a great novelist seems almost beside the point to many of his critics. Robert Liddell, for example, regards him as one of the great masters of fictional technique but takes that as a secondary achievement. Proust's intellectual work makes him no less than "the greatest man of this century."[2]

Extravagance of this sort illustrates a curious aspect of Proust's rep- utation. He is one of a small number of novelists widely accepted as a major thinker. In his lifetime, Camille Vettard compared him to Einstein.[3] François Mauriac, a man seldom noted for his giddiness, credited Proust with "conquering and mastering" time.[4] Nor are such remarks restricted to journalistic froth. Since his death, Proust's intel- lectual stature seems to have grown. He is routinely treated by aca- demic philosophers and literary critics as a major exemplar of literary and philosophic concepts: by Georges Poulet on "human time" and "Proustian space," by Paul de Man on "allegory," by Paul Ricœur on time and narrative.[5] But there is a further dimension to his reputation in which he is himself treated as an academic or scientific intellectual.

Theodore Zeldin, in a major historical work on modern France, examines Proust's work and credits him with raising "the analysis of the individual ... to a new plane."[6] Henri Ellenberger evaluates Proust's place in the history of psychology.

> Marcel Proust's work is of particular interest because its subtle analyses were not influenced by Freud and the other representatives of the new dynamic psychiatry. His academic sources went no further than Ribot and Bergson. It would be quite feasible to extract from his work a treatise of the mind, which would give a plausible picture of what the first dynamic psychiatry would have become had it followed its natural course.[7]

But what does it mean to speak of Proust's "academic sources"? Sources for what? A reader of this passage who does not know that Proust was a novelist might conclude that he was a pathologist whose "subtle analyses" are to be found in learned articles or textbooks. Indeed, *A la recherche du temps perdu* has been described as a "living textbook," not by an overenthusiastic amateur but by a professional psychiatrist.[8]

Just what it is about Proust's book that elicits such response is not easy to determine. Some commentators seem to regard the book as social history. It seldom is claimed unambiguously, however, that social history is the purpose of the book. Usually the "value" of *La recherche* as social history is claimed to be more or less incidental to its original conception.[9] A second view holds that *La recherche* is best understood as autobiography. George D. Painter advances this thesis without qualification. Indeed, for Painter *La recherche* is not a work of fiction at all but a "creative autobiography."[10] A third view sees *La recherche* as an unconventional but genuine contribution to the study of human psychology—not a "psychological novel," such as Henry James or Dostoyevsky are sometimes said to have written, but an original contribution to an academic discipline expressed in a work of fiction.

Proust followed no profession and had no direct contact with psychological research—which was in significant ferment during his lifetime.[11] Some of his scientific admirers offer these facts to explain the unconventional form that Proust chose to express his thought. It is taken for granted by most of them that he was his own data, and that his book is the result of an almost uniquely interesting and thorough self-analysis.

Even if all these views are mistaken, they are all plausible mistakes that deserve to be examined. It is hardly possible to read the book without noticing that the Narrator often discusses material proper to social history and psychology. He frequently refers to "laws" and to such exotic entities as the "algebra of desire," "the psychology of Time," and the more prosaic "process of oblivion." There are knowledgeable if not learned observations on homosexuality scattered through the book and even a kind of treatise on the subject at the beginning of *Sodome et Gomorrhe*.[12]

Proust was eager to claim any kind of intellectual distinction for his book and was anything but reticent about what he was and was not trying to accomplish. He seems to have spent a fair amount of time trying to manage the public reception of *La recherche* even while he was engaged in an irresistible romantic race with death to finish it. But an investigation of his plans and claims raises unexpected puzzles.

His book has a history almost as complicated as its form. Ideally, it was to be published as a single unit with no internal divisions. As this proved to be impractical, the book was divided into parts, given one general title and two, later three, finally seven part titles. When *Du côté de chez Swann* was published by Bernard Grasset in 1913, the rest of the book already existed in various stages of revision.

But *this* book was never published. When Proust resumed publication in 1919 with Gallimard, he had substantially altered and expanded the remaining text. Unfortunately, no direct comparison with the original sequence is possible. The situation is further complicated by the fact that Proust died in 1922, five years before *La recherche* was completely in print. He did not see the last part of *Sodome et Gomorrhe*, nor any of *La prisonière*, *La fugitive* (*Albertine disparue*), or *Le temps retrouvé* through the press. Because he normally added substantially to his text even after it was in proof, and the manuscript was not in an orderly state at his death in any case, the last three main parts are almost certainly not what they would have been had Proust lived a few years longer.

Perhaps the kind of problems the text offers can be illustrated by the ending of *Du côté de chez Swann*. That ending as Grasset published it in 1913—and as Gallimard re-issued it in 1919—is a publisher's convenience. Although *La recherche* is not, like *La comédie humaine*,[13] a series of novels, Proust, apparently as a concession to his publisher, did provide *Swann* with a plausible ending so it could stand alone.[14] This ending, brilliant as it is, sits very awkwardly with the rest of the text as we now have it. It is difficult to conceive its being appropriate to any continuation. Proust apparently took it from a later point in the narrative and used it to give *Swann* the appearance of a single, finished text, thinking that the section could later be restored to its original place. However, the drastic changes in what follows *Swann*—made at indeterminate dates between 1912 and 1919—eliminate its original context. It is inconceivable that Proust would not have made some changes in *Swann* had he lived long enough to establish a definitive text. As things now stand, *Du côté de chez Swann* is the first installment of two distinct works, the original text of 1912 and the text we now have as *A la recherche du temps perdu.* [15]

As a consequence of this history of the text, it is not altogether certain what Proust is talking about in his letters prior to 1919. We cannot know if he would have stood by his statements after his change of plan, since it is impossible to determine the extent and nature of the change.[16] Exceptionally sensitive readers sometimes notice that the text of *La recherche* is not perfectly coherent. Vladimir Nabokov, for example, includes "the first half of Proust's fairy tale *In Search of Lost Time*" fourth and last on his list of "greatest masterpieces of twentieth-century prose."[17]

But investigating the history of the text forces us to face another problem. The idea that *La recherche* is a kind of autobiography is difficult to maintain in view of what we learn from the letters. The image of Proust as the brilliant, insightful, occasionally profound intelligence supremely in command of massive and diverse materials is difficult to locate in the correspondence, or even to reconcile with it. To read the letters is to understand why André Gide, as Gallimard's reader, rejected *Swann* for publication after flipping through a few pages to confirm his belief that it was a dilettante's work. Gide, writing to Proust in 1914 after he realized his mistake, said gallantly,

> The rejection of this book will remain the most serious mistake made by the N.R.F.—and (because I bear the shame of being largely responsible) one of the most poignantly remorseful regrets of my life. Without doubt I think that we must see in it an implacable act of fate, for my error is certainly not adequately explained by my saying that the picture of you in my mind was based on a few meetings in "soci-

ety" twenty years ago. For me you were still the man who fre-
quented the houses of Mmes. X and Z, the man who wrote for the
Figaro. I thought of you, shall I confess it, as "du côté de chez Verdurin"; a snob, a man of the world, a dilettante—the worst thing possible for our review.[18]

Gide's letter is a very generous one. There can be no doubt that his
regret was genuine, but no reader of Proust's correspondence will
need to refer to an act of fate, implacable or otherwise, to understand
what happened.

At first sight, it is difficult to believe that the man who wrote *La
recherche* was anything like what we know of Marcel Proust. To anyone who knew him—especially to anyone who knew him well—his
achievement must have been all but incredible. Proust *was* a snob, a
man of the world and a dilettante in so many respects that it is hard to
imagine him capable of the extraordinary emotional range, the rich interior life, and the formidable discipline shown by the author of his
book. Indeed, this almost grotesque contrast must be the starting point
of any attempt to understand the force of *La recherche* as an individual's action. For Proust was well aware of the contrast. His book was
designed to be an achievement massive enough to cast the rest of his
life into a permanent and impenetrable shadow.

Consider for a moment the progress that Gide's letter represents,
strictly from a professional point of view. Proust was not utterly unknown as a writer, even as a writer of fiction, before he began his
search for a publisher. He would have been far better off if he had
been. As things were, he was attempting to find a publisher for a novel
three to seven times longer than "ordinary" novels, difficult in style,
unconventional in subject matter—a novel whose organizing principle
remains obscure for six hundred or so pages.

Only a writer with a name commanding a large and devoted following can expect to publish a novel of this description without cuts and
compromises. But Proust had a reputation as a dilettante and a snob—
a reputation established on the pretentious appearance of *Les plaisirs et
les jours* (1896), the society he kept, and his bizarre hours. His first
difficulty was simply to get an editor to wade through that seemingly
endless manuscript. Gide's letter represents the first offer to do so, for
Proust had been reduced to the humiliation of bearing the publication
expenses of *Du côté de chez Swann* himself. So Gide's letter represents
a dramatic reversal. Proust had gone to every likely publisher in

France and was treated as a pariah. Now one of the most prestigious of them began to court him.

Once in the bosom of the *Nouvelle revue française*, Proust's future was secure. Within about ten years after he began writing *La recherche*, Proust commanded the means for revealing his genius. Once his book was properly circulated, he was free of reputations that had fettered him for most of a lifetime. He overcame parental opposition to his literary ambitions; an unfortunate debut as a writer; an even more unfortunate reputation as a protégé of the decadent poet and virtuoso snob, Robert de Montesquiou; and a bizarre phase as a translator of Ruskin innocent of English.

If it was not clear by the time of his death that he would be considered the most important figure in French fiction since Flaubert, it was clear very soon after. Journal entries as late as 1938 show Gide still trying to understand how the society columnist of the *Figaro* managed to transform himself into the magisterial author of *La recherche*. This apparent miracle is a little easier to understand now that Proust's notebooks and the manuscript of an earlier, abandoned novel are accessible. They reveal that he worked on most of the material in *La recherche* for as long as sixteen years before he could recast a lifetime of personal anxieties into material for a landmark of novelistic literature. Not many writers can say with as much authority as Proust, "art is the perpetual sacrificing of inclination to truth."[19]

If the manuscripts reveal nothing else, they reveal that Proust became a novelist to deal with problems he did not choose. Chief among them was the problem of finding an acceptable use for his past. Its importance to him can be established by observing that he could turn to no new activities until he had solved that problem. Writing *La recherche* was his means to a solution. He pursued his project despite illness and recklessly attempted to finish the book rather than receive urgent medical treatment, which might have forced an indefinite postponement of his work.

To whatever extend *La recherche* satisfied the extraordinary demands of its author, the public recognition accorded to him as something more than a writer was essential. The effort Proust put into directing his book's reception is instructive. He conducted a careful campaign built around the insistently reiterated claim that his work was "scientific." Recognition as a great prose stylist was not enough to satisfy him. To be taken as the author of an autobiography or a confession—of whatever merit or distinction—was positively repellent.

Proust sought to justify his past, not merely to express it. He was convinced that, properly seen, his own past experience revealed "laws" and, on that ground, justified public attention. By showing something about the effect of time on passion, he would reveal something significant about the nature of truth and where it is—and is not—to be found. This project would not necessarily seem strange to his original readers. The way for *La recherche* as a scientific work was prepared by the popularity and prestige of Henri Bergson, whose books Proust read with care. They are the main source of Proust's ideas about time and memory, the intellect and intuition.[20]

Contemporary ideas about psychology and "spiritual pathology" greatly affected Proust's notion of what he was doing in *La recherche*. These "sciences" are not essential to the book's continued vitality, any more than Vincent of Bauvais's *Speculum majus* is essential to the continued vitality of the Cathedral of Chartres. But it is impossible to understand Proust's project without them, just as it is impossible to understand what the Cathedral of Chartres was built to *do* without knowing the ideas in the *Speculum majus*.

"PSYCHOLOGY IN SPACE AND TIME"

Unless one understands Proust's concepts of science, psychology, and significant intellectual work, his claims about the way *La recherche* is to be seen may appear simply to be unintelligible. For Proust, *La recherche* has no special connection with his life at all. Indeed, its value would be seriously compromised if it did. In 1919 he wrote to Paul Souday, "I can picture readers thinking that I am writing the history of my life, relying on an arbitrary and fortuitous association of ideas."[21] Less than a year before he died, he was still trying to correct the same misimpression.

> I was unfortunate enough to start a book with the word "I," and immediately it was assumed that instead of trying to discover universal laws, I was "analysing myself, " in the personal and odious sense of the word. I shall therefore, if you are willing, replace the term "analytical novel" by "introspective novel." As for the "adventure novel," certainly there are in life, in external life, great laws, too, and if the adventure novel can unravel them, it is as good as the introspective novel. Everything that can help discover laws, to throw

light on the unknown, to bring a more profound knowledge of life, is equally valuable.[22]

It is not easy to follow Proust's thinking because he expresses it in undocumented fragments, and his sources are now obscure. The manuscripts that came to light after his death, especially the ones originally published as *Contre Sainte-Beuve* are helpful, but even more helpful are two items that precede the original *La recherche* of 1912 and relate directly to the pivotal crisis of Proust's life, the death of his mother.[23] These two items, "*Sur la lecture*" and "*Sentiments filiaux d'un parricide*," show Proust struggling to define the "work" that will make his life significant by allowing him to put his past to practical use.

The first of these items, "*Sur la lecture*," was written during the early months of 1905 when Proust was considering taking a "cure" for his asthma. It was used as the preface to his translation of Ruskin's *Sesame and Lilies*, but it is, in effect, the best historical introduction to *A la recherche du temps perdu*. Like everything else in Proust's mature voice, it is at once astonishing, eccentric, and profound.

Its eccentricity is not limited to the fact that it is related to *Sesame and Lilies* only as a contradiction is related to a statement. Ruskin's book praises reading. Proust's preface is a warning against its abuse—and it is what Proust calls an abuse that Ruskin has praised.

The further eccentricity of this preface lies not so much in its argument as in its assumption about what ought to be sought in reading. The trouble, it seems, is that literature can give no answers to practical questions; it merely stimulates our desire to know what it cannot tell us. Proust describes himself as a child reading Théophile Gautier's *Capitaine Fracasse*, at once both admiring the wisdom of this author and wanting Gautier to apply his wisdom to the problems then troubling him. This seemed so simple for Gautier to do: "Above all, I would have wanted him to tell me whether I had more chance of arriving at the truth by repeating my first year at the lycée, and thus being a diplomat later, or a lawyer at the Court of Appeals."[24] It is a feeling that most people will recognize and smile at, but Proust never changed his mind about the practical role that reading should have to claim the importance Ruskin assigns it. Reading ought to reveal the truth. Instead it becomes a substitute for what the reader ought to be doing—writing. For Ruskin reading is a way to escape from one's self; Proust warns that the only way to learn the truth is to plunge profoundly into the self—for which, of course, reading is a substitute.

This apparently philistine insistence on practicality, combined with great sensibility, is characteristic of the mature Proust, whose thought is anything but that of an "esthete." In his own way, Proust is like an illiterate who stands before Vermeer's *Maid Pouring Milk* and says, It is all very beautiful, but the milk quenches no thirst and the bread satisfies no hunger; only a fool would stand here and look at it because it is the surest way to starve. However, we must imagine this illiterate to have the ability to appreciate minutely the great beauty he finds so useless. The hunger of which Proust was always painfully aware is psychological, and if reading, or what he refers to as "the psychological act called reading," does not *cure* him, it "should not play the preponderant role in life assigned to it by Ruskin."[25]

Yet reading is not completely useless. Although it is not what Ruskin took it to be—it does not "constitute" the spiritual life—it is "at the threshold of the spiritual life." Besides, there are "certain pathological cases of spiritual depression" for which the stimulus of reading is prescribed.[26] This diagnosis evidently is based on Théodule Ribot's analysis of depression in *Les maladies de la volonté* to which Proust refers in the notes to "*Sur la lecture.*" According to Ribot's analysis, people are often incapable of doing what seems to be within their power because they cannot will to do what they desire. The pathology of the will in these cases is the result of a physiological defect that renders the will incapable of receiving sufficient stimulation from the usual sources.[27] Some of Ribot's terms, or echoes of them, can be found in Proust's later writing, but the physiological basis of Ribot's psychology makes it too material to have retained Proust's interest for long.

In "*Sentiments filiaux d'un parracide,*" which follows "*Sur la lecture*" by about two years, Proust expresses ideas more congenial to his temperament. "*Sentiments*" appeared as a news analysis in the *Figaro*.[28] It deals with the sensational matricide and subsequent suicide of Henri van Blarenberghe, a man Proust knew slightly and with whom he had recently corresponded. The article was written in haste. Proust had no time to consult books. He mentions no psychologists, although he quotes from Euripides, Sophocles, and Shakespeare and alludes to Dostoyevsky and Cervantes. These references and allusions lend dignity and even a sort of nobility to the figure of the dead van Blarenberghe. For he, not unlike Oedipus, is a man whose action has revealed something "universal." What is significant about van Blarenberghe's terrible act of matricide is that it dramatically articulates a universal phenomenon.

All men kill their mothers, but the act is usually invisible because it is diffused over time. Like all passionate actions, van Blarenberghe's, when it is deeply probed, reveals a universal significance. Undoubtedly the commonplace that the intensive investigation of a single "case" has general scientific significance had great appeal for Proust. It probably provided the rationale that convinced him to write his novel.

Proust considered that he knew something about psychology and the laws of the mind when he began *La recherche*. Like van Blarenberghe's matricide, *La recherche* makes "laws" accessible by showing their action telescoped in time. "The law of mental optics" that Proust had announced in *"Sur la lecture"* is his own warrant for considering himself a savant. "We can receive the truth from nobody . . . we must create it ourselves."[29] He did not "analyze" himself in an "odious sense." He demonstrated the operation of laws in materials near at hand. That these materials are drawn from his own life is insignificant. What is significant is that they show the operation of the laws.

The idea that there can be a kind of literature that demonstrates psychological laws, if indeed it does not reveal them for the first time, gave Proust his rationale for writing *La recherche*. It also accounts for the book's unconventional shape and organization. "There are novelists . . . who envisage a brief plot with few characters. This is not my conception of the novel. There is a plane geometry and a geometry of space. And so for me the novel is not only plane psychology but psychology in space and time."[30]

I return to the subject of what this concept of the novel has to do with the actual achievement of *La recherche* after first investigating the illness and recovery of its Protagonist. Such an investigation is a necessary preliminary to an evaluation of Proust's achievement; his concept of psychology and the goal of the spiritual life are not only essential for the understanding of his project, they are equally essential to an understanding of the spiritual history of his protagonist—who is perhaps the greatest *invented* writer in the history of fiction since Cid Hamete Benengeli.

THE SYLLABUS OF ERRORS

Perhaps the statement most generally agreed upon by Proust's interpreters is that *La recherche* is the "story of a writer's discovery of his vocation." Robert Vigneron, who has offered one of the most detailed expositions of the book's structure, qualifies this view only by adding that there is a simultaneous "plot" about the organization of society running parallel to the story of the Protagonist's discovery of his vocation.[31] The thesis is plausible and can even claim the Narrator's support.[32] "I felt ... an enthusiasm which might have borne fruit had I remained alone and would thus have saved me the detour of many wasted years through which I was yet to pass before the invisible vocation of which this book is the history declared itself."[33]

But the description cannot stand. In addition to the irony of the masterful Narrator of this book recounting the stages of his conviction that he had no "gift" for writing, there is another progress, prior to the writer's progress and more fundamental. It is the story of that very "detour of many wasted years" which stands in the way of his invisible vocation.

That progress—a round of obsessions that will end only with the Protagonist's collapse and prolonged hospitalization—begins with his earliest memories of childhood. The Narrator's first description of himself as a child refers to his "melancholy and anxious thoughts." The magic lantern that introduces the subject of the French aristocracy was someone's attempt to distract the child on evenings when he seemed "abnormally wretched." But he is so dependent on the "familiar impression" of his room, which the change of lighting destroyed, that his "sorrows were only increased."[34]

The impression of the child's extraordinary sensitivity and even morbidity is confirmed by the very first remark that any character in the book makes about him. His grandmother criticizes his father's practice of sending him in the house with a book on wet days. "That is not the way to make him strong and active ... especially this little man who needs all the strength and will-power that he can get."[35] A few pages later we are told that his "lack of will-power ... delicate health, and the consequent uncertainty as to [his] future" weighed heavily on his grandmother's mind.[36]

The Protagonist's lack of will power and delicate health dominate his childhood. His family tries incessantly to overcome his apparently groundless but pervasive anxiety. This is the background for the narration of the first great crisis in the Protagonist's life.

That the Protagonist was ill even before he was allowed to think of himself as ill is effectively the first thing we know about him. His own father is not aware of the extent of his wretchedness because his mother and grandmother refuse to allow anyone to regard him as ill. They impose a strict regime on him, one that requires him to resist his impulses under threat of severe punishment in order to "reduce my nervous sensibility and to strengthen my will."[37]

This regime is recommended in *L'Hygiène des neurasthéniques* (1897), a book written by Marcel Proust's father, Dr. Adrien Proust, in collaboration with Dr. Gilbert Ballet, his colleague on the Paris *Faculté de Médecine*. In attempting to thwart the development of neurasthenia, Proust and Ballet suggest "holding [the patients'] hereditary tendency in check by reinforcing as much as possible their nervous centers' energy to resist."[38]

One night the child determines not to do without his mother's evening kiss, despite his anticipation of severe punishment. But in the moment of crisis, his father inadvertently destroys the hygienic regime. The Protagonist's mother tries to maintain her course, but she is overruled. "You can see quite well that the child is unhappy," his father says, "after all, we aren't gaolers."

> And thus for the first time my unhappiness was regarded no longer as a punishable offence but as an involuntary ailment which had been officially recognized, a nervous condition for which I was in no way responsible: I had the consolation of no longer having to mingle apprehensive scruples with the bitterness of my tears; I could weep henceforth without sin.[39]

But relief from his mother's regime of forced resistance brings the Protagonist new and worse misery.

> It struck me that my mother had just made a first concession which must have been painful to her, that it was a first abdication on her part from the ideal she had formed for me, and that for the first time she who was so brave had to confess herself beaten. . . . I had succeeded, as sickness or sorrow or age might have succeeded, in relaxing her will, in undermining her judgment. . . . this evening opened a new era, would remain a black date in the calendar.[40]

Changing his mother in such a way was the last thing that this wretched child wanted to do, especially since the extraordinary concession that breaking his mother's will brought did not satisfy his real desire: "the strongest desire I had in the world, namely, to keep my mother in my room through the sad hours of darkness, ran too much counter to general requirements and to the wishes of others for such a concession as had been granted me this evening to be anything but a rare and artificial exception."[41] The pattern of this first anxiety and crisis can be traced through the Protagonist's major experience until the day his will is restored and he ceases the pursuit of phantoms in exchange for the reality of the real past. On that day something like the *"cercle parfait"* to which Vigneron refers is completed. It is a circle recognized by the Narrator, who recalls the crisis provoked by the irresistible desire for his mother's kiss.

> the night that was perhaps the sweetest and saddest of my life, when I had alas! (at a time when the Guermantes still seemed to me mysterious and inaccessible), won from my parents that first abdication of their authority from which, later, I was to date the decline of my health and my will, and my renunciation, each day disastrously confirmed, of a task that daily became more difficult—and rediscovered by me to-day, in the library of these same Guermantes, on this most wonderful of all days which had suddenly illuminated for me not only the old groping movements of my thought, but even the whole purpose of my life and perhaps of art itself.[42]

It is important too to recall that the introduction of the important figure of Charles Swann into the narrative is made not in connection with the Protagonist's "vocation" but in connection with his anxiety over his mother's kiss. It is Swann who has inadvertently been the occasion of the crisis—a fact of crucial importance to the Protagonist's later dealings with Swann, his wife, his daughter, and "society." Swann is called "the unwitting author of my sufferings."[43] It is through his suffering and not his "vocation" that he is most significantly related to Swann.

In telling the story of the night he forced his mother's recognition of his "nervous condition," the Narrator makes a special point of the then-unknown link between the Protagonist and Swann. When the Protagonist has sent his note asking his mother for her evening kiss, the story is interrupted for the Narrator's comment: "As for the agony through which I had just passed, I imagined that Swann would have laughed heartily at it if he had read my letter and had guessed its purpose; whereas, on the contrary, as I was to learn in due course, a similar anguish had been the bane of his life for many years, and no one perhaps could have understood my feelings at that moment so well as he."[44] The crisis of the mother's kiss is the first specific event represented in *La recherche*. It is the pattern for a number of other crises that together constitute the main body of the whole book. Moreover, the Narrator dates the decline of his will—and it is a lack of will or a weakness of will that he says prevents his working—from this first crisis.

The story of his illness, then, is prior to and more fundamental than the discovery of his vocation.

According to the Narrator, the morbid attachment of the Protagonist to his mother, his fixing on the ceremony of her evening kiss, is a symptom of a deep disturbance. In Swann's case, the anguish "that comes from knowing that the creature one adores is in some place of enjoyment where oneself is not and cannot follow . . . came through love."[45] But the Protagonist's anguish is said to have possessed his soul before there was anything for it to fix itself upon. It is a truly primitive characteristic of his personality, an anxiety "vague and free, without precise attachment, at the disposal of one sentiment to-day, of another to-morrow, of filial piety or affection for a friend."[46]

The early descriptions of anxiety induced by the change in the appearance of his room when the "magic lantern" was used, and the momentary loss of time, place, and identity that marked the process of waking up and the process of falling asleep are prior to his dependence on his mother's kiss. That kiss became a kind of fixed point holding together a precarious and capricious world. The need for such a fixed point is the need for protection from being cast adrift in a Heraclitian world of experience with no fixed points—a world stronger than the Protagonist's very identity, which itself always seemed to him on the verge of being carried away.

During all the years of the "temps perdu" the Protagonist seeks another point of permanence after the pattern of his mother's kiss. This point is identified with "Truth," the real object of his quest. He is alternately frightened and fascinated by change and assumes until the moment of his great illumination that Truth is itself static and to be found outside of the self. This is why the experience of the *"temps perdu"* is divided into a series of episodes in which the Protagonist attempts to possess something that he takes to be the depository of Truth. This is how the episodes, some as long as most novels and very fully represented, are connected to the whole work. The Protagonist's illness is the most fundamental "beginning," and his recovery consists in abandoning a search for Truth where it never can be found. An insight into the nature and *locus* of Truth allows the Protagonist to overcome his illness and establish his identity in the only place any identity can be established—the real world of time.

Precisely how many attempts he makes to locate a Truth that lies outside of himself is difficult to determine. Like the number of moments of illumination, which differs in different accounts, the number of phantoms the Protagonist chases depends on the principle of inclusion we choose.[47] Some episodes are represented very fully; some are summarized in a few pages. The list I offer will seem too long to some readers, too short to others. I cannot claim it is complete, but I hope there are no important omissions. At least no whole "category" of errors has been left out of account. Here, then, is my list.

The Mother's Kiss
The Name "Swann"
The Name "Guermantes"
The Theatre
Bergotte's Books
Italy
Gilberte
Balbec
The Little Band
The Duchess de Guermantes
"Society"
The Vintueil Septet
Albertine

The difficulty of seeing that something like this list of "errors" actually organizes the narrative is very considerable because of the great disparity in their representation. The problem is compounded by the fact that the various titles, and especially the volume divisions, correspond to nothing internal to the narrative. Proust's original idea of publishing the entire text at once and without any divisions was obviously impractical, but he managed to make the worst of the practical requirement of dividing the text.

His extreme and reiterated anxiety that no one would ever grasp his "architecture" comes close to being justified. Once his search for a publisher was over, this anxiety vies with his illness as the major topic of his correspondence.[48] That aspect of Proust's personality which prompted Samuel Beckett to refer to "the garrulous old dowager of the Letters" is very much in evidence in his scattered discussions of the organization of La recherche. For the original novel, which he thought would be published in three parts, he once suggested the part titles "The Age of Names," "The Age of Words," and "The Age of Things." The distinction between "names" and "words" in these part titles is not clear, but the errors of the "temps perdu" fall into distinct categories.

My list of "errors" can be grouped into "names," "places," "things," and perhaps "persons," although the Narrator regards both love and friendship as illusions[49] so that perhaps "persons" and "things" ought not be distinguished. Arguments, too, might be made on behalf of Elstir, and perhaps the Champs-Elysée, Madame Swann, and Combray itself deserve headings of their own. It is difficult to decide whether Gilberte and the Champs-Elysée are separate objects in the Protagonist's mind; it is clearer that Balbec meant something to him as an object of desire before he encountered either the Little Band or Albertine.

Swann occupies a special place in the Protagonist's life, but the knowledge of Swann's early life discussed in *"Un Amour de Swann"* apparently is not the product of conscious "research" as the indirect knowledge of Albertine's life is. Swann is a kind of precursor for large parts of the Protagonist's experience, but, unlike the Protagonist, Swann finally succumbs to his phantoms. The baron de Charlus, too, represents a personality lost at a stage of illusion through which the Protagonist passes, as do the duc de Guermantes and Madame Verdurin. But these characters, unlike Swann, come into the story because of their close connections with various of the Narrator's obsessions; they are not direct objects of his "errors."

What all the "errors" have in common is that they are asked to do something for the Protagonist that he must do for himself. They are asked to do the impossible—protect him against incessant change and preserve him as an unchanging, integrated personality against all the chances of life. They are all in turn thought to contain Truth, which in his childhood the Protagonist conceived of as one, immutable, and outside of the self. Many—and perhaps originally all—of the "errors" come into the Protagonist's life in two parts. The first consists of his obsessive meditation on them as "names" or "words," the second of his encounters with them as objects.

Following the pattern established by the ritual of his mother's kiss, each encounter with a new object ends with its destruction as a *locus* of Truth. But with each new object, the Protagonist makes more elaborate and more desperate efforts at control. Possession becomes more important even than pleasure with the last of them, Albertine. And it is with this "prisoner" who becomes a "fugitive" that the pattern reaches its "logical" end. When she is killed in an accident, the Protagonist completely withdraws from active life to a sanitarium. It is a second and more terrible accident, the Great War, that occasions his return to the world.[50]

119

There are many indications in the text that the similarities between the errors are carefully planned, especially in those sections dealing with the Protagonist's love for Albertine. In the earliest volumes it is the theater, Italy, the Persian church at Combray, Gilberte, the Little Band, and Albertine that successively stand as objects of obsessive interest replacing his mother's kiss. Later, beginning with the Protagonist's fascination with Oriane de Guermantes, the aristocratic society of the "côté de Guermantes" supplants all the rest. Albertine gradually encroaches on this society and suddenly becomes a compulsive obsession of even greater intensity.

Through this long "detour of many wasted years" the fantasy of being a writer rises periodically to the surface only to disappear again. The "vocation" of writing is never viewed realistically by the Protagonist. In his fantasies it serves whichever of his obsessions happens then to be dominant.

Here, for example, is one of his fantasies about writing during the first heat of his fascination with the name "Guermantes"—"invariably wrapped in the mystery of the Merovingian age, and bathed, as in a sunset, in the amber light which glowed from the resounding syllable 'antes.' "[51]

> I used to dream that Madame de Guermantes, taking a sudden capricious fancy for myself, invited me there [to Guermantes], that all day long she stood fishing for trout by my side. . . . She would make me tell her . . . all about the poems that I intended to compose. And these dreams reminded me that, since I wished, some day, to become a writer, it was high time to decide what sort of books I was going to write. But as soon as I asked myself the question, and tried to discover some subject to which I could impart a philosophical significance of infinite value, my mind would stop like a clock, my consciousness would be faced with a blank. . . .[52]

Only after the Protagonist has finally conceded that he will never write that poem with "philosophical significance of infinite value" and surrenders to the flux of time, where no value is infinite, is the crisis at length resolved. It is true that he is able to write, apparently for the first time, in a serious and sustained manner. But we are speaking of a man who had become an invalid and retired from active life in society. His problem was more fundamental than an inability to write. He had been at war with the "psychology of space and time" since that

120

point in childhood when his mother's kiss had served as the fixed point in a world of perpetual change.

His life had been a succession of replacements for that original attempt to find a static "truth" more real than himself. He had tried to transform Madame de Guermantes into the "substance" of the tapestry at the church of Combray.[53] He had definitively fallen in love with Albertine when he grew convinced that there was an important part of her life from which he was excluded.[54] Somehow, he thought, the truth is *there*, and he sought entrance with the same kind of desperation that he felt so many years before when he sent his note to his mother in the garden at Combray.[55]

Before he can become a writer, this round of obsessions must be broken. The lifelong effort to control his experience by holding fast to an image of the ideal is finally abandoned at the final reception of the princesse de Guermantes.[56] His ability to write follows, with fairy tale rapidity. But the "discovery of his vocation as a writer" is subordinate to his discovery of philosophical truth, a truth accessible only in time and that comes only from introspection.

This summary, of course, does not prove my claim about the organization of the text. I cannot finally establish the priority of something like my list of errors over the story of the Narrator's discovery of his vocation in any way short of a full and minute analysis of all of the episodes and an investigation of their connections to one another and to the whole work. Such analysis and investigation would require an exposition of impossible length. Nevertheless, I hope I have established that what I have designated a "syllabus of errors" runs through the narrative and that while the desire to work punctuates the narrative, it is always subordinated to the search for something more fundamental, which the Narrator calls Truth.

What remains to be seen is how the Narrator overcomes his errors. For at the point when the Narrator is cured of his spiritual depression the syllabus of errors, but not *La recherche*, comes to an end.

The Triumph of the Will

The Narrator's errors are not so much symptoms of what he first calls his "nervous condition" (*un état nerveux*) as they are its cause.[57] His mother's early efforts to control it could have been suggested by

121

L'Hygiène du neurasthétique, in which neurasthenia is described as "a *neurosis* [*une névrose*], that is to say a disease of the nervous system without known organic lesion" whose cause is largely hereditary.[58]

Proust himself hints at Ribot's well-known book, *Les maladies de la volonté*, which had gone through eight editions by 1893, as one source for his own conception of his character's illness. Some of Ribot's patients who suffer from dysfunctional "wills" have, like the Narrator, odd regimes shaped by primitive fears. Ribot mentions one whose fears came to him as a voice. He had suffered from agoraphobia that developed into total paralysis at the behest of a whispered voice that said, "Don't move or you're dead."[59]

In *La recherche*, the Protagonist first cannot go to sleep without his mother's kiss, later cannot bring himself to write for years on end, and finally, after Albertine's death, must be confined to a sanatorium. All through the years of the "*temps perdu*" his identity appears to be so fragile a thing that he fears it simply will fly apart if it is not secured in something or someone more permanent than himself.

The Protagonist's illness has interested many of Proust's readers, most of whom find Adrien Proust, Gilbert Ballet, and even Théodule Ribot a good deal less illuminating than Sigmund Freud. Heroic efforts have been made to establish an intellectual as well as a chronological connection between Proust and Freud, despite the discouraging paucity of evidence.

That such a connection exists is most unlikely. Even among professional psychologists, Freud was all but unread in France before about 1920. While it is not, of course, impossible that Freud's books could somehow have found their way into Proust's hands, it is hard to imagine what he could have done with them. Proust could read Latin and even a little Greek; he somehow managed to be both learned and illiterate in English, but for practical purposes he knew no German. At least once, in a letter to Robert Curtius, he suggests that he does, but the circumstances suggest even more strongly that this is a more or less innocent deception quite typical of Proust.[60] Curtius, an eminent Romance philologist, was the first well-established academic figure to write about Proust—in a language the *grand auteur* was too embarrassed to admit he could not read.

There are, to be sure, indirect ways to learn the content of books and even the possibility, which Miller seems to suggest, of parallel discovery.[61] But I think Ellenberger—who flatly rejects an affinity between

Proust and Freud—is right. Their concepts of psychology and mental pathology belong to different intellectual worlds.

If we consider Proust's education and what we know of his later reading, these differences should not surprise us. In all but name Proust's academic formation ended with the *classe de philosophie*, the final year of the French lycée. He spent his final year at the Lycée Condorcet studying philosophy under the direction of a teacher he admired, Alphonse Darlu, and he distinguished himself in the subject, winning the *prix d'honneur en dissertation française* or first prize in philosophy at the end of the academic year 1888–1889.

The program M. Darlu followed is defined in the relevant sections of the *lois et actes de l'instruction publique* of 1885. The philosophy curriculum is divided into four parts: logic, ethics, elements of metaphysics, and psychology.[62] One of the topics to be studied under psychology is the *"méthode sujective: la réflexion."* Two of the three main divisions of the subject are *"Intelligence"* and *"la volonté"*—the other is *"sensibilité."* *La volonté* includes the subheading *"les rapports du physique et du moral."*[63] Later, Proust took private lessons from M. Darlu to prepare for the *licence ès lettres*. What these lessons included is now impossible to recover, but while he was taking them he read Henri Bergson, apparently rather carefully.

Freud was a physician who conceived of psychology as a branch of medicine, not of philosophy. He specifically distinguished it from the study of ethics. After 1920 psychology is almost universally considered as either a branch of medicine or one of the "social sciences." In either case no writer's ideas are more fundamental to the conception of the subject than Freud's. But Proust conceived of psychology as part of philosophy, touching on ethics at certain points. He was introduced to this conception by M. Darlu at the Lycée Condorcet, and his reading of Bergson can only have reinforced it. Ribot was the most clinical and "advanced" author he is known to have read on the subject.

Proust was attracted to the idea that what he sometimes calls "spiritual depression" is a pathology of the will. He certainly borrowed the term from Ribot, but he did not adopt Ribot's thesis that such pathologies are physiological. In Proust they are philosophical, the result of the intellect *(intelligence)* trying to usurp the role of the will *(la volonté)*.

Involuntary memory is an agent of the will. It remembers the operation of time on the self. The involuntary memory records the "real past." The voluntary memory is controlled by the invariably transitory desires of the intellect, desires that the intellect cannot, at the moment of attraction, perceive as transitory. Only the involuntary memory ignores all the fads of the intellect. In doing so, it preserves the real continuity of the self, provides the self with a foundation in time, and protects it from the erosion and disintegration that all conscious desires undergo.[64]

Proust never moved very far from the concepts he acquired during his year of philosophy at the Lycée Condorcet. The conflict between intellectual constructs and unintellectualized apprehension that Bergson describes in the preface to his *Essai sur les données immediates de la conscience* belongs to the same universe of discourse as the psychology Proust already knew. It is true that the Protagonist's disorientation can also be accounted for by Freud, or Ribot, or, for that matter, by Adrien Proust and Gilbert Ballet. Freud's concept of what causes such disorientation, however, precludes the possibility of the Protagonist's sudden recovery.

The Protagonist's illness is caused by his repeated attempts artificially—that is, intellectually—to fix his experience in order to make it correspond to an invented past. The invented past is itself constructed from ideas, but the "real past" is constructed from all the "meaningless" sensations too fine to be captured in the coarse net of the intellect. This "real past" can be thought of as the mark of direct experience on the self. The account of the Protagonist's first direct encounter with the duchesse de Guermantes offers a particularly clear example of the intellectual distortion of the real past. She had come to Combray to attend the wedding of Dr. Percepied's daughter. As she followed the nuptial Mass from the chapel of Gilbert the Bad, the Protagonist got his first glimpse of her. "My disappointment was immense. It arose from my not having borne in mind, when I thought of Mme. de Guermantes, that I was picturing her to myself in the colours of a tapestry or a stained-glass window, as living in another century, as being of another substance than the rest of the human race."[65] At this point the Protagonist's idea, "the Duchesse de Guermantes," and his simple apprehension of the woman before him are in conflict: "I was endeavouring to apply . . . to this fresh and unchanging image the idea: 'It's Mme. de Guermantes'; but I succeeded only in making the idea pass between me and the image, as though they were two disks moving in separate planes with a space between."[66]

The Mme. de Guermantes whose existence is independent of the Protagonist's idea of her does not, however, overcome that idea. The intellect, paralyzed for a moment, regroups and reacts like an army refusing to be routed by a powerful and unexpected assault. His imagination recites these words: "Great and glorious before the days of Charlemagne, the Guermantes had the right of life and death over their vassals; the Duchesse de Guermantes descends from Geneviève de Brabant. She does not know, nor would she consent to know, any of the people who are here to-day."[67] At the moment of crisis, the involuntary memory is cut off from the impressions it gathers. Instead the intellect manufactures an image to suit itself, "my eyes resting upon her fair hair, her blue eyes, the lines of her neck, and overlooking the features which might have reminded me of the faces of other women, I cried out within myself, as I admired this deliberately unfinished sketch: 'How lovely she is! What true nobility! It is indeed a proud Guermantes, the descendant of Geneviève de Brabant, that I have before me!' "[68]

The intellectual distortion of experience, of which this encounter with the duchesse de Guermantes is a model, repeated over a lifetime turns the Protagonist into an invalid. He cannot write so long as he keeps up his search for a "worthy" subject—one that can reveal the truth that he thinks exists somewhere outside of himself. He cannot love so long as he loves only what he thinks embodies "truth" because he is driven to strip away everything that stands between him and a face to face encounter with that truth. Only when the idea of the Guermantes has lost its magic can the princesse de Guermantes's reception become the setting for a revelation.

The recovery of "lost time" is the result of two circumstances, one normal and, so to speak, inevitable, the other fortuitous. The normal one is a result of the fact that forcing the world to conform to the intellect is a demanding and exacting task. Sooner or later, it results in exhaustion. After Albertine's death and the Protagonist's subsequent attempts to learn the definitive truth about her, he collapses. He gives up all attempts to attach himself to the intellectual inventions he mistakenly considered to be more firmly rooted in reality than he is. He does not yet understand his error, but he is no longer actively pursuing it. His recovery, at this point, entirely depends on fortuitous circumstances—as miraculous and as natural as the fertilization of the duchesse's orchid by the timely visit of a particular and rare sort of bee.

At the reception the Protagonist's involuntary memory is stimulated by a series of sensations that recall trivial and unintellectualized but authentic memories. Within a few minutes, he is transformed. By the time he leaves, he has had his real past restored to him and is ready to begin writing a book. This book will be quite different from the books he used to imagine he would write. He will not try to discover a subject to which he can "impart a philosophical significance of infinite value." Any subject not abstracted from its existence in time is infinitely valuable because it is real.

The value of Proust's work does not rest on the validity of his psychology. Nevertheless, it is important to understand his concept of psychology because it plays a considerable role in the organization of his book and determines the way he presents both large and small episodes. Without it, the Protagonist's illness cannot be properly understood and his recovery is unintelligible.

The Historical Author, the Narrator, and Their Books

Once we have come to understand the concepts that organize Proust's text, we are ready to consider the relationship between Proust and the Narrator and to ask what sort of book each of them has written.

Many of Proust's readers assume that the Narrator represents Proust, and the Narrator is called "Marcel" by many critics and interpreters. Even the important differences between Proust and the Narrator—who is probably not given any name in the novel[69]—have not always been considered good reasons to rule out the identification. Some of the differences, however, are quite important. Unlike Proust, the Narrator is not Jewish, is not homosexual, has no brother, and is prevented from writing by a philosophic error until he is "old."

Proust once made a point of the fact that he had been confirmed by the archbishop of Paris as a way of denying that his position during the Dreyfus Affair was founded on a religious or "racial" affinity. But there is persuasive evidence that having one Catholic and one Jewish parent caused, in his case, a kind of conflict of cultural loyalties that his confirmation certificate left unresolved. There is no need to argue that Proust's homosexuality caused him crippling problems all his adult life.

Having a brother is not a necessary source of lifelong anxiety, but Proust's brother Robert, who was born less than two years after the writer, inadvertently sharpened Proust's personal anxiety and sense of failure. Proust can hardly be called conventional either as a man or as an artist, but his standards of conduct and success were, in most respects, those of his time, place, and social class. His family, and particularly his eminently successful and respectable father, regarded him as a painful disappointment. Years of conflict with his parents over his way of life and his inability to follow an acceptable profession can only have been made worse by his brother's easy and brilliant success as a surgeon.

Finally, there is the question of literary "vocation." Proust's in literature and writing began as early as the Narrator's. Dr. Proust urged his son to choose a profession, but he could not bring himself to consider the "profession of letters" an eligible choice. Proust himself seems never to have doubted either his desire or his ability to write, and it is a simple historical fact that he wrote a great deal.[70]

Beginning with his days at the lycée, he did just what might be expected of someone who wants to write. He contributed to a little magazine, which he had founded with a few of his friends; he won a prize for French composition; and he established a reputation for being well read. Nor did his writing ever stop. Considering that he was barely past fifty when he died, his output is remarkable. What is more, it would not be insignificant, at least in quantity, had he never written a word of La recherche. All the time that "the garrulous old dowager of the Letters" complained of not being able to work, he was writing. Evidently what he wrote did not meet his requirements, but that is beside the point.

He had published a book by the time he was twenty-five, and, during the next ten years, he published over fifty items in reviews and in Le Figaro as well as two book-length translations from Ruskin. Except for the war years, 1915–1918, there is no year between 1892 and 1922, the year of Proust's death, in which he failed to publish something.[71]

What he did not publish is even more impressive as evidence for his literary activity. Sometime between 1896 and perhaps 1909, he worked on and abandoned a long novel, first published in 1954 by Bernard de Fallois as Jean Santeuil. Fallois also gathered some of Proust's other papers and published them as Contre Sainte-Beuve.

Proust had stringent requirements for his fiction, and they went well beyond technical points. He wanted to write a book that would "bring harmony to disturbed minds and calm to troubled hearts," first of all his own.[72] This is, of course, a great deal to demand of a book. So when he complains in his letters—as he often does—that he cannot work, we must understand him to mean that he is not meeting his standards. The evidence of his manuscripts makes it impossible to take his words literally.

Proust did not become a great writer overnight, but even a cursory glance at his early writings, both those he published and those issued only after his death, shows that he did not change his mind about what the appropriate subject matter for his fiction was to be. Proust mastered the techniques of sustained narrative in order to redeem his past. He did not find his true subject matter as late as 1909 or whenever he began to write *Du côté de chez Swann*. If Proust had a philosophic *mirabile*, it occurred at least eight years before the publication of *Swann*. There are no ideas in that book about the nature of time or the *locus* of truth that he did not have by 1905 at the latest. Wherever he got these ideas, the manuscript of *Jean Santeuil* proves that he did not experience a revelation that changed him from a man who had given up even the ambition to write to one who had, at last, set to work. The documented facts are that he had the ambition to write for many years and that he wrote for many years.

In all of these important respects Proust is different from the Narrator of *La recherche*. We do not learn much about the character's relationship to his father after his early adolescence. The father drops out of the novel as an active character before the end of *A l'ombre des jeunes filles en fleurs*. At any rate, he seems to be persuaded by M. de Norpois to allow the Narrator to pursue a literary career. The problem is not his family's disapproval of his choice of a vocation, but his own inability to follow it effectively. Indeed, it is difficult to decide if *La recherche* itself *is* the book the Narrator talks about wanting to write.

The difficulty is undoubtedly compounded by the fact that the end does not dovetail perfectly into the beginning, whatever may have been true of the "original" version of 1912. A still more puzzling question of authorship concerns *"Un Amour de Swann."* Despite the fact that it is not quite perfectly self-contained as a narrative, it is difficult to avoid regarding it as a work of the Narrator—composed when? Is *this* the book he determines to write at the end of *Le temps retrouvé*? There are some difficulties in answering yes without qualification, but it meets the Narrator's theoretical requirements embarrassingly well and could hardly have been written before the final reception of the princesse de Guermantes.

The Narrator's problems, unlike Proust's, are at root philosophical. Because he is mistaken about where truth is to be found, he thinks he has no literary ability. His early obsessions create serious love problems, but those problems are not compounded by homosexuality and concomitant feelings of guilt.

Various attempts have been made to dismiss as superficial these differences between Proust and the Narrator. Miller, with the kind of ingeniousness that is characteristic of his profession, maintains that Robert de Saint-Loup is a symbolic representation of Robert Proust, and George Painter elaborates the thesis that *La recherche* is a "creative autobiography" in his well-known biography of Proust. But these and other attempts to maintain that Proust was engaged in self-analysis or that the book is an autobiography, however creative, rest on special theories of "meaning" or theories about the structure of the mind that are immaterial to historical inquiry because they beg the historical question.

There is no point in asking whether Proust wrote a work of self-analysis if, like Miller, one holds to a theory that he must have written a work of self-analysis whether he wanted to or not, whether he knew it or not. All the differences I have cited are disguises, from Miller's point of view, because the theory guarantees they cannot be anything else.

Painter's interpretation, which rests on the assumption that *La recherche* is a special kind of autobiography, is so well protected by a tacit theory that none of the obvious differences between the Narrator and Proust, which Painter surely knows as well as anyone, can be seen as evidence that the work is not autobiographical. For Painter, Proust's life had "the shape of a work of art," a shape that Proust simply expressed in literature. To understand his life is to understand his book.[73]

Once we are willing to treat the differences between Proust and the Narrator as something to explain instead of something to explain away, I think it is impossible to regard *La recherche* as autobiography or as self-analysis. So far, Proust's disclaimers seem to be true. Can we go a step further and accept his positive claim that *La recherche* is a "scientific" work, written to demonstrate laws, with no special connection to his life? Are the invented characters and situations to be regarded as elements of a "thought experiment" like Einstein's famous clocks?

Not, I think, unless we apply a double standard and give a warrantless privilege to an author's claims—for surely Proust's claims are not true simply because he made them. As historical interpreters we should be foolish to ignore the author's claims and equally foolish to think we have no choice but to accept them. To do so would be to confuse a claim with an intention, surely an error if not a fallacy.

It is not that Proust's claims make no sense placed against the evidence of the text. Given sufficient ingenuity and commitment to theory, any positive claim will find support. Do we need better examples than Miller and Painter? The trouble with adopting someone's theory in this kind of inquiry is not that it cannot be proven but that it cannot fail to be proven. If we accept Proust's claim that the author of *La recherche* is simply a different "self" from the man who was born to Mme. Proust on 10 July 1871, his claim is unassailable.[74] Yet if we refuse to accept Miller's theory, or Painter's, there is no reason to accept Proust's. Knowing what he believed is, nevertheless, helpful in trying to understand what kind of thing he wrote and might help to establish that his action in writing was purposeful.

It is true that the Narrator has theories about human psychology, about the structure of the mind, about time, society, love, and a great many other things. It is also true that characters in novels seldom proffer theories that their creators take seriously as contributions to recognized fields of knowledge. Proust's book contains both tacit and articulated theories, but that does not make it a treatise.

If Miller is impressed with Proust as a psychologist, it may be that the theories have merit. But even if, as I do, a reader concludes that there is not a single "theoretical idea" in the whole book that Proust did not borrow from Henri Bergson, that their worth is problematic in any case, or even that they suggest the character of a literary hoax,[75] Proust's achievement is unaffected.

There is another side of Proust's work that suggests autobiography. It is true that he had a compelling personal interest in most of the subject matter of his book. Painter persuasively suggests that most of the important characters and events in the book are the result of the simple incorporation, hardly disguised, of people Proust actually knew and things he actually did. Proust's disclaimers are not at all convincing. Certainly he did not want his former mentor, Montesquiou, to see himself as the source for Charlus's traits and even his speeches. He wrote letters to Montesquiou denying that Charlus bore any similarity to him.[76] Montesquiou decided to make the best of things by accepting the denials. But Painter's claim that Montesquiou is the principal model for Charlus is about as well supported as any such historical claim can be.

The Albertine material is very closely related to Proust's experiences with Albert Agostinelli. Even many of the minor scenes have real life sources. Bergotte's death takes place in the Jeu de Paume as he studies the little patch of yellow wall in Vermeer's *View of Delft*. What gave

Proust the idea for that setting? Who can doubt that it is just as Painter says? Proust went to the exhibit of Dutch masters in the Jeu de Paume in July of 1921 because he was interested in seeing the Vermeers, some of which he had seen years before in the Netherlands. He became ill while he was in the gallery.

But even if every last character and event in the book could be connected in this fashion with Proust's actual experiences, that would not make the book an autobiography. We cannot decide what kind of book he wrote by discovering where he got his material. We are asking not where his material came from but what he made of it.

He said often enough that he did not want to write an autobiography. Certainly he spent a great deal of energy concealing important things about himself, and it must mean something that a reader who knows nothing about Proust's life except what he learns from this presumed autobiography will have a very inaccurate knowledge of Proust's life.

Self-analysis, we can well believe, seemed "odious" to Proust. He did not want to reveal what he regarded as defects in his character, and how could he have engaged in self-analysis without doing that? He was choking with guilt and had no reason to believe that self-analysis would do anything to relieve his condition. Freud and Miller might disagree, but their notion of the value of analysis simply was not Proust's.

Miller is right, however, to stress that Proust's personal problems incessantly demanded relief. I think he is also right in seeing *La recherche* as an effort to obtain relief. Robert Vigneron's historical work in *"Genèse de Swann"* has established the overwhelming urgency of Proust's predicament after his mother's death. Vigneron is also persuasive when he points to this predicament as the practical origin of the novel.[77] But I cannot accept his suggestion that Proust attempted to solve his problem with an autobiographical novel. As Vigneron himself so firmly establishes, Proust did not want to reveal his life; he wanted to replace it. Such a thing may not be possible, but Proust thought it was. He hoped that in writing *La recherche* he would bring about the change.

Perhaps as early as his year of study with Darlu (1888–1889), Proust accepted the idea that something he called the "spiritual life" was the only one worth leading. The goal of the spiritual life is "truth." The method of achieving truth is to plunge profoundly into the self because the general laws of truth are instanced in the self. Truth cannot come from anywhere but the self because study of the self is the only way to arrive at knowledge of general laws.

It is important to recognize that Proust is attempting not merely to illustrate general laws but to demonstrate them. He compared his book to a telescope[78]–an instrument that allows us to see what cannot be seen without it. The inventor of the telescope can see stars invisible to the naked eye. He cannot directly communicate what he has seen, but he can offer the instrument. Proust's telescope looked inward. He did not believe it was possible to communicate specific knowledge. Everyone must learn the truth for himself, but the laws are instruments of knowledge.

There are two consequences of these ideas for Proust's life. The conviction that he had wasted his life and perhaps killed his mother—a conviction that was driving him to despair in 1905—is disproven by the discovery of the general laws. He used his wasted time as the source for knowledge of general laws, the only "public" knowledge there is. This solved the urgent practical problem of replacing his previous "self" with one he could accept. He was not a failure but a successful *savant*. The second consequence is the confirmation of his new identity. The book forced people who had known him for years to regard him in a new way. But it was not enough for Proust to have changed; he wanted to destroy the past and replace it with another past.

It is one thing to say he failed to achieve any such thing and another to deny that this was the book's purpose. The historian who chooses to deal with Proust does not choose to deal with a reasonable person. It is not a joke to say that no reasonable person would have written *La recherche*.

Of course, Proust, for all his pretensions and perhaps his madness, was a serious person gifted with an acute moral sensitivity. It would be unjust as well as untrue to deny that he redeemed himself and his past in writing *La recherche*. The instrument of his redemption is an enduring and magnificent work, but Proust's book is not "scientific" in the way the Narrator says *his* book will be. Proust's book is not a demonstration of general laws but a representation of passion and change—as specific and, given its proportions, as perfect as the patch of yellow paint that seemed to Bergotte more valuable than all his books.

Historical Interpretation:
The Face of the Muse and the Baker's Daughter

Il reste qu'en littérature comme en astrophysique la singularité,
jalouse de ses droits, ne se laisse pas si aisément refouler.
(Thomas Pavel, *Le Mirage Linguistique*)

IN THE COURSE of discussing the concept of historical interpretation in the opening chapter, I quoted R. G. Collingwood on the proper way to understand "what a man means." This phrase was conventional in 1939, the publication date of Collingwood's book. This nuance of his discourse helps to date him by placing him within a set of conventions about gender. Such conventions have changed so much in the ensuing fifty years that if an Oxford professor of philosophy were to use this phrase today in a similar context, it would seem pointed.

To be sure, Collingwood's text is dated by more than nuances of discourse. His very conception of interpretation as a discipline as well as his conception—not just his expression—of its object are more radical today than they were in 1939. The notion that we read a text to understand its meaning is now regarded in most elite circles of the academic study of literature as something fit for a glass case in the Concept Museum. It is, if anything, even quainter to speak of an *author's* meaning. As a result of the wide diffusion of theories that were beginning to make an impression on academic critics in the United States as early as 1939, texts were declared to be autonomous. When the interpreter's question became, What does the autonomous text mean? it was discovered first that such texts are fundamentally ambiguous and then, some decades later, that they are literally meaningless. The concept of texts as fundamentally ambiguous is characteristic of the New Criticism. Perhaps the fullest expression of this concept among the original New Critics is given by Cleanth Brooks in *The Well-Wrought Urn* (1947). William Empson, another of the original generation of New Critics, advanced the idea that literature should be valued because of its ambiguity. The discovery that texts are meaningless is an extension of the discovery that they are ambiguous: possible interpretations of texts are not merely many and supplementary, they are in fact infinite and ungovernable. Meanings are construals of marks on the page, and the ineradicable feature of construal is slippage. There is no way to make interpretations reliable or unitary and no limit to the play of signification. Thus to the question, What does this text mean? or What does this phrase mean? the answer became that the question makes no sense. So the text is literally meaningless. This is one difference between the original New Critics and the Deconstructionists.

In my interpretations I have spoken neither of the texts' meaning nor of their authors' meanings as conceived separately from the writer's action. I have considered individual writers' claims and purposes as if they had a legitimate place in the understanding of specific works because what I addressed directly was what individual writers did. What they did determines the status of the text as part of a strategy. The status of the text as part of the writer's strategy is inseparable from the writer's meaning, but that strategy must be addressed in order to construe the writer's meaning. *Saint Joan* is not incoherent or incomprehensible if the interpreter knows nothing about Shaw's politics. It can be understood to mean *something*, but that something is not what Shaw did. So it is a question of addressing the text as a writer's action in the writer's own context of action or placing the text in another context—Derrida's, for example, where the context is one of language looked at in a certain way, or Northrop Frye's, where the context is a mode, a symbol, a myth, or a genre.

I have looked at texts as actions, human actions, and therefore "historical" in Collingwood's sense. Texts, when they are considered in isolation—apart from any context, as just marks on a page—are literally meaningless. They acquire meaning when someone brings them a context. What we are discussing here is whether that context will be one derived from the common concepts we bring to human action or one derived from a theoretical warrant that separates writing or certain kinds of writing from the commonplace context of human action. Meaning belongs to a person, not an autonomous text. Historical interpreters want to understand a text in the light of its history, so if it was conceived by its writer as a way to solve a problem or answer a question, for example, that conception determines the status of the text and allows us to construe its meaning as its writer's action.

Claims and purposes play no role whatsoever when the object of interpretation is "the text," whether we adopt the now old-fashioned view in which the surface presents a kind of simulated meaning that is systematically related to the genuine meaning, or the more up-to-date view in which texts are incoherent, since there is no genuine meaning behind the simulated meaning. In either of these broad alternatives, we cannot use common experience to formulate a concept of a text; we need a theory to establish either the systematic relationship between the surface meaning and the genuine meaning or to establish that there is no genuine meaning to which the surface meaning can have a systematic relationship.

The nature of a text is not, in either of these alternatives, within a writer's power to affect, regardless of the writer's claims or purposes, regardless of the writer's concept of what he is doing. It is for this reason that, in both of these alternatives, to speak of a writer's intention is irrelevant to interpretation. Intention, as I have said following Austin, is the defining mark of an action. If the writer's action is irrelevant because the text is autonomous, there is no point in talking about an individual writer's intention. The text will have an agent, but the agent will not be an individual writer.

To the extent that an interpreter defines the object of interpretation as an autonomous text considered separately from the presumed fact that texts come into being because writers write them, we leave the domain of the humanities as traditionally conceived and enter into the study of language and literature viewed as natural phenomena like the circulation of the blood. I do not say that such a view is impossible—clearly it is not, since it actually has been adopted by many academic writers—nor that it is without value. It merely has nothing to do with literary interpretation when we take the object of interpretation to be not an autonomous text or a text whose agent is something other than the writer, but a writer's action.

The selection of what the object of interpretation shall be is the interpreter's since only the interpreter, not the text, can have a concept of literature. The interpreter must decide whether to investigate the writer's concept of literature or to place the text in some context that the writer never gave a moment's thought to or even rejected out of hand. From time to time, certain alternatives become fashionable enough to exercise a dominance, not to say tyranny, that discourages any other selection, but there is no way absolutely to establish what the object of interpretation shall be.

I think it is best to recognize this situation frankly and consider some consequences. One consequence is that the study of literature has ceased over broad areas of the field to advance by accretion. One group of its professors denies the ground on which "traditional" questions make sense. A second consequence is that for those who have broken with tradition, in this sense, it is necessary to discredit the way most Western writers since the Middle Ages have understood their role and the way in which most of their readers understood their work. These writers and readers have established a conventional concept of literature that must be regarded as naive precisely because it assigns the role of agent to individual writers.

The sophisticates must accept a huge gap between the conventional concept of literature and their own. Their concept of literature is inaccessible to ordinary experience. It is sophisticated because it requires theory to overrule the presumptive truth of experience. It is sophisticated in another way too: it cannot form the basis of elementary education. Children cannot, in general, be taught to read texts if they are told it is impossible to determine what those texts mean and nonsensical even to ask the question.[1] The fact that the conventional concept of literature and the sophisticated ones are not located on a gradient leads to some weird confrontations.

Let us consider a specific example. For a writer such as Bernard Shaw, writing is a formal representation of speech. It is, in most respects, a kind of impoverished speech. As he wrote with characteristic penetration and economy, there are fifty ways of saying "yes" but only one way to write it.[2] Shaw wrote much of his work ostensibly for the stage. He was always aware that the actors, by their gestures and intonations, could turn his plays into something different from what he wrote. When his plays were produced, he fought over authorship with actors and actresses, producers and directors, and he renewed these fights at each production if not each performance.[3] When we read the published versions of his plays, it is not easy to miss the fact that he used his considerable resources as a writer to make sure that the reader does not mistake his meaning in writing the play—not merely the dramatized author's meaning, but *his*, Bernard Shaw's. He is careful to help his readers meet Collingwood's requirements of establishing each play as the answer to a carefully defined question. He does not ask his reader to understand what his text means as if it were autonomous, or a natural product of language working behind the writer's back, so that the writer becomes an instrument of the language, or of culture, or of society. Instead he asks his readers to understand what he means, not apart from his work but precisely as the writer of a work that is his in a special sense because he presumes, and expects his readers to presume, that the writer—not the language, or the culture, or God, or the reader—is the effective author. He asks his readers, then, to interpret a human action, *his* action in writing this play; he does not ask them to interpret an autonomous text and find it, as the most intelligent of them must, literally meaningless. Many readers have accepted Shaw's invitation to interpret a human action and, while these readers do not necessarily agree when they compare their interpretations, by 1939 only a handful claimed that the invitation itself was based on a fundamental misunderstanding about the very nature of writing and reading.

Twenty years later their number had increased manyfold. In 1957 Northrop Frye published his immensely influential *Anatomy of Criticism*, in which he dismissed the idea that writers have any defining relationship to what they write. They are, in his four theoretical perspectives, instruments of historical modes, ethical symbols, archetypal myths, and rhetorical genres. It makes little difference what writers think they are doing in any of these perspectives since, in Frye's view, criticism is a science addressing what amounts to a natural phenomenon, literature as a whole. Since then the academic study of literature has seen a succession of influential theories about the nature of language and culture that treat works of literature as the natural by-products of these institutions. If Northrop Frye, in effect, tells Bernard Shaw that there might be a peculiar interest in hearing how he thinks *Saint Joan* ought to be understood, but that his interpretation has no peculiar authority,[4] Jacques Derrida tells him that he is entirely wrong even about the nature of writing—which is not, to begin with, a representation of speech at all.[5]

This situation represents a notable progress from Samuel Johnson's criticism of Shakespeare. Dr. Johnson was a moralist; he knew what dramatists ought to do. Frye and Derrida—standing here for many others—are naturalists; they know what literature does. Shaw has given vigorous expression to what he thinks of Dr. Johnson's morality.[6] How would he have responded to Derrida? If we think Shaw would conclude that Derrida builds theoretical structures with no particular relevance to what people actually do when they read or when they write, I suppose he would dismiss him as an articulate and clever crackpot. If we are more imaginative and think he would conclude that Derrida has discovered something fundamental about the nature of language and the possibilities of literature, I suppose he would have stopped writing, since what he sought to accomplish by writing is quite impossible according to Derrida.

Shaw's concept of how *Saint Joan* is to be understood—and Collingwood's and mine—cannot be modified by what Derrida has to say; it can be only annihilated. Shaw might say something like, I wrote the play; I know what I meant to do in writing it; now I don't want every actor, actress, and director to rewrite the damned thing and make it a vehicle for what *they* mean to do. Frye would accuse him of unbecoming imperialism since he, Northrop Frye, has a view of literature warranted by a theory in which *Saint Joan* is an autonomous text, not a writer's action. Derrida would accuse him of simple futility since he, Jacques Derrida, has another view of literature also warranted by a theory in which *Saint Joan* is a natural product of language, not a writer's action.

Both Frye and Derrida must dismiss Collingwood and me as wrong in seeing what they call a text as a writer's action; our notion of the object of interpretation is wrongheaded because it ignores the nature of both writing and language. This is a situation that admits of no compromise. If I may put it this way, Frye and Derrida accuse Shaw, Collingwood, and me of dealing with a fantasy, one that by *nature*—the nature of literature, the nature of language—cannot exist. That fantasy is a text conceived as a writer's action, a text that comes to be what it is not by nature but by an individual writer's intention. Shaw, Collingwood, and I accuse Frye and Derrida of a sort of willful blindness. They categorically refuse to see the text that we see, the text that generations of readers and writers have seen. Instead they insist in the manner of Aristophanes' Socrates on hanging from the ceiling in a basket and taking a higher view of things, armed with a theory that says, appearances to the contrary, texts are autonomous, have no connection with human writers except in the most superficial sense, and are by nature incoherent and meaningless. Anyone who says anything else is ignorant of the nature of language and literature and ought to go to school, *our* school, and be initiated into the mysteries.

In the perspective I share with Collingwood and Shaw, language and its relationship to reading, writing, readers, and writers is not a world apart from common experience; it is central to human culture and self-understanding on a quotidian and pervasive scale. The programmatic claim that texts are natural objects is based on what we might call a gratuitous theory. It is a theory that exists for no other reason than to perceive something in a manner different from the way it is already perceived independent of the theory. When I account for, let us say, the six scenes in *Saint Joan*, the account may be adequate or inadequate, but the fact and order of the scenes—there are six of them, not three or thirteen, and they come in a certain sequence—require no theory to be perceived. Once we are this far, we do not need a theory to tell us that someone decided on the sequence, that there is a presumptive purpose behind the ordering, that this purpose belongs to someone's action; we need only a commonplace concept based on experience. We do need a theory, of course, if we want to maintain that the sequence is merely apparent, as it must be if the text is autonomous and meaningless. We have to know that texts are by nature autonomous in order to know that the sequence is merely apparent, and there is no way to know these interesting aspects of the nature of texts except by the warrant of a theory.

Sophisticates like Frye and Derrida want to claim that writing is something like the human body fighting bacterial infection. It can seem like a purposeful activity, but it really is not. Texts have a "nature" in the sense that white corpuscles or the immune system has a nature. Frye and Derrida want us to alter our standing presumptions about the scope and nature of human agency. There seems to be no adequate reason for doing so, and, as M. H. Abrams and many others have pointed out, they require an awkward and apparently ad hoc disjunction between the way they want to treat the kind of texts traditionally studied by literary scholars and their own texts or texts that affect them in their ordinary activities—activities they share with people who are not literary theorists or natural philosophers.[7]

Let us consider this disjunction and some of its consequences in the form of an Aristophanic fantasy. I am thinking especially of Pseudartabas in *The Acharnians*, an Athenian who gets himself up in a Persian costume as the Persian king's ambassador ("The Great King's Eye"), pretends he can't speak Greek, and mumbles unintelligible "Persian" until Dikaoipolis catches his gestures, which reveal him to be "local talent." Let us imagine, then, a sort of American academic Pseudartabas, a noted ambassador of French deconstructionists whose discourse is as unintelligible as Pseudartabas's Persian and for whom no text is determinate, the eminent professor H. John Baker.

Baker has been lured to the golden West at a salary of over ninety thousand dollars payable from September to May. His teaching duties are limited to one seminar—enrollment severely limited—each academic year. The university has offered him a mortgage on favorable terms, allowing him to buy a house beside a private marina in nearby Newport. He has a secretary, a graduate assistant, free access to the university's computing system, and generally all the usual fringe benefits, material and social, of academic celebrity—which in his case go far beyond the traditional ones of long vacations and access to great libraries.

In addition to his well-known books, which, for dozens of canonical texts, have demonstrated the consequences of the death of authors, the abandonment of the distinction between text and commentary, the irrelevance of such metaphysical ghosts as intention and purpose, the recognition that "facts" are illusions, and the consequent futility of bothering about historical context, Baker's work is to be found in the long and growing list of articles, commentaries, and speeches that are promptly published at full length in leading journals and reviews. The death of authors notwithstanding, editors acknowledge that Baker's writing cannot be evaluated in the same way as those of some obscure lecturer at Northeast Dogpatch State. An article by Baker may fail to make much sense, may seem self-indulgent or even wrongheaded, but the fact that Baker wrote it gives it an overriding significance that makes it unthinkable to reject it or submit it to the caprice of publishers' readers.

Let us imagine that one afternoon Baker returns to his house to find a group of people he doesn't know acting as if they live there. Could he have forgotten about an afternoon reception perhaps arranged by his wife? He parks his BMW in the garage and walks toward the house feeling a bit confused. He can remember nothing about a party this afternoon and the "guests" are not the sort of people his wife would be likely to invite. They are making very free with his food, with his best wine. They are using the most attractive of the Villeroy & Boch dishes.

They are not in the least disturbed by his arrival. In fact, they greet him by name, for although he is sure he does not know them, they know him. At this point he recognizes one of them, Justine Citizen, a teaching assistant (thirty-nine hundred dollars a course) now in her fifth dissertation year ("*Mansfield Park*: Incest and *Aporia*") at the university. She is about to hand him a glass of his own best *premier crû* from a particularly charming *climat* just at the southern border of Meursault when he can contain himself no longer. "What are you doing in my house, drinking my wine and eating my food?"

"*Your* house?" Justine Citizen responds, with every sign of being genuinely surprised. "Really, Professor Baker, to hear you talk, anyone would think you'd never *read* 'The Critic as Host,' let alone assigned and taught it." She gets almost to "Old Norse" *gestr*, from *ghos-ti*, the same root as for 'host.' A host is a guest and a guest is a host"[8] in her recitation of this article when Baker, outraged by this invasion of teaching assistants and their companions (who are, moreover, working on the last of the Meursault), begins loudly asserting that they are in his house, that he has a deed to prove it, and that he will call the police if they don't clear out in five minutes.

Justine Citizen and the other hosts or guests are, of course, ready to set off the infinite play of signification with Baker's deed, but he adamantly refuses to accept his own practice and insists on an old-fashioned interpretation of the deed that contradicts everything that has made him the academic celebrity he is and gained him the handsome salary that allows him to afford such a house.

Baker retreats to his study as the others continue to register surprise and protest at his troglodyte claims about the univocal meaning of "host" and the determinate meaning of his deed. He encounters there his bewildered wife, who tells him that she found the house overrun on her return from a frustrating morning at the bank. The university failed to deposit his salary check. Their account is overdrawn, and the cash machine refuses to give them any money.

Baker, feeling as if he is suspended over a void, calls the payroll office to find out what has happened to his check (hitherto always deposited automatically every month). Payroll tells him he is no longer scheduled to receive a check. Eventually he speaks to the vice-president for personnel, who tells him that the recent seminar on "The Deconstruction of Legal Texts"[9] showed the university the way out of a budget crisis. "We've deconstructed your contract, and we're not paying you anymore."

Baker, who in his critical practice rejects the possibility of determinate meaning, will nevertheless be on the phone to his lawyer as soon as he recovers from the initial shock of this uncanny moment and will instruct that unregenerate upholder of naive tradition to argue that the determinate meaning of his contract is that the university must pay him. He will ignore his own professional practice in this case, thereby demonstrating that, although that practice is the source of his professional prestige and allows him to command a salary roughly thirty times that of Justine Citizen, it has no authority in his practical life.

At this point I shall let Professor Baker enjoy the exhilarating endless play of signification between host and guest as he tries to reclaim his house and get his finances in order as best he can, while I try to sort out a few of the issues in this *aporia*, where theory collides with practice and things start to unravel.

In the Aristophanic fantasy we are looking at a central and recurring dispute in interpretation. It is a dispute about what object shall be interpreted. Professor Baker, like Jacques Derrida, shifts back and forth. Sometimes he chooses to treat a text as having a determinate meaning. Sometimes he does not. The dispute arises because a text cannot determine how it will be regarded by an interpreter. It is the interpreter who chooses the object of interpretation. The fact that the *words* are the same does not mean the object of interpretation is the same. When I look at *Saint Joan* I see a political sermon addressed to people who share some of Shaw's goals but, in his view, do not understand that they must work through established institutions to effect them. If Derrida were to look at it, he would see the same words, of course, but he would not bother with all the stuff I have looked at in order to place it in Shaw's failed project to transform the political institutions of Great Britain. So the object of his interpretation would be not an individual person's action as it fits into a larger context of that same person's action, but an endless play of significations suspended over a void. I cannot see any particular reason for treating writing as if it belonged to a conceptual universe different from the one in which we understand other human actions. Since I do not find Derrida's conception of language compelling, I do not see why it should replace our commonplace concept of writing as a human action like other human actions, or even be considered somehow superior to or more profound than our commonplace concept of writing. I have, therefore, chosen to ignore Derrida's theory and avoid the *aporia* and unravelling he would be sure to find in *Saint Joan*.

Disputes over which object the interpreter selects and the value placed on some possible objects by particular academic guilds recur in the history of interpretation. The contest, like the one I considered in the fantasy, frequently is between an object of interpretation that is removed from the quotidian and one that is connected to ordinary experience in many and complex ways by commonplace concepts. When an object of interpretation is isolated from this network of commonplace concepts, it needs an articulated theory to exist because it cannot otherwise be conceived at all. Derrida's isolated text *déjà écrit* cannot be encountered without the theory of language that not only makes it intelligible but is the ground of its existence. Commonplace concepts are not grounded in academic theories because those concepts are indispensable to the commonplace experience of people in the culture. In the order of human experience, they have priority. This is why, I think, critics such as Wayne Booth can talk about deconstruction as parasitical on a prior *kind* of understanding.[10]

It might be useful in closing to step back and look at an analogue to contemporary disputes about literary interpretation. The dispute I would like to look at was conducted long ago by Netherlandish painters, literal guild members, and the academic theorists of their day who assigned values to the subjects that painters chose to represent. The dispute between interpreters over the object of interpretation, a text *déjà écrit* or a text as its writer's action, for example, has recurred as a dispute among writers, among painters, and among musicians over the proper concept of each of these "arts."

Should the subject of the most valuable kind of painting be something that never occurs in ordinary visual experience, or should its subject be precisely our ordinary visual experience? Each of these alternatives is not merely represented but actually addressed in canonical masterpieces of northern European painting. I have chosen to look at examples of two paintings directly representing each of these conceptions of painting. The concept of painting as something concerned with a world apart from our ordinary visual experience is represented in *Saint Luke Painting the Virgin* by Rogier van der Weyden (1400–1464) [plate 1]; the concept of painting as something closely connected with ordinary visual experience is represented in *The Art of Painting* by Johannes Vermeer (1632–1675) [plate 2].

Painters in the Netherlands, as elsewhere in Europe from the late Middle Ages until the dissolution of the guild system, were members of guilds named for Saint Luke, who was, according to legend, himself a painter who left portraits of the Virgin.[11] In the middle of the fifteenth century, when Philip the Good was the virtual sovereign of the Burgundian Netherlands, Rogier van der Weyden made, for the headquarters of the Guild of Saint Luke in Brussels, capital of Philip's duchy of Brabant, a picture that expresses a concept of painting thoroughly established in theory and, as far as we can tell today, widely true to actual practice.[12]

Rogier's picture shows the Virgin giving suck to the infant Christ. She is sumptuously dressed and sits under a splendid canopy. Saint Luke, in what appears to be a half-kneeling posture, is drawing the Virgin and Child apparently with a silverpoint. In the background, through an open gallery punctuated by three columns, is a walled enclosure containing a garden. A man and a woman lean over the wall and look at a receding townscape divided by a river. In a further room,

Plate 1: Rogier van der Weyden, *Saint Luke Painting the Virgin* (Boston: Museum of Fine Arts).

to the right of Saint Luke, we see a hand-copied book, almost certainly meant to be an attribute of the painters' patron, his gospel with its uniquely detailed "portrait" of the Virgin.

This picture represents a concept of painting that continued to have academic force long after practice had changed. It is a concept that assigns the highest dignity to a particular kind of subject, which the academic theorists called "historical."[13] History paintings represent important and unusual things: religious subjects, subjects from mythology, and the great events of national history. In this convention, the most important purpose of painting—and its ultimate justification—is to extend human vision beyond the world of ordinary visual experience. Rogier, one of the greatest masters to work within this convention, represents, in most of his surviving works, the sacred world that is inaccessible to ordinary vision. Among them are several panels of the Virgin giving suck to the infant Christ that are wholly congruent with the subject that the great evangelical patron of painters is seen to be working on in Rogier's guild picture.[14]

This concept of painting is like many of the concepts of literature I have cited. Like "history painting," these literary concepts remove literature from ordinary human action. Sometimes this removal is seen as a way of dignifying literary activity, and its corollary situates agency in something more permanent and less fragile than an individual's action. This kind of painting puts a high premium on technique and learning and a low premium on the way an individual painter looks on the world. Literary theory of the sort advanced by Frye and Derrida also places a high premium on technique and learning and pretty much ignores the way an individual writer conceives of writing. The completed pictures, in this convention, do not draw attention to the fact that they are *made* at all. They are, so to speak, *déjà peints*. Jacques Derrida's followers, too, cannot draw much on their ordinary experience when they "deconstruct" a text *déjà écrit*, but what they do requires considerable technical skill and specially acquired learning.

About two centuries later in the independent Republic of the Netherlands the dominant subject matter of painting had long since ceased to be "historical." In a Calvinist culture, religious painting of the sort Rogier had done was an anachronism. The most popular kind of painting, with the possible exception of portraits, showed scenes from everyday life in contemporary surroundings, something that later came to be called "genre painting." Popular as these pictures were, they were not accorded by academic theory the same level of importance as "history painting."[15]

In about 1660 Johannes Vermeer of Delft, at the height of his powers as a painter and a leading member of the local painters' guild, just then building a new guild house, painted a picture that amounts to an allegorical editorial on the proper "subject" of painting. It is an argument in the form of a picture. Vermeer's claims for the power of commonplace concepts as opposed to specialized academic concepts and his estimate of their value in painting are precisely analogous to my own claims for the commonplace concept of texts as their writers' actions as opposed to the autonomous texts severed from human writers and ordinary experience and resting on arcane academic theories.

Vermeer's picture is sometimes called *The Art of Painting* and sometimes *The Artist in His Studio* (plate 2). Despite the considerable literature devoted to it in art historical scholarship, it has never, to my knowledge, been treated in the scholarly literature as a (very funny) argument, meant both to ridicule academic theory and to promote the "unworthy" commonplace subjects that Vermeer himself ordinarily painted.[16] It cannot be established that this picture was painted for the Delft painters' guild, which Vermeer twice served as an officer, but it is a painting about painting addressed in the first instance to practitioners of the art and an obvious counterpart to Rogier's guild picture.

Vermeer's argument is made up of a complex series of comparisons—some immediately evident, others ingenious—summarized by the contrast between what he has painted and what the painter he represents is painting. In keeping with this summary contrast, then, the curtain on the left emphasizes that everything we see behind it *is* a painting. The curtain is to Vermeer's painting what the canvas on the easel is to the figure of the painter in the painting. We see just enough of the represented painter's subject to understand how it will contrast with Vermeer's.

The painter is painting a subject that belongs to the highest academic category. Not only is he working on a "history" painting, he is painting Clio, the Muse of History, herself. We see him working on the model's crown of laurel leaves. It is important to understand that this painter is a very broad caricature and figure of fun, something no seventeenth-century Dutch painter or connoisseur could possibly miss. First of all, he is wearing a kind of Halloween costume. No seventeenth-century Dutch painter would actually paint in such a get up.[17] The costume, for one thing, is out-of-date, implying that the subject he is painting is as out-of-date as his costume. His procedure is archaic as well. No seventeenth-century Dutch painter, certainly not Vermeer, would start by painting *only* the crown in full detail with no other color anywhere on the canvas. Finally, no painter would ask his model to pose in full costume holding the props in the manner that this model poses.

One reason for claiming that history painting is superior to the

Plate 2: Jan Vermeer, *The Art of Painting* (Vienna: Kunsthistorichesmuseum).

painting of common objects that are part of daily visual experience is the supposed universality and permanence of such subjects. Clio belongs to no particular human place; her "art" is of high and unchanging significance. But the model in Vermeer's painting is standing in front of a map. Her head is positioned so that part of it is superimposed on a map of the Netherlands; the rest is touching two "town views" of Netherlandish towns that form part of the left border of the map. In this unmistakable way Vermeer emphasizes what he makes clear in several other ways as well; the dope of a painter in the goofy costume may be painting the universal and unchanging Muse of History, but Vermeer is painting a Dutch town girl dressed up in a costume and holding props.

When one looks closely at her [plate 3], it is difficult to miss that, besides being unmistakably Dutch, she is young, innocent, and naive. She has none of the gravity or dignity that is characteristic of engravings of Clio and the other muses that figure among Vermeer's likely sources. It is impossible now to know if Vermeer expected at least part of his audience to be able to identify the girl in the picture. It is more likely that he expected her to be identified with a stereotype that is obviously inappropriate for the muse. It is as if an American advertising director today were to ask a modeling agency to send a cheerleader type and then cast her as, say, a Supreme Court justice. Whether or not Vermeer expected any part of his audience to have recognized the specific girl, it is part of his joke to have picked an incongruous stereotype.

Since the single surviving seventeenth-century commentary on any of Vermeer's paintings informs us that one of them was to be seen at a baker's shop or home,[18] I have come to think of the Dutch girl incongruously dressed up as the Muse of History as the baker's daughter, and I refer to her as such in the remainder of my discussion of this picture. I do this not merely whimsically but because I am quite confident that the young model is meant to convey a particular kind of incongruity. It is not simply that she does not look grave and magisterial enough to conform to the established iconography of Clio.[19] Equally important, although she is trying her best to impersonate the Muse of History, she has no clue about what might be appropriate to such a performance because she belongs to Vermeer's own society of Delft artists and artisans.[20] The Muse of History is a character quite remote from her experience. Anyone who has seen American school girls in the 1990s celebrate Purim by trying to impersonate Queen Esther in what they imagine to be appropriate costume, bearing, gesture, and expression will have an excellent idea of what Vermeer was up to with the baker's daughter.

In short, Vermeer shows us a painter who doesn't know what he's doing and a model who doesn't know what *she's* doing. I think Vermeer expects us to have confidence that the incompetent painter is not

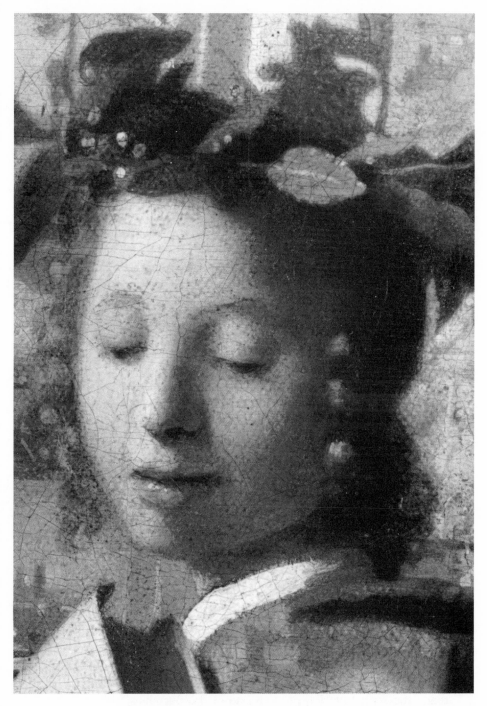

Plate 3: Jan Vermeer, detail: the face of the muse from Jan Vermeer, *The Art of Painting* (Vienna: Kunsthistorichesmuseum).

going to paint the map in *his* picture, nor will he paint the face of the baker's daughter. He will not represent the baker's daughter in a silly costume; he will be sure to have a proper muse in his picture. In other words, he will paint something he does not see rather than the girl in front of him; inasmuch as muses don't walk the streets of Delft or any other town, he will paint something no one can see outside of a picture. This extension of vision from the everyday to the "eternal" will be the dignity of his picture because he is wrong-headed enough to think that showing people what they never can otherwise see is the highest function of painting.

And Vermeer? No one can doubt his competence as a painter. No reproduction can recreate the effect of looking at this painting. It is a visible exemplar of what Vermeer values in painting and cannot fail to make an impression on almost anyone with a working optic nerve, whatever concept of painting and its proper subject may be closest to the observer's heart. And what is it that Vermeer paints instead of the imaginary muse whom no one has ever seen? Why, what he *can* see, of course, and what anyone with conventional vision unobstructed by academic theories about muses and "history" painting can see. That is, he paints not merely the baker's daughter and the map (to which I shall return in a moment) but also, to contrast with the represented painter's exalted and superdignified subject, that worthy man's ample rump as contained in his baggy black trousers, a characteristically Dutch way of bringing things back to earth.

It is clear enough that the represented painter working on his picture of the muse would hardly think of his ass in baggy black trousers as a valuable subject for painting, but that is only part of the joke. No reproduction can do justice to the tones of black Vermeer has used.[21] The passage is a virtuoso demonstration of skill that succeeds in drawing admiration and attention of the sort that suggests a whole new dimension of what might be seen in ordinary black cloth worn by a particular individual at a particular moment, with the resulting complex play of light and shadow. Only a master with Vermeer's concept of painting and his characteristic sense of humor would select such a subject for such treatment, but it demonstrates the proposition that it is not the subject-in-itself that makes a painting interesting but a combination of the painter's "eye" (selection and conception of subject) and technical mastery. The passage develops from a tradition that made the representation of cloth one of its specialties, although the subject of this passage is deliberately coarse in conventional terms.

The concept of painting that Vermeer argues for here does not supplant ordinary "subjects" and does not isolate itself from normal visual experience. In fact, he accuses his represented painter of just such an attempt to supplant and isolate. This accusation is analogous to my objections to autonomous texts understood apart from the way we understand other human actions. The disjunction that sophisticated critics must accept between the texts they approach as professional critics and commonplace texts, such as deeds and contracts, is analogous to the contrast between the muse—sophisticated and accessible only with the help of academic theory—and the girl, who anyone can see without any need of academic theory.

The represented painter, in his role as a painter, sees a muse. He sees the trumpet and the book she holds not as the unlearned might see them, but as Clio's attributes. How does he see the objects in the room that are not part of his depiction of Clio, including things as simple as the wall behind her and the map? I have already explained that one conventional iconographic use of the map is simply to identify the model as Dutch, surely an incongruous thing for Clio to be. Clio, after all, exists somewhere beyond everyday human experience. She has no nationality; she does not grow old; she does not change: these are all aspects of her more-than-human dignity.

Just as we can be sure that Vermeer's painter never paid as much attention as Vermeer does to a pair of baggy black trousers, we can be sure that while the represented painter is alert to the Dutch "muse," he is oblivious to the sunlight on the wall behind her. This is another passage like the black trousers, but on a "neutral" rather than a "low" subject. For the kind of history painting we see the painter at work upon, the wall is not so much incongruous as simply not worth noticing. Like the black trousers passage, this passage retains only a small fraction of its power in reproductions. In Vermeer's painting it demonstrates both the inherent possibilities of oil paint to represent nuances of color tone and technical mastery—Vermeer's, of course, but also that of the whole Netherlandish tradition of painting for the past two centuries. That he has chosen an ordinary, basically white, wall for this demonstration of what the art of painting can do says something about what he conceives this art's proper subject to be.

The map has been identified and analyzed in detail by James A. Welu.[22] It is one of the most famous passages in seventeenth-century Dutch painting. Welu has pointed out that it is an example of decorative cartography; that is, it was sold in much the way people today might sell posters advertising nineteenth-century consumer products or cabarets of the 1930s and used much as such posters are used today, as decorative art. It is an out-of-date map of the seventeen provinces defined by earlier political boundaries. It is not an old map but a deliberately anachronistic "modern" edition of an old map.

As many others have remarked, this map is itself something like a history painting. An allegorical figure of a woman, paint brushes in hand, is represented back to back with a geometer in the upper left corner to indicate that cartography is both a science and an art.[23] The map is itself a picture; it is a simulated surface—the surface of the earth and the sea—over a literal surface of paper. The *painting* of the map is a simulated surface, a piece of paper wrinkled in a certain way, over a literal surface—a piece of linen stretched in a certain way. The map is casually taken at first as a representation of a geographic space, something "serious," but it is an out-of-date map, the Netherlands in an old-fashioned costume being used as a decoration, something "not serious." The muse, once an allegorical figure representing serious art, is similarly old-fashioned and, as seen here, "not serious."

The girl dressed as a muse has something more in common with the map and especially with the "town views" that constitute the map's borders. The map, like the painting-in-progress of the muse, is a kind of bogus document. It provides a sort of evidence for what does not exist in ordinary experience. The Netherlands (*Germania Inferior*, as it is called on the map) exists, of course, and so do the towns, yet the map represents a Netherlands that has been officially out-of-date since 1648 and, for all practical purposes, for much longer than that. Nor is the map merely politically out-of-date; it adopts a special tone and point of view through the "town views" that are, in effect, attributes of the country and that help to give it a particular cultural interpretation.[24] There are eighteen "views" that represent whole towns and two others that represent the courts of Holland and Brabant.[25] The towns and the courts are real, but the "views" are abstractions, clichés really, like the contemporary iconographic shorthand seen in advertisements of Paris as the Eiffel Tower and of London as Big Ben. It is not merely that these towns are much more complex than the "views"; the views are static and depict the town as a cultural invention, an invention that, moreover, makes all towns the same in important respects. Perhaps the most important of these respects is that all the towns are, in effect, attributes of the country. One starts with a concept of "The Netherlands," and this concept is reinforced by the town views. They are a

152

set. It is very similar to the sort of thing Erich Auerbach does in *Mimesis*. There the texts he discusses are attributes of "Western Literature"; as attributes they have a common function and a common point of reference. We could say much the same for Derrida's *textes déjà écrits*, which are similarly attributes of *écriture*.[26]

Because of the map's special relationship with the model, we can see that both the girl-as-muse and the Netherlands-as-map are treated in the same transcendent and idealized way. Every problem raised in the picture as a whole is mirrored in both the map and the girl-as-muse. The muse stands for a concept of "history painting" of which the map is an example. For all their imposing cultural weight, they are both much more fragile than the ordinary things that Vermeer himself takes as suitable subjects for painting. These ordinary things—the wall reflecting the sunlight, the curtain, the painter's trousers—are part of the commonplace visual experience of everyone who belonged to the culture. The muse, who is the subject of the represented painter's picture, is quite different. Muses are not part of commonplace visual experience. The muse, as opposed to a girl dressed in a costume, requires special academic concepts to be seen at all. Not everyone can see a muse, and muses can disappear if the academic theories that make them possible are forgotten. The concept of a model is much less arcane, but it too is a special concept belonging to certain conventions of visual representation. The concept of "girl" is quite different. It really cannot be undercut by something more basic; it does not depend on academic theory or conventions of artistic practice. Muses are dispensable; girls are not.

If we compare Vermeer's painting with his imaginary painter's, we see a contrast between a muse in an undefined place and a Dutch girl posing in a costume in a painter's house. I think Vermeer suggests that we consider which is more "eternal" or "permanent," muses or girls. It is the same suggestion offered by the comparison between the room itself—a little piece of the Netherlands but a real and enduring one (what can we imagine happening to Dutch culture to make rooms obsolete?)—and the cultural interpretation of the Netherlands as represented by the out-of-date map. What is the status of the Court of Brabant in 1660? To Vermeer the eternal or enduring subjects are not mythic ones but commonplace ones, those things we cannot conceive of the world without: inside and outside, light and shadow, women and men, walls and floors.

In this concept of painting, the painter's role is not to supplant ordinary visual reality or supersede it but to represent it. The muse stands for a concept of "history painting" given every honor by academic theory, but common experience can be neither created nor annihilated by theory. In contrast, the subjects that belong to "history painting" are wholly dependent on "theory" of a sort that is wholly unnecessary to anything else. It is not Clio standing in front of this decorative depiction of one mythology of the Netherlands; it's the baker's daughter dressed up in a costume. The picture as a whole, with all its obvious and subtle contrasts, framed by the pulled back curtain, is Vermeer's comment on the question of the great and acceptable subject of painting.

Vermeer's selection of subject is enduring because it rests on the most fundamental of commonplace concepts. We can make the muse disappear by seeing the baker's daughter in a costume because the muse disappears as soon as the observer is ignorant of or chooses to ignore the theoretical world that gives her her very fragile mode of existence. But no one can make the baker's daughter disappear with a theory.

In 1939, when Collingwood suggested that understanding a text involves more than understanding language, that it involves understanding the text as its writer's action, academic criticism was already moving in other directions. One group of critics advanced a theoretical model of poetic (or literary) language distinct from other kinds of language. Others advanced special academic concepts of literature as the product of natural impulses or unchanging archetypes. More recently a theoretical concept of language that writes itself and can be seen as an infinite and unstoppable play of signification suspended over a void has achieved acceptance at the highest academic levels. There is no place in these theoretical perspectives for Collingwood's commonplace concept of an individual writer's action of writing. For the past fifty years the most prestigious guilds of critics have tried to see writing in its minute particulars and as a vast sequence of texts. In doing so most of them have superseded commonplace concepts with academic theory. To see the evolution of style or the play of language or the cycle of unchanging archetypes, they have tried to dispense with writers, who are, from their perspectives, more temporary and less essential. They have tried to make Shaw and Proust disappear with a theory.

❖ *Notes* ❖

PREFACE

1. Quoted in *World Authors 1950–1970: A Companion Volume to Twentieth-Century Authors*, ed. John Wakeman (New York: Wilson, 1975), 7–8.

2. Clifford Geertz, *Local Knowledge: Further Essays in Interpretive Anthropology* (New York: Basic Books, 1983).

3. See Clifford Geertz, *Works and Lives: The Anthropologist as Author* (Stanford, Calif.: Stanford University Press, 1988), 6–7, 17–20.

CHAPTER ONE
THE WRITER WRITING

1. John M. Ellis makes a similar point in his analysis of the deconstructive term *textuality* by considering the opposition between "text" and "author." Ellis, *Against Deconstruction* (Princeton, N.J.: Princeton University Press, 1989), 114.

2. Henry James, "Gustave Flaubert," introduction to *Madame Bovary* by Gustave Flaubert (New York: D. Appleton, 1902), v–xliii, revised for *Notes on Novelists with Some Other Notes* (New York: Charles Scribner's Sons, 1914). Reprinted in Henry James, *Selected Literary Criticism*, ed. Morris Shapira (New York: McGraw-Hill, 1965), 212–39. "Our complaint is that Emma Bovary, in spite of the nature of her consciousness and in spite of her reflecting so much that of her creator, is really too small an affair" (222).

3. [Charles-Augustin] Sainte-Beuve, *Causeries du lundi*, 15 vols. (Paris: Garnier, 1857–1862), 13:283–97.

4. Baruch Spinoza, *Tractatus Theologico-Politicus* (1670) [*Caput VII: "De Interpretatione Scripturae"*] in *Spinoza Opera*, ed. Carl Gebhardt, 5 vols. (Heidelberg: C. Winter, 1925), 3:97–117. The standard English translation is by R. H. M. Elwes, *A Theologico-Political Treatise* and *A Political Treatise* (New York: Dover, 1951), "Of the Interpretation of Scripture," 98–119.

5. One reader of an earlier draft of this chapter asked if I had ever heard of Leo Tolstoy. I have, but do not believe he is a parallel case. Late in his career Tolstoy embraced a "practical" concept of novelistic fiction, one that influenced Shaw's own thinking. But Tolstoy's reputation as a major writer in a traditional art form—in place well before 1880—was established by works that were not "practical," as Shaw's drama was from the beginning. Tolstoy himself denounced what were—and are—normally considered his greatest novels precisely because they were merely "literature" (what he came to consider "bad art") and apparently unable to help readers achieve sanctity.

6. R. G. Collingwood, *An Autobiography* (London: Oxford University Press, 1939), 31–32. For a characterization of Collingwood's concept of history as including "all interpretation of ourselves and others," see "Against False Divisions," Simon Blackburn's review of David Boucher, *The Social and Political Thought of R. G. Collingwood*, and of Boucher's edition of Collingwood's *Essays in Political Philosophy* (*TLS*, April 6–12, 1990, 370).

7. See Eric Cochrane, *Historians and Historiography in the Italian Renaissance* (Chicago: University of Chicago Press, 1981), especially his discussion of Leonardo Bruni and humanist historiography, 3–9. "Since he [Bruni] limited causality in history to the intentions, desires, passions, and personal idiosyncracies of the individual actors, the causes were most appropriately expounded in the very words that were, or might have been, pronounced by the agent" (4).

8. Gustave Flaubert, *Madame Bovary* (1857; Paris: Garnier-Flammarion, 1966), 83. My translation.

9. Barry Paris, *Louise Brooks* (New York: Knopf, 1989), 481.

CHAPTER TWO
'INTENTIONS' AND 'PURPOSES'

1. James Boswell, *Life of Johnson* (1791), ed. R. W. Chapman, new edition corrected by J. D. Fleeman (London: Oxford University Press, 1970), 333.

2. Samuel Johnson, "Preface to Shakespeare" (1765) in *Johnson on Shakespeare*, ed. Arthur Sherbo, 2 vols. (New Haven, Conn.: Yale University Press, 1968), 1:71, 80.

3. Robert Marsh makes this point in his discussion of the history of English neoclassical criticism in *Four Dialectical Theories of Poetry: An Aspect of English Neoclassical Criticism* (Chicago: University of Chicago Press, 1965). "Real intellectual characteristics frequently exist in an unstable and unpredictable relation to the commonplace verbal elements and structures in which they may be found, and this reflects the further assumption . . . that the 'theories' which we seek to examine and understand are the products of individual human intellectual *actions*, not of 'natural processes,' divine providence, general linguistic development, or racial myth" (3).

4. Jorge Luis Borges, *"Pierre Ménard, Autor del Quijote"* (1944), in *Ficcionees*, trans. Anthony Kerrigan (New York: Grove Press, 1962), 48–49, 51, 52–53. For the Spanish text see Borges, *Obras Completas* (Buenos Aires: Emecé Editores, 1974), 446, 448, 449.

5. Henry James, preface to *The Golden Bowl*, in *The Novels and Tales of Henry James*, 24 vols. (New York: Charles Scribner's Sons, 1907–1909), 23:xxv.

6. Eugène Vinaver, *Form and Meaning in Medieval Romance* (Cambridge: Modern Humanities Research Association, 1966), 4.

7. Erich Auerbach, *Mimesis: The Representation of Reality in Western Literature*, trans. Willard R. Trask (Princeton, N.J.: Princeton University Press, 1953), 353–54. This item is identified on its copyright page as a translation of *Mimesis: Darstellte Wirklichkeit in der Abendländischen Literatur* (Bern: A. Francke, 1946). However, the German text has nineteen—not twenty—chapters, none of which corresponds to the English text's chapter on Cervantes. I have, therefore, been unable to check the German text for Auerbach's own words, given here as "intention" and "interpret" in key phrases.

8. For a survey of some current discussions of this issue, see Lorna Sage, "Trouble at the Theory Carnival," *TLS*, May 18–24, 1990, 523–24, especially the quotations from Joseph Natoli and Barbara T. Christian (523).

9. This paragraph, including the allusion to Montaigne and the quotations from Chapelain and Cervantes, is a summary of parts of three different items by Eugène Vinaver: *The Rise of Romance* (Oxford: Oxford University Press, 1971), 70—where Montaigne and Chapelain are quoted (n. 2); *Form and Meaning*, 9—where Montaigne is quoted, and 95—where the canon of Toledo is quoted; and the introduction to *The Works of Sir Thomas Malory*, 2d ed., 3 vols. (Oxford: Clarendon Press, 1967), 1:lxv—where the canon is quoted again at greater length. The translation of Cervantes is Vinaver's; that of Chapelain is mine.

10. Vinaver, *Rise of Romance*, 69–70.

11. Vinaver, *Form and Meaning*, 8–9.

12. Vinaver, *Works of Malory*, 1:lxv.

13. Madame de Lafayette, *La princesse de Clèves, tome troisième*, in *Romans et nouvelles*, ed. Emile Magne (Paris: Garnier, 1970); the "avowal scene" is on 332–34.

14. For the composition and publication of *La princesse de Clèves*, see Antoine Adam, *Histoire de la littérature française au XVIIe siècle*, 5 vols. (Paris: Domat, 1949–1956), 4:183–94; Adam's preface to *La princesse de Clèves* (Paris: Garnier-Flammarion, 1966); Alain Niderst, introduction to *Romans et nouvelles*; and André Beaunier, *L'Amie de La Rochefoucauld* (Paris: Flammarion, 1927), 184–91.

15. Madame de Sévigné, *Correspondance*, ed. Roger Duchêne, 3 vols. (Paris: Gallimard [Bibliothèque de la Pléiade], 1972–1978), 2:617.

16. Ibid.

17. Madame de Lafayette, *Romans et nouvelles*, 337. The English edition is *The Princesse de Clèves*, trans. Nancy Mitford, rev. Leonard Tancock (Harmondsworth: Penguin Books, 1978), 134.

18. Ibid., 349; 147.

19. This phrase is a variation of Max Beerbohm's. See *A Christmas Garland* (London: Heinemann, 1912), 162.

20. Georges Poulet, *Etudes sur le temps humain* (Paris: Plon, [1950]), 122.

21. For the term *intention* in literary criticism, see Michael Hancher, "Three Kinds of Intention," *Modern Language Notes* 87, no. 7 (December 1972): 827–51. The common use of the word *intention* to mean "a plan" was given wide currency in seventeenth-century casuistry. The classic analysis is in Pascal's seventh *Lettre écrite à un provincial* (1656). See also Kenneth Burke, "Pascal on 'Directing the Intention,' " in Burke, *A Rhetoric of Motives* (1950) (Berkeley and Los Angeles: University of California Press, 1969), 154–58.

22. J. L. Austin, *Philosophical Papers*, ed. J. O. Urmson and G. J. Warnock, 2d ed. (Oxford: Oxford University Press, 1970), 282.

23. Ibid., 285–86.

24. This point is similar to one made in Steven Knapp and Walter Benn Michaels, "Against Theory," *Critical Inquiry* 8 (1982): 723–42. "We have argued that what a text means and what its author intends it to mean are identical" (731). I am not addressing "meaning" directly, but "being." My question is not, What does the text mean? but What is it? If we regard a text as a writer's action, then the thing intended and the thing done are identical.

25. All quotations from *Macbeth* are from the text edited by J. Dover Wilson (Cambridge: Cambridge University Press, 1946).

26. C. B. Young, "The Stage-History," in Wilson, ed., *Macbeth*, lxix–lxxxii, esp. lxxii–lxxiv.

27. See Wilson's note to 1.7.22, p. 114.

28. This is a basic doctrine of the New Criticism of the 1930s, what might be called the old New Criticism. It returns in an altered form in the new New Criticism of the Deconstructionists: the nature of a text is to be incoherent. A less popular but widespread analogous doctrine belongs to one version of pluralism: the nature of literary art is to be plural, that is, two or more conflicting things at once.

CHAPTER THREE
'PARODY' OR THE IMITATION OF DISCIPLINES

1. The career of parody as a literary term is exceptionally complex. It designates, for example, an important concept in the criticism of Mikhail Bakhtin. His is a quite different concept from the one I put forward here, and one that I cannot address within the scope of this chapter—whose purpose is to identify a technique, not to establish a "true definition." For a more general discussion of parody see Gary Saul Morson, *The Boundaries of Genre: Dostoyevsky's* Diary of a Writer *and the Traditions of Literary Utopia* (Austin: University of Texas Press, 1981), esp. 107–115; for a discussion of Bakhtin's concept of parody, see Morson and Caryl Emerson, *Mikhail Bakhtin: Creation of a Prosaics* (Stanford, Calif.: Stanford University Press, 1990), esp. 433f.

2. *Oxford English Dictionary*, 12 vols. (Oxford: Clarendon, 1933), 7:489. *OED*, 2d ed., 20 vols. (Oxford: Clarendon, 1989), 11:247.

3. Max Beerbohm, "G.B.S. Republished," *Saturday Review* 103 (27 April 1907): 519.

4. Max Beerbohm, *A Christmas Garland* (London: Heinemann, 1912), 161.

5. Vladimir Nabokov, *Ada* (New York: McGraw-Hill, 1969), 471.

6. For Proust's parodies see Jean Milly, *Les Pastiches de Proust: édition critique et commentée* (Paris: Colin, 1970); for an analysis of his parody of Saint-Simon see Jean Milly, "Un pastiche de Proust: 'L'affaire Lemoine dans les *Mémoires* de Saint-Simon,' " *Cahier Saint-Simon* 5 (1977): 17–22.

7. *Nouveau Larousse Illustré*, 8 vols. (Paris: Larousse, [1898–1901]), 6:715.

8. Milly, *Les Pastiches*, 37.

9. James Thurber, "The Macbeth Murder Mystery," *New Yorker* 13 (2 October 1937): 16–17.

10. Antoine Adam, *Histoire de la littérature française au XVIIe siècle*, 5 vols. (Paris: Domat, 1949–1956), 2:85–86.

11. Although parody *is* a common baroque technique, it has been widely neglected until quite recently. I have not been able to find the term properly explained in any English or American reference work. *Grove's Dictionary of Music and Musicians*, 5th ed., 9 vols. (London: Macmillan, 1954), contains no entry for "parody," although it does include an entry for "parody mass" (5:359). *The New Grove Dictionary of Music and Musicians*, ed. Stanley Sadie, 20 vols. (London: Macmillan, 1980), has two entries for "parody," both by Michael Tilmouth (14:238–40). "Parody (i)" (14:238–39) associates the technique almost exclusively with the sixteenth century and with masses. Tilmouth thinks the term describes Bach's parodies poorly, but by grounding the term in the sixteenth century as he does, he does not give a clear picture of what is involved. The *Harvard Dictionary of Music*, 2d ed. (Cambridge: Harvard University Press, 1969) includes an entry for "parody," although it is incomplete and, in certain respects, misleading. The best short treatment of "parody" as a musical term is in the *Riemann Musiklexikon*, 3 vols. (Mainz: B. Schottis Söhne, 1967), 3:704–6; this article includes an excellent bibliography.

12. For Bach's parodies see Werner Neumann, "Über Ausmass und Wesen des Bachschen Parodieverfahrens," *Bach-Jahrbuch* 51 (1965): 63–85, from which I have taken my figures.

13. Pieter Geyl, *Use and Abuse of History* (New Haven, Conn.: Yale University Press, 1955), 12–13.

14. Ibid., 12.

15. The current vogue for the word *paradigm*—and my use of it here—derives from its appearance in Thomas S. Kuhn, *The Structure of Scientific Revolutions* (Chicago: University of Chicago Press, 1962). I tried to avoid it because, like all such vogue words, its meaning becomes less precise as its application becomes broader. But in the end I found it irresistible. I use the term to name concepts that define a discipline by organizing its subject matter, identifying problems proper to it, and offering a technique or a group of techniques for

solving them. Thus "psychology" is the name of a group of disciplines; Freud's analytic psychology is a paradigm.

16. J. M. Robertson, *Mr. Shaw and "The Maid"* (London: Richard Cobden-Sanderson, [1925]), 114.

17. Johan Huizinga, "Bernard Shaw's Saint" (1925), in *Men and Ideas: History, the Middle Ages, the Renaissance*, trans. James S. Holmes and Hans van Marle (New York: Meridian, 1959), 207–8.

18. "Mais je vous envie aussi de pouvoir si jeune avoir ainsi tribune et cimaise." Proust, *Correspondance*, 19 vols. to date, ed. Philip Kolb (Paris: Plon, 1970 [vol. 1: 1880–1895]–1991 [vol. 19: 1920]), 11 [1912]: 68. See Kolb's note on *"cimaise"* (n. 6, 69).

19. There is considerable dispute about Proust's sources. Elisabeth Czoniczer makes a case for Frédéric Paulhan and is doubtful about Bergson: "bien plus qu'entre Bergson et Proust, il semble y avoir des correspondances entre Proust et Frédéric Paulhan." *Quelques antécédents de "A la recherche du temps perdu"* (Geneva: Droz, 1957), 109.

20. Milton L. Miller, *Nostalgia: A Psychoanalytic Study of Marcel Proust* (Boston: Houghton Mifflin, 1956), and Henri F. Ellenberger, *The Discovery of the Unconscious* (New York: Basic Books, 1970).

21. Richard H. Barker, *Marcel Proust: A Biography* (New York: Criterion, 1958), vi.

22. Proust expresses this distinction most forcefully in the fragmentary essay *"La Méthode de Sainte-Beuve,"* unpublished until long after his death. See *Contre Sainte-Beuve*, ed. Pierre Clarac and Yves Sandre (Paris: Gallimard [Bibliothèque de la Pléiade], 1971), 219–32, esp. 225.

23. Proust used such analogies, read Mâle's *L'Art religieux du XIIIe siècle en France* (1898) soon after its publication, and corresponded with its author. See Philip Kolb, "Marcel Proust et Emile Mâle (Lettres la Plupart inédites)," *Gazette des Beaux-Arts* 108 (September 1986): 75–88. See also Marcel Muller, *Préfiguration et structure Romanesque dans A la recherche du temps perdu* (Lexington, Ky.: French Forum, 1979), 12ff; and Vincent Descombes, *Proust: Philosophie du Roman* (Paris: Minuit, 1987), 45–46.

CHAPTER FOUR
EXPLANATIONS

1. Quoted in William Dray, *Laws and Explanation in History* (London: Oxford University Press, 1957), 77.

2. Ibid., 72.

3. In "The Concept of Purpose," *Ethics* 72 (April 1962): 157–72, Francis E. Sparshott writes, "it is indeed the most notorious fault of prescientific attempts at explanation that they proffer identically the same explanation for widely

differing phenomena" (162). "Scientific" explanation has narrowed its scope by declaring certain kinds of differences to be irrelevant, but it does not differ in method from what Sparshott describes as prescientific.

4. Among the prominent champions in this contest are, on one side, Carl G. Hempel, "The Function of General Laws in History," *Journal of Philosophy* 39 (15 January 1942): 35–48; Karl Popper, *The Open Society and its Enemies*, 4th ed., 2 vols. (New York: Harper and Row, 1962), chap. 25; A. C. Danto, *Analytic Philosophy of History* (Cambridge: Cambridge University Press, 1965); and Morton G. White, *Foundations of Historical Knowledge* (New York: Harper and Row, 1965). Opposing them are Michael Oakeshott, *Experience and its Modes* (Cambridge: Cambridge University Press, 1933); William Dray, *Laws and Explanation in History* (London: Oxford University Press, 1957); J. H. Hexter, *Reappraisals in History* (London: Longmans, 1961); and Hexter, *The History Primer* (New York: Basic Books, 1971).

5. Popper, *The Open Society*, 2: 262.

6. ῥαββί, τίς ἥμαρτεν, οὗτος ἢ οἱ γονεῖς αὐτοῦ, ἵνα τυφλὸς γεννηθῇ; . . . . Οὔτε οὗτος ἥμαρτεν οὔτε οἱ γονεῖς αὐτοῦ, ἀλλ ' ἵνα φανερωθῇ τὰ ἔργα τοῦ θεοῦ ἐν αὐτῷ. (John 9:2–3). *Novum Testamentum Graece*, 26th ed., ed. Kurt Aland, Matthew Black et al. (Stuttgart: Deutsche Bibelgesellschaft, 1979), 278.

7. Herbert Spencer's attempt to replace a religious framework with a scientific one had a wide influence among both English and French intellectuals, as did his concept of science. *On the Origin of Species by Means of Natural Selection* (1859) became a landmark in British intellectual history in large part because of the implications for religious belief it was thought to have. But perhaps the publication of *Essays and Reviews* (1860) and the ensuing debate within the Anglican church and in the influential journals of opinion is the signal "occasion" of the controversy in England.

8. Bernard Shaw, *Complete Plays with Prefaces*, 6 vols. (New York: Dodd, Mead, 1962), 3:xiii.

9. Ibid., xxxv.

10. Ibid., lxix.

11. Ibid., 486.

12. Oakeshott, *Experience*, 106.

13. Shaw, *Everybody's Political What's What* (London: Constable, 1944), 146.

14. Ibid., 181.

15. Shaw, *The Collected Works of Bernard Shaw*, Ayot St. Lawrence Edition, 30 vols. (New York: Wm. H. Wise, 1930–1932), 17:45.

16. Shaw, *What's What*, 186.

17. Shaw, *Complete Plays*, 2:cxxx.

18. Oakeshott, *Experience*, 34.

19. Hexter, *Reappraisals in History*, 189.

20. Hexter, *History Primer*, 151.

21. Ibid., 172.

22. Oakeshott, *Experience*, 141.

23. Hexter, *History Primer*, 152–55. Dray makes the same point in *Laws*, 67–69, where he argues that "there is an irreducible pragmatic dimension to explanation."

24. Marcel Proust, *Remembrance of Things Past*, trans. C. K. Scott-Moncrieff and Terence Kilmartin [the final section, *Time Regained*, trans. Andreas Mayor], 3 vols. (New York: Random House, 1981), 1:465. For the French text see Proust, *A la recherche du temps perdu*, ed. Pierre Clarac and André Ferré, 3 vols. (Paris: Gallimard [Bibliothèque de la Pléiade], 1954), 1:431; hereafter cited as *RTP*. This text has now been superseded by the edition of Jean-Yves Tadié et al., 4 vols. (Paris: Gallimard [Bibliothèque de la Pléiade], 1987–1989), hereafter cited as Tadié. For this passage, see Tadié, 1:423.

25. For these stories see Proust, *Remembrance*, 2:766–67; 3:32–35; 2:264–72, 127–28. For the French text see *RTP*, 2:739–41; 3:39–42; 2:256–63, 127. Tadié, 3:137–38, 548–51, 2:553–60, 425–26.

26. Proust to Louis de Robert in Robert, *Comment débuta Marcel Proust* (1925), rev. and enlarged ed. (Paris: Gallimard, 1969), 59–63. "j'omets . . . tous détail, tout fait, je ne m'attache qu'à ce qui me semble . . . déceler quelque loi générale" (60). Also in Proust, *Correspondance*, 12 (1913): 230–31.

27. This story is found in *Remembrance*, 1:427–56; *RTP*, 1:383–413; Tadié, 1:376–405.

28. Saint-Simon, *Mémoires Additions au journal de Dangeau*, ed. Yves Coirault, 8 vols. (Paris: Gallimard [Bibliothèque de la Pléiade], 1983–1988), 1:5. My translation.

29. Hexter, *History Primer*, 151.

30. Miller, *Nostalgia*, 205–23.

CHAPTER FIVE
BERNARD SHAW

1. René Wellek and Austin Warren, *Theory of Literature*, 3d ed. (New York: Harcourt, Brace, and World, 1963), 24–25.

2. Bernard Shaw, *The Quintessence of Ibsenism*, in *Collected Works*, 19:160.

3. Shaw, preface to *On the Rocks*, in *Complete Plays*, 5:510.

4. Shaw, "Mainly About Myself," preface to the first volume of *Plays: Pleasant and Unpleasant*, in ibid., 3:xxviii.

5. Edmund Wilson, *The Triple Thinkers* (New York: Harcourt, Brace, 1938), 228–29.

6. Elder Olson, *The Theory of Comedy* (Bloomington: Indiana University Press, 1968), 120–21.

7. R. S. Crane, "Critical and Historical Principles of Literary History," in *The*

Idea of the Humanities, 2 vols. (Chicago: University of Chicago Press, 1967), 2:149.

8. Marvin Mudrick, *On Culture and Literature* (New York: Horizon Press, 1970), 108, 116.

9. Shaw, "Epistle Dedicatory to Arthur Bingham Walkley," preface to *Man and Superman*, in *Collected Plays*, 3:513–14.

10. Ibid., 514.

11. Shaw, "Preface on the Prospects of Christianity," in ibid., 5:361.

12. Ibid., 3: x–xi.

13. Meisel, "Shaw and Revolution: The Politics of the Plays," in Norman Rosenblood, ed., *Shaw: Seven Critical Essays* (Toronto: University of Toronto Press, 1971), 108. This is an exceptionally important article.

14. Shaw, *Complete Plays*, 3:ix.

15. Quoted in Stanley Weintraub, *Private Shaw and Public Shaw* (New York: George Braziller, 1963), 157.

16. Shaw, preface to *Immaturity*, in *Collected Works*, 1:xlviii.

17. Ibid., xliii.

18. Shaw, *Collected Letters: 1898–1910*, ed. Dan H. Laurence (New York: Dodd, Mead, 1972), 479–94, esp. 484–92.

19. Shaw, *Collected Works*, 29:306.

20. Valency, *The Cart and the Trumpet: The Plays of George Bernard Shaw* (New York: Oxford University Press, 1973), 9.

21. Morris W. Croll, "Attic Prose in the Seventeenth Century," *Studies in Philology* 18 (April 1921): 89; reprinted in *Style, Rhetoric, and Rhythm: Essays by Morris W. Croll*, ed. J. Max Patrick, Robert O. Evans et al. (Princeton, N.J.: Princeton University Press, 1966), 51–101.

22. Jorge Luis Borges, "A Note on (toward) Bernard Shaw," in Borges, *Labyrinths*, ed. Donald A. Yates and James E. Irby (New York: New Directions, 1964), 215; for the Spanish text see "Nota sobre (hacia) Bernard Shaw," in Borges, *Otras Inquisiciones (1937–1952)* (Buenos Aires: Sur, 1952), 196.

23. Shaw, *Complete Plays*, 3:x–xi.

24. Ibid., xv.

25. For Shaw's thinking about the published version of the plays, see Michael Holroyd, *Bernard Shaw: A Biography*, vol. 1, *1856–1898: The Search for Love* (New York: Random House, 1988), 400–405.

26. S. N. Behrman, *Portrait of Max: An Intimate Memoir of Sir Max Beerbohm* (New York: Random House, 1960), 24.

27. On this point see Erwin Panofsky, *Early Netherlandish Painting: Its Origin and Character*, 2 vols. (Cambridge: Harvard University Press, 1953), chap. 5, "Reality and Symbol in Early Flemish Painting: 'Spiritualia Sub Metaphoris Corporalium,' " 1:131–48.

28. Shaw, *Complete Plays*, 5:190.

29. William Butler Yeats, *The Autobiography of William Butler Yeats* (New York: Macmillan, 1953), 169.

30. Shaw, preface to Charles Dickens, *Great Expectations* (Edinburgh: R. and R. Clark, 1937), xxi–xxii.

31. Shaw, *Complete Plays*, 2:10.

32. Ibid., 5:324.

33. Shaw, *Collected Works*, 17:3.

34. Herbert Spencer, *Education: Intellectual, Moral, and Philosophical* (New York: D. Appleton, 1862), 69–70.

35. Shaw, *Collected Works*, 17:3.

36. Ibid., 49.

37. Ibid., 31.

38. Ibid., 27.

39. This point is made frequently in Shaw's prefaces and non-dramatic writings. For some representative expressions of it see *Complete Plays*, 5:191–92, 522–24.

40. Shaw, *Collected Works*, 17:158.

41. Ibid., 19:159.

42. Shaw, *Complete Plays*, 6:457.

43. Shaw, *What's What*, 186.

44. Ibid., 1.

45. Shaw, *Collected Works*, 17:57.

46. Ibid., 62.

47. Ibid., 61.

48. Ibid., 57.

49. Ibid., 59.

50. Ibid., 71.

51. Ibid.

52. Ibid., 75.

53. Ibid.

54. Ibid., 77.

55. Ibid., 78.

56. Ibid., 76.

57. Ibid., 81–82.

58. Ibid., 72, 75, 82.

59. Ibid., 87.

60. Ibid., 103.

61. Ibid., 106.

62. Ibid., 105.

63. Ibid., 106–7.

64. Ibid.

65. Ibid., 107.

66. Ibid., 108.
67. Ibid., 113.
68. Ibid., 112.
69. Ibid., 115–16.
70. Ibid., 128.
71. Ibid., 143.
72. Ibid., 145.
73. Ibid., 40.

CHAPTER SIX
MARCEL PROUST

Marcel Proust, *Remembrance of Things Past*, trans. C.K. Scott-Moncrieff and Terence Kilmartin [the final section, *Time Regained*, trans. Andreas Mayor], 3 vols. (New York: Random House, 1981), will be referred to in these notes as *Remembrance*. Marcel Proust, *A la recherche du temps perdu* (1913–1927), ed. Pierre Clarac et André Ferré, 3 vols. (Paris: Gallimard [Bibliothèque de la Pléiade], 1954), will be referred to in these notes as *RTP*. Marcel Proust, *A la recherche du temps perdu*, ed. Jean-Yves Tadié et al., 4 vols. (Paris: Gallimard [Bibliothèque de la Pléiade], 1987–1989), will be referred to in these notes as Tadié.

1. Early reviewers were almost bound to be confused about the form of *La recherche* because of the serial mode of its publication. Proust's attempts to control the response of his critics can be seen in his letters to Paul Souday and others. See Proust, *Correspondance générale*, 6 vols. (Paris: Plon, 1930–1936), 3:61–102, and Proust, *Correspondance*, 12 (1913): 380–81. Richard H. Barker gives an extended account of this subject in *Marcel Proust*, 202–37, 266–01.

2. Robert Liddell, *A Treatise on the Novel* (London: Jonathan Cape, 1947), 78.

3. Vettard, "Proust et Einstein," *Nouvelle revue française* 19 (August 1922): 246–52. Proust was so pleased with this comparison that he sent Vettard a telegram thanking him. "Votre magnifique article ... est le plus grand honneur que je puisse recevoir." *Correspondance générale*, 3:191.

4. François Mauriac, *Proust's Way*, trans. Elsie Bell (New York: Philosophical Library, 1950), 46.

5. Georges Poulet, *Etudes sur le temps humain* (Paris: Plon [1950]), *Etudes sur le temps humain IV* (Paris: Gallimard, 1968), and *L'Espace proustien*, 2d. ed. (1963. Paris: Gallimard, 1982); Paul de Man, *Allegories of Reading: Figural Language in Rousseau, Nietzsche, Rilke, and Proust* (New Haven, Conn.: Yale University Press, 1979); Paul Ricœur, "*A la recherche du temps perdu: Le temps traversé*," in *Temps et récit*, 3 vols. (Paris: Seuil, 1983–1985), 2:194–225.

6. Theodore Zeldin, *France: 1848–1945*, 2 vols. (Oxford: Clarendon, 1973, 1977), 2:816.

7. Henri Ellenberger, *The Discovery of the Unconscious* (New York: Basic Books, 1970), 167–68.

8. Miller, *Nostalgia*, 21.

9. This view is less common than it once was. Barker accepts it to some extent. It is also advanced as a claim for Proust's value in Howard Moss, "One Hundred Years of Proust," *New Yorker* 47 (18 December 1971): 124–35.

10. George D. Painter, *Marcel Proust: A Biography*, 2 vols. (London: Chatto and Windus, 1958, 1965), 1:xiii.

11. For a well-documented account of French schools of psychology contemporary with Proust see Czoniczer, *Quelques antécédents*, 35–57.

12. The project that finally became *A la recherche du temps perdu* initially may have been conceived as a serious novel on the general subject of homosexuality. See Robert Vigneron, "Genèse de Swann," *Revue de la philosophie et d'histoire générale de la civilisation* (15 January 1937): 67–115, esp. 73–76; reprinted in Vigneron, *Etudes sur Stendhal et sur Proust* (Paris: Nizet, 1978), 308–51, esp. 314–17. Despite the fact that many relevant documents were not accessible to Vigneron in 1937 so that certain details stand in need of correction, it remains an essential starting point for any serious study of the origins of *La recherche*.

13. There was almost inevitable confusion on this point during the original publication of the work and for at least ten years thereafter. Indeed, it had not altogether disappeared almost fifty years later. William H. Gass perpetuates it in "Marcel Proust at 100," *New York Times Book Review* (11 July 1971): 1, 14–16. For one of many clarifications see Robert Vigneron, "Structure de Swann: Balzac, Wagner et Proust," *French Review* 19 (May 1946): 370–84 [*Etudes sur Stendhal et sur Proust*, 414–29].

14. What I call the "ending" is indicated only by a space in the text. It is found in *RTP*, 1:421–37, beginning, "Cette complexité du Bois de Bologne" (Tadié, 1:414–20). In Kilmartin's revision of Scott-Moncrieff's translation, it begins, "That sense of the complexity of the Bois de Bologne" *Remembrance*, 1:456. On this point see Vigneron, "Genèse de Swann," 92–93 [*Etudes sur Stendhal et sur Proust*, 331–32]. See also Proust, *Correspondance*, 12 (1913): 14. "Proust a ajouté à la fin de Swann 'cinq ou six pages qui se trouve au milieu du second volume et qui feront un couronnement un peu plus étendu.' "

15. On this subject see Alison Winton, *Proust's Additions: The Making of "A la recherche du temps perdu,"* 2 vols. (Cambridge: Cambridge University Press, 1977). This book is based on materials acquired by the Bibliothèque Nationale in 1962 and supersedes the original and still interesting discussion in Albert Feuillerat, *Comment Proust a composé son roman* (New Haven, Conn.: Yale University Press, 1934). See also Douglas W. Alden, *Marcel Proust's Grasst Proofs: Commentary and Variants*, North Carolina Studies in the Romance Languages and Literatures, no. 193 (Chapel Hill: University of North Carolina at Chapel Hill, Department of Romance Languages, 1978).

16. In a letter that Proust wrote to Madame Emile Strauss—at the end of August 1909, according to Vigneron's chronology—he said, "Et avant vous me lirez—et plus que vous ne voudrez—car je viens de commencer—et de finir—tout un long livre." *Correspondance générale*, 6:116, and *Correspondance*, 9 (1909): 163. Kolb dates this letter "vers le 16 août 1909." Proust's words do not support the construction Painter places on them in *Marcel Proust*, 2:150. See Vigneron, "La méthode de Sainte-Beuve et la méthode de M. Painter," *Modern Philology* 63 (November 1967): 146.

17. Vladimir Nabokov, *Strong Opinions* (New York: McGraw-Hill, 1973), 57.

18. Proust, *Letters of Marcel Proust*, trans. Mina Curtiss (New York: Random House, 1949), 259. For the French text see Proust, *Lettres à André Gide* (Neuchatel and Paris: Ides et Calenders, 1949), 9–10, and Proust, *Correspondance*, 13 (1914): 50–51.

19. *Letters*, 328. *Correspondance générale*, 3:10. Proust, *Correspondance*, 18 (1919): 296.

20. Proust denied the influence of Bergson in what was published as an "interview" in *Le temps*, 13 November 1913. This item is reprinted in Philip Kolb and Larkin B. Price, *Textes retrouvés* (Urbana: University of Illinois Press, 1968), 215–30: "mon œuvre est dominée par la distinction qui non seulement ne figure pas dans la philosophie de M. Bergson, mais est même contredite par elle" (217). This "interview" consists largely of a letter Proust sent to Antoine Bibesco as part of his publicity for *Du côté de chez Swann*. Proust was anxious to avoid being swallowed up in Bergson's reputation, of course, and this anxiety probably accounts for his bringing up Bergson in order to dismiss his importance for his own work. See also Proust, *Correspondance*, 12 (1913): 14–15.

21. *Letters*, 331; *Correspondance générale*, 3:69; Proust, *Correspondance*, 18 (1919): 464.

22. *Letters*, 381–82; for the French text see *Les Annales politiques et littéraires* 26 (February 1922): 236.

23. There are several excellent accounts of this crisis. For one of them see Robert Vigneron, "Marcel Proust ou l'angoisse créatrice," *Modern Philology* 42 (May 1945): 212–30 [*Etudes sur Stendhal et sur Proust*, 387–413]. An English translation was published as "Marcel Proust: Creative Agony," *Chicago Review* 12 (Spring 1958): 33–51.

24. Proust, *On Reading*, ed. and trans. Jean Autret and William Burford (New York: Macmillan, 1971), 35, French text on facing page. "Sur la lecture" under the title "Journées de lecture" has been published in a critical text: *Contre Sainte-Beuve*, 160–94.

25. *On Reading*, 31.

26. Ibid.

27. Ribot, *Les maladies de la volonté*, 8th ed. (Paris: Alcan, 1893), 35–71.

28. *Le Figaro*, 1 February 1907: 1; for the critical text see *Contre Sainte-Beuve*, 150–59.

29. *On Reading*, 35.

30. *Letters*, 381–82; *Annales politiques et littéraires*, 26 February 1922: 236.

31. Robert Vigneron, "Structure de Swann: Combray ou le cercle parfait," *Modern Philology* 45 (February 1948): 188 [*Etudes sur Stendhal et sur Proust*, 471–72].

32. Throughout this discussion I have found it necessary to distinguish the Narrator from the Protagonist. Vigneron puts the reason as well as anyone: "Pour en bien comprendre l'architecture et les perspectives, il est indispensable de discerner l'essentielle dualité du personnage qui dit je, et qui tantôt évoque du fond du passé le protagoniste tel qu'il était au moment de l'action et tantôt represents le narrateur dans le présent, au moment où il compose son récit et tel qu'en lui-même enfin le temps incorporé et l'eternité entreuve l'ont changé" (ibid., 189). [*Etudes sur Stendhal et sur Proust*, 472–73].

The most thorough and sophisticated discussion of this point that I know is Marcel Muller, *Les voix narratives dans la Recherche du temps perdu* (Geneva: Droz, 1965). See also Pascal Alain Ifri, *Proust et son Narrataire dans A la Recherche du temps perdu*, Histoire des idées et Critique Littéraire, no. 216 (Geneva: Droz, 1983).

33. *Remembrance*, 2:412; *RTP*, 2:397; Tadié, 2:691. In a note to this passage published in 1988, Thierry Laget and Brian Rogers support this thesis. "Noter [*sic*] la mention capitale du véritable sujet du roman, indiqué par anticipation et comme en passant." (Tadié, 2:1733).

34. *Remembrance*, 1:9–10; *RTP*, 1:9; Tadié, 1:9.

35. *Remembrance*, 1:11; *RTP*, 1:11; Tadié, 1:11.

36. *Remembrance*, 1:13; *RTP*, 1:12; Tadié, 1:12.

37. *Remembrance*, 1:40; *RTP*, 1:37; Tadié, 1:37.

38. Adrien Proust and Gilbert Ballet, *L'Hygiène du neurasthénique* (Paris: Masson, 1897), 126.

39. *Remembrance*, 1:39, 41; *RTP*, 1:38; Tadié, 1:36, 37–38.

40. *Remembrance*, 1:41; *RTP*, 1:38; Tadié, 1:38.

41. *Remembrance*, 1:46; *RTP*, 1:43; Tadié, 1:42.

42. *Remembrance*, 3:922–23; Tadié, 4:465.

43. *Remembrance*, 1:46; *RTP*, 1:43; Tadié, 1:43.

44. *Remembrance*, 1:32; *RTP*, 1:30; Tadié, 1:30.

45. Ibid.

46. *Remembrance*, 1:32–33; *RTP*, 1:30; Tadié, 1:30.

47. See, for example, Samuel Beckett, *Proust* (New York: Grove Press, 1957), 23, for a list of eleven "fetishes"; Howard Moss, *The Magic Lantern of Marcel Proust* (New York: Macmillan, 1962), 98–99, for a list of eighteen "mnemonic resurrections"; and Roger Shattuck, *Proust's Binoculars* (New York: Random House, 1963), 70–74, for a list of eleven *"moments bienheureux."*

48. For André Gide's observations on this subject see *Journal, 1889–1939* (Paris: Gallimard [Bibliothèque de la Pléiade], 1951), 1322.

49. This is a view he apparently shares with his creator. On this subject see

the article by Proust's friend of many years Antoine Bibesco, "The Heartlessness of Marcel Proust, " *Cornhill* (Summer 1950): 421–28.

50. No events in the sanitorium are represented in the novel. But see *Remembrance*, 3:885; *RTP*, 3:854; Tadié, 4:433, for a summary reference to the two different sanitoria in which the Narrator was a patient.

51. *Remembrance*, 1:187; *RTP*, 1:171; Tadié, 1:169.

52. *Remembrance*, 1:188; *RTP*, 1: 172–73; Tadié, 1:170.

53. *Remembrance*, 1:190–94; *RTP*, 1:174–78; Tadié, 1:172–76.

54. *Remembrance*, 2:1150–69; *RTP*, 2:1112–31; Tadié, 3:497–515.

55. The Narrator twice makes this connection explicitly. *Remembrance*, 2:1162; *RTP*, 2:1124; Tadié, 3:508–9, also *Remembrance*, 2:759; *RTP*, 2:733; Tadié, 3:130–31.

56. There is a kind of overture to this abandonment in the Narrator's comments on the prince de Guermantes's new mansion. *Remembrance*, 3:889; *RTP*, 3:857; Tadié, 4:436.

57. *Remembrance*, 1:41; *RTP*, 1:38; Tadié, 1:37.

58. Proust and Ballet, *L'Hygiène*, 1.

59. Ribot, *Maladies*, 63.

60. *Letters*, 403–4; *Correspondance générale*, 3:312–13 (see also 311–12).

61. Miller, *Nostalgia*, vii, 153.

62. *Recuil des lois et actes de l'instruction publique . . . Année 1885* (Paris: Delalain, 1885), 120–21.

63. Ibid.

64. Scott-Moncrieff's translation causes confusion at a key point: "since the facts which I should then have recalled would have been prompted by an exercise of *the will* [my emphasis], by my intellectual memory, and since the pictures which that kind of memory shews us of the past preserve nothing of the past itself, I should never have had any wish to ponder over this residue of Combray. To me it was in reality all dead" (*Remembrance of Things Past*, 12 vols. [1922–1931; London: Chatto and Windus, 1967] 1:57). This translation seems to indicate that the will and the intellectual memory are the same thing. They are not.

There is no such indication in the French text: "comme ce que je m'en serais rappelé m'eût été fourni seulement par la mémoire volontaire, la mémoire d'l'intelligence, et comme les renseignements qu'elle donne sur le passé ne conservent rien de lui, je n'aurais jamais eu envie de songer à ce reste de Combray. Tout cela était en réalité mort pour moi" (*Du côté de chez Swann* [Paris: Editions de la Nouvelle Revue Française, 1919, 45]). The text is identical to the critical text of Clarac and Ferré, *RTP*, 1:44.

Kilmartin's 1981 revision of the Scott-Moncrieff translation corrects this confusion: "since the facts which I should then have recalled would have been prompted *only by voluntary memory, the memory of the intellect*" (*Remembrance*, 1:47). My emphasis. This confusion would not have been introduced if Scott-

Moncrieff had been familiar with the lycée curriculum in philosophy that Proust studied.

Proust seems to refer to this passage in a letter to Louis de Robert that explains what he conceives of himself as doing in his book: "c'est toute une théorie de la mémoire et de la connaissance ... non promulguée directement en termes logiques" (*Correspondance*, 12 [1913]: 231; see Kolb's n. 7, p. 232).

65. *Remembrance*, 1:190–91; *RTP*, 1:174–75; Tadié, 1:172.

66. *Remembrance*, 1:191–92; *RTP*, 1:175; Tadié, 1:173.

67. *Remembrance*, 1:192; *RTP*, 1:176; Tadié, 1:173.

68. *Remembrance*, 1:193; *RTP*, 1:177; Tadié, 1:174.

69. On this point, see Michihiko Suzuki, "Le 'Je' Proustien," *Bulletin de la Société des Amis de Marcel Proust et des Amis de Combray* 11 (1959): 69–82; see also Muller, *Les voix narratives*, 164–65.

70. "Ce n'est pas que je ne croie toujours que toute autre chose que je ferai autre que les lettres et la philosophie, est pour moi du temps perdu" (Proust to his father, 1893, in *Correspondance*, 1 [1880–1895]: 236).

71. See Kolb and Price, *Textes retrouvés*, 264–75 for a list of Proust's publications, 1892–1922.

72. Proust, *Letters*, 394; *Correspondances générale*, 3:44.

73. Painter, *Proust*, 1:xiii.

74. See especially Proust, *Contre Sainte-Beuve*, 221ff.

75. Barker, *Proust*, vi.

76. *Correspondance générale*, 1:281–83.

77. Vigneron, "*Genèse*," 78–79 [*Etudes sur Stendhal et sur Proust*, 318–19].

78. Proust, *Letters*, 381–83; *Les Annales politiques et littéraires*, 26 February 1922: 236.

Chapter Seven
Historical Interpretation

1. See Bruno Bettelheim and Karen Zelan, *On Learning to Read: The Child's Fascination with Meaning* (New York: Vintage, 1982), esp. chap. 12, "Empty Texts—Bored Children," 235–64.

2. Shaw, "Mainly About Myself," in *Complete Plays*, 3:xxvi.

3. For detailed accounts of some of these fights, see Holroyd, *Shaw*, 1:383–92.

4. Frye's specific example is Shakespeare, not Shaw, but the point is general and applies to all individual writers. "Critics of Shakespeare are often supposed to be ridiculed by the assertion that if Shakespeare were to come back from the dead, he would not be able to appreciate or even understand their criticism. This in itself is likely enough: we have little evidence of Shakespeare's interest in criticism, either of himself or anyone else. Even if there were such evidence, his own account of what he was trying to do in *Hamlet*

would no more be a definitive criticism of that play, clearing all its puzzles up for good, than a performance of it under his direction would be a definitive performance." *Anatomy of Criticism: Four Essays* (Princeton, N.J.: Princeton University Press, 1957), 5–6.

5. Jacques Derrida, *De la grammatologie* (Paris: Minuit, 1967). The opening chapter, "La fin du livre et le commencement de l'écriture," addresses the relationship of writing to speech and defies summary citation. Gayatri Chakravorty Spivak's English translation, *Of Grammatology* (Baltimore, Md.: Johns Hopkins University Press, 1976), offers a phrase—not quite in the original text—that may serve as a trace of the absent: "And thus we say 'writing' for all that gives rise to an inscription in general, whether it is literal or not and even if what it distributes in space is alien to the order of the voice" (9). The English sentence is a slightly rearranged excerpt from a French original that begins, *"On tend maintenant à dire"* (*De la grammatologie*, 19).

6. Bernard Shaw, "Parents and Children," preface to *Misalliance*, in *Complete Plays*, 4:20–21.

7. M. H. Abrams, "The Deconstructive Angel," *Critical Inquiry* 3 (1976): 425–38, esp. 437–38; reprinted in Abrams, *Doing Things with Texts: Essays in Criticism and Critical Theory* (New York: Norton, 1989), 237–52. Frederick Crews makes the same point in *Skeptical Engagements* (New York: Oxford University Press, 1986), 116–17; he notes that Gerald Graff has named this disjunction the "Poststructuralist Two-Step" (xvii–xviii).

8. J. Hillis Miller, "The Critic as Host," *Critical Inquiry* 3 (1976): 442; reprinted in Miller, *Theory Now and Then* (Durham, N.C.: Duke University Press, 1991), 141–70.

9. At this seminar, organized by Baker, one of the guest speakers, Christopher Norris, in glossing Paul de Man's *Allegories of Reading* showed that de Man's analysis of Marcel Proust "has the effect of breaking down the conventional assumption that draws a firm line between private and public activities, the world of thought and the world outside." See Norris, *Deconstruction: Theory and Practice* (London: Methuen, 1982), 100–101.

10. Wayne Booth, "M. H. Abrams: Historian as Critic, Critic as Pluralist," *Critical Inquiry* 2 (1975–1976): 441; reprinted in Booth, *Critical Understanding: The Powers and Limits of Pluralism* (Chicago: University of Chicago Press, 1979), 170–71.

11. For the legend of Saint Luke and his patronage of the painters' guilds, see Louis Réau, *Iconographie des saints II, G–O*, vol. 3 of *Iconographie de l'art chrétien* (Paris: Presses Universitaires de France, 1958), 827–32.

12. There are a number of fifteenth-century copies of this painting. The version at the Boston Museum of Fine Arts, illustrated in plate 1, is sometimes thought to be the original.

13. For the concept of history painting see Peter C. Sutton, "Masters of

Dutch Genre Painting," in *Masters of Seventeenth-Century Dutch Genre Painting* (Philadelphia: Philadelphia Museum of Art, 1984), xiv–xvi.

14. See Erwin Panofsky, *Early Netherlandish Painting: Its Origins and Character*, 2 vols. (Cambridge: Harvard University Press, 1953), 2: nos. 368, 372. See also nos. 317, 370, 374, 375.

15. Sutton, *Masters*, xiv–xvi.

16. I have learned most of what I know about the details of this painting from the published work of art historians, for whom I have a great deal of respect. I am puzzled, however, by these scholars' interpretations of the painting as a whole. None of them sees in it a deliberate contrast between academic theories of painting and Vermeer's practice. None of them mentions humor. The consensus seems to be that it is a painting in praise of painting in general. Albert Blankert thinks it is a painting in praise of history painting.

Lawrence Gowing, *Vermeer*, 2d. ed. (1952; London: Faber and Faber, 1970) considers its subject to be "the glory of painting, its undying fame. . . . The girl has a radiance, an aura of intact divinity, which reminds us that of the studio pictures of the time none follows so closely as this the traditional iconography of St. Luke and the Virgin" (140).

Madlyn Millner Kahr, *Dutch Painting in the Seventeenth Century* (New York: Harper & Row, 1978) says that "its allegorical meaning claims higher status for the painter [i.e., for painters in general, not the represented painter] by associating painting with the liberal arts" (12).

Albert Blankert, *Vermeer of Delft: Complete Edition of the Paintings*, trans. Gary Schwartz and Hinke Boot-Tuinman (Oxford: Phaidon, 1978), says that "Vermeer has . . . expressed in symbolic guise the idea that history painting was an artist's noblest calling" (48).

Svetlana Alpers, *The Art of Describing: Dutch Art in the Seventeenth Century* (Chicago: University of Chicago Press, 1983), is closer to my position. She says that "the argument that this depiction of history's Muse shows that, despite his own art, he still honored the noblest art in the traditional sense is unpersuasive." (166). She sees "History [raising] her trumpet to praise such descriptive painting" (ibid.) and thinks that Vermeer depicted himself in the represented painter (168). While I see contrasts where she does not, and do not imagine for a moment that Vermeer represented himself in this painting, I do agree with her remark that Vermeer celebrates "the world seen" (ibid.).

H. Miedema, "Johannes Vermeers 'Schilderkunst,' " *Proef* (September 1972): 67–76, says that the allegory is about the artistic calling that produces history painting and about the nature of the subject of history painting, but Miedema sees neither a contrast with another kind of painting nor humor.

17. Compare this costume with Rembrandt's working costume (note especially the head covering) in the late self-portraits, almost exactly contemporary with this picture, that show him paused in the act of painting. The Louvre's

"Self-Portrait of Rembrandt Painting" (INV 1747) makes the point especially well. Miedema, "Vermeers 'Schilderkunst,' " observes that the costume is an unlikely working outfit and also that it is out-of-date (74).

18. Balthazar de Monconys, *Journal des Voyages* . . . , 3 vols. (Lyon: H. Boissat et G. Remeus, 1665–1666): "[11 août 1663] A Delphes ie vis le Peintre Vermer qui n'auoit point de ses ouurages: mais nous en vismes vn chez vn Boulanger qu'on auoit payé six cents liures, quoyqu'il n'y eust qu'vne figure, que i'aurois creu trop payer de six pistoles" (2:149). [(11 August 1663) At Delft, I saw the painter Vermeer who had none of his works at all: but we saw one of them at a baker's, which had cost six-hundred livres, although there was only one figure in it, that I would have believed cost too much at six pistoles."] The value of a pistole was fixed at ten livres in 1652.

19. On the iconography of Clio and for a reproduction of an important seventeenth-century Dutch example, see Hermann Ulrich Assemissen, *Vermeer, L'Atelier du Peintre ou l'image d'un métier* (Paris: Adam Biro [Collection "Un sur Un"], 1989), 41–48, fig. 30:55.

20. This society has been described and documented by John Michael Montias in his *Artists and Artisans in Delft in the Seventeenth Century: A Socio-Economic Study of the Seventeenth Century* (Princeton, N.J.: Princeton University Press, 1982), and in his *Vermeer and his Milieu: A Web of Social History* (Princeton, N.J.: Princeton University Press, 1989).

21. This is one of those passages that reminds us that wonderful as reproductions are, it is impossible to maintain the highest standards in interpreting paintings without working with the originals directly. I hope those readers who have not seen this picture, or who have not seen it recently, or who did not pay attention to the tones of black when they saw it, will have an opportunity to check what I say here against the original. In the spirit of the *Guide Michelin*, let me say that, in my opinion, it is worth the trip. There is an attempt in Ludwig Goldscheider, *Johannes Vermeer: The Paintings, Complete Edition*, 2d ed. (1958; London: Phaidon, 1967), to give some idea of the "richness of the gradation of tones" (131) in this passage. See plate 59 (monochrome with two inks).

22. James A. Welu, "The Map in Vermeer's Art of Painting," *Imago Mundi* 30 (1978): 9–30.

23. Ibid., 17–19, fig. 12:22. This detail is reproduced more clearly in Assemissen, *Vermeer*, 27.

24. Simon Schama makes this point in *The Embarrassment of Riches: An Interpretation of Dutch Culture in the Golden Age* (Berkeley and Los Angeles: University of California Press, 1988): "it may be that Vermeer . . . expressed . . . a nostalgic view of the old Netherlands and its art in his *Allegory of Painting*. . . . In the map that appears so prominently above the figure of the painter (once thought to be a self-portrait) the Fatherland is represented, not in its new

guise, as the seven provinces of the Republic, but the seventeen of the humanist Renaissance" (57).

25. For the town views, see Welu, "Map," figs. 13–15:23–25; Assemissen, *Vermeer*, 26–27.

26. M. H. Abrams points out that every text *déjà écrit* turns out to be the same endless play of significations over the same old void once properly "deconstructed." "Constructing and Deconstructing," in *Doing Things with Texts*, 330–31.

⁘ *Index* ⁘

decor: in *Pale Fire*, 50; in 'parody', 51; in political debate, 50–51, 55
Defaux, Gérard: *Montaigne: Essays in Reading*, 3
de Man, Paul, xxi, 104, 171n.9
Derrida, Jacques, xxi, 134, 137–39, 142, 145; *De la grammatologie*, 171n.5
Descombes, Vincent, 160n.23
detail: in Proust, 67, 71; in Shaw, 64, 68, 70
discovery, xxiv–xxv
disjunction, 139, 151
doing: writing as, 12, 26, 51, 134, 138
done: writing as act, 11, 22, 27
Dray, William, 58, 65, 69, 71; *Laws and Explanation in History*, 57, 161n.4, 162n.23

écriture, 3, 153
Ellenberger, Henri F., 55, 105, 122–23
Ellis, John M., xxi, 155n.1 (chap. 1)
Emerson, Caryl, 158n.1
Empson, William, 133
errors: Emma Bovary's, 14; Emma Bovary's, contrasted to the Narrator's (in Proust), 14–15; Narrator's, 117–21, 125
Essays and Reviews, 161n.7
evaluation and interpretation in Samuel Johnson, 22
evidence, historical, 32, 44, 94–95, 101
experience: common, 138; ordinary, 20, 146
explanation, xvii, 15, 16, 57–71; acts of, 57; as philosophic act, 57; pragmatic dimension of, 162n.23; prescientific attempts at, 160–61n.3; "processive," 57, 58, 64–71; rhetorical aspects of, 57, 58; "scientific," 57, 58, 59–63, 160–61n.3; through stories, 66, 71
Eyck, Jan van, 82; *Virgin of Autun*, 10

fact, 43, 101
facts, 52, 63, 64, 70, 86, 89–90, 91; local, 60; made intelligible by fiction, 62, 91; mere, 61, 62, 89–90; "real," 52

fallacy, the intentional, 20, 24
fantasy, Aristophanic, xxi, 139–42
Ferré, André, 169–70n.64
Feuillerat, Albert , 166n.15
fictions, conscious, 63
Figaro, Le, 108, 112, 127
Flaubert, Gustave, 4, 24, 109; and his concept of literary art, 5–9; contrasted to Proust, 12–15; *Madame Bovary*, 5–9, 14, 24
Foucault, Michel, xxi, xxii
French, Thomas, 70–71
Freud, Sigmund, 55, 122–23, 124, 131
Frye, Northrop, 134, 145; *Anatomy of Criticism*, 137–39, 170–71n.4

Gallimard. See *Nouvelle revue française*
Gass, William H., 166n.13
Gautier, Théodule: *Capitaine Fracasse*, 111
Geertz, Clifford, xxii, 155n.3 (preface)
genre, 134; as agent, 24, 38
genre painting, 145
George, Henry, 77
Geyl, Pieter: *Use and Abuse of History*, 50–51, 55
Giants (New York baseball team), 64–65
Gide, André, 107–8, 109, 168n.48
girl: concept of, 151–53
girls compared to muses, 151–53
Goldscheider, Ludwig: *Johannes Vermeer*, 173n.21
Gowing, Lawrence: *Vermeer*, 172n.16
Graff, Gerald, xxi, xxii, xxiii, 171n.7
Grasset, Bernard, 106
Greenblatt, Stephen, 18
Gröber, Gustav, 31, 44
guilds, 143; academic, 142, 154; of Saint Luke, 143

Hancher, Michael, 158n.21
Hempel, Carl G., 161n.4
heresy in Shaw, 53, 82, 83, 87, 89, 91, 92, 93, 99, 101, 102, 103
Hexter, J. H., 62, 63, 65, 69, 70, 71; *The History Primer*, 57, 64, 161n.4; and

Welu, James A., 151–52

Weyden, Rogier van der, 82; *Saint Luke Painting the Virgin*, 143–45, 144 (pl. 1), 146, 171n.12

"what actually happened," 62, 63

"what-did-you-expect" explanation, 63, 86

White, Morton G., 71, 161n.4

whole and the part: epistemological problem of, 63

Wilde, Oscar, xvii, 10

will, 112, 122, 123; and intellectual memory, 169–70n.64

Wilson, Edmund: *The Triple Thinkers*, 73, 81

Wimsatt, William K., Jr., 19–21

Winton, Alison, 166n.15, 170n.71

writer, xviii, 25–26; in *A la recherche du temps perdu*, 121; contrasted with author, xix, 20, 29; writing, 4, 12–13

writing, xxii, 15, 20, 138–39; act of, 3, 4, 19; image of, 19; in Proust, 120; and speech, 136

Yeats, William Butler: and Shaw, 12, 83–84

Zelan, Karen, 170n.1

Zeldin, Theodore, 105